PRAISE FOR *THIS IS YOUR CAPTAIN SPEAKING*

"What a wonderful walk down memory lane with one of my favorite people! Not only did Gavin safely helm the ship to all the great ports of the globe, but he calmed the 'seas of egos,' old and young. But I was the lucky one—I got to marry the captain."

—MARION ROSS, Mrs. C. from *Happy Days*

"*Incredible* is a word used to describe the amazing, as well as something we don't believe to be true. Gavin's book demands the first interpretation! That's an unqualified assertion made on the grounds of knowing him well—in triumph or through trial, at both high and low points of life's ebb and flow. I have been Gavin and Patti's pastor for over thirty years. Thus, I endorse a man of character and kindness: the Captain of the *Love Boat* was, and is, a gracious, thoughtful, reliable, and trustworthy man of accomplished professionalism. So as you meet the host of personalities he introduces from his life experience, or read his interactions with life and people, you can believe you're hearing the real story—not a puff job or schmooze treatment. Gavin's real! And his story is amazing! And it's both a fun and heart-touching read."

—DR. JACK W. HAYFORD, chancellor,
The King's University-Los Angeles/Dallas

"From struggling on the wrong side of the tracks in poverty to sailing the seven seas in luxury, from hot dog lunches to ship launches, Gavin MacLeod's life is a story of an American dreamer and his dream, and it shows how tenacity, faith, and talent (and a gorgeous smile doesn't hurt) can get you where you need to go, with or without hair. Reading his book has been a little unnerving for me because I know Gavin as my friend and neighbor and love him dearly, but now, after reading about his sometimes difficult journey, I treasure him even more. What a wonderful man, a true American ambassador."

—NANCY SINATRA, SINGER, ACTOR, AND AUTHOR

"When *The Love Boat* set a 'course for adventure' in 1977, who could have predicted the enormous impact this TV show would have on the then-nascent cruise industry, let alone how it would introduce Princess Cruises to a wonderful ambassador? I've had the privilege of calling Gavin my friend and inspiration for over two decades. Like a rising tide that lifts all boats, I've seen him lift the spirits of all he comes into contact with. His enthusiasm for life, for people, for storytelling—and also for cruising—is infectious. I don't think there's ever been a better spokesperson for a company or industry, ever. Sailors set their course by the stars, and Gavin has been our shining star."

—JULIE BENSON, VICE PRESIDENT OF
PUBLIC RELATIONS, PRINCESS CRUISES

"I just got back from the most delightful cruise and I never got seasick! I just cruised through Gavin MacLeod's wonderful book *This Is Your Captain Speaking*, and only a real cruise on the real *Love Boat* would equal it. Like everyone else in America, I knew he was a great actor and always seemed like the kind of man you'd love to live next door to and have as a friend. After reading his compelling and candid story, I understand why I felt this way. Gavin's life story is fascinating just to read, but I found it far more than another book about a celebrity's life. It's a book about life, period, and the insights, lessons, and life experiences he so honestly shares will leave you inspired, refreshed, and encouraged. Whether you feel like your ship is setting sail or sinking, you will be in good hands with *this* Captain! This book is like the midnight buffet without the calories!"

—MIKE HUCKABEE, SYNDICATED TV AND
RADIO HOST AND BEST-SELLING AUTHOR

"Who wouldn't love to spend an intimate evening or two with one of the most beloved actors in the country? A few hours in which he tells of his countless experiences with a who's who of show business and then takes you behind the curtain into his own checkered, almost unbelievable life, with its highs and lows and remarkable accomplishments. Best of all, he shares how he came to know and love and devote his life to his own Captain, the Creator of the Universe.

"I love it. It's a modern-day *Pilgrim's Progress*."

—PAT BOONE, ENTERTAINER

"Gavin epitomizes the old-fashioned concept of a gentleman. He is a loving, generous, and authentic seeker of God's truth. His life story speaks for itself."

—KATHIE LEE GIFFORD, COHOST OF THE *TODAY* SHOW

"You will love this book. It's filled with fun, faith, and hope. Just like my friend Gavin MacLeod!"

—FLORENCE HENDERSON, ACTOR, SINGER, AND AMERICA'S FAVORITE TV MOM

"With his characteristic, contagious exuberance, Gavin recounts his life story with unvarnished candor—beginning as a young boy from the 'wrong side of the tracks' who goes on to reach the pinnacle of acting success while encountering a lot more than just bumps and bruises along the way. Inspirational and richly evocative, Gavin's story isn't simply a celebration of his life and those with whom he's worked— it's a heart-lifting, encouraging celebration of that often forgotten American dream itself."

—JOHN TINKER, EMMY AWARD- WINNING TELEVISION PRODUCER

THIS IS YOUR
CAPTAIN SPEAKING

THIS IS YOUR CAPTAIN SPEAKING

My Fantastic Voyage Through Hollywood, Faith & Life

GAVIN MACLEOD
WITH MARK DAGOSTINO

W PUBLISHING GROUP

AN IMPRINT OF THOMAS NELSON

Published in Nashville, Tennessee, by W Publishing Group. W Publishing is a registered trademark of Thomas Nelson.

Thomas Nelson titles may be purchased in bulk for educational, business, fund-raising, or sales promotional use. For information, please e-mail SpecialMarkets@ ThomasNelson.com.

Author is represented by the literary agency of Alive Communications, Inc., 7680 Goddard Street, Suite 200, Colorado Springs, CO 80920; alivecommunications.com

ISBN: 978-0-8499-4762-9 (HC)
ISBN: 978-0-7180-3745-1 (TP)

Library of Congress Control Number: 2013941972

Printed in the United States of America

15 16 17 18 19 RRD 7 6 5 4 3 2 1

This book is dedicated to the Captain of my life, who came that I might have life and have it more abundantly.

CONTENTS

CONTENTS

PREFACE

ONE DOOR CLOSES . . .

I REMEMBER IT LIKE IT WAS YESTERDAY. I WAS SO excited. Here I was, this young actor with a single Broadway credit to his name, newly planted in Los Angeles with my beautiful wife, ready to take on the world. It was my first day shooting on a new television sitcom pilot with Hal March. *Hal March!* The incredibly popular host of *The $64,000 Question*! I couldn't have been happier if I'd been called to sing opera at the Met straight out of glee club, or to pitch for the Mets straight out of the minor leagues. I went out and bought myself a new sweater at Bullock's. (I wanted to look good for my first day.) I didn't own a car then, so I rented a car to drive to the studio. I was flying.

My call wasn't until late morning, around eleven o'clock. All the other actors were already rehearsing as I walked onto the set as quietly as I could. I'll admit I was delighted when one of them spotted me and everyone stopped to say hello.

"Gavin, how are you?" they said. I met Hal March right away, and he didn't seem all that friendly, but that was okay. It was just great to meet him and to think that I was about to work with him. The great comedic actor Stubby Kaye was there. I knew Stubby from New York, so I said, "Great to see you!" And the talented actress Jeanne Bal was on set too. "I loved you in *Guys and Dolls*," I said. She was so gracious. They gave me a desk where I could lay my sweater and my script, behind a canvas lean-to where I could get changed if I wanted to. I was just buzzing. I was raring to go.

Finally we started rehearsing. Hal and I did a scene and there was a sofa between us. Hal said, "I think it would be fun if you go down on that line and I'll go up, and then I go down—like a see-saw."

I said, "Oh, that sounds good. Okay!" So we started to get into it when someone called, "Lunch!"

Union rules are strict, so we broke and went to lunch even though I'd barely begun. I was watching my weight at the time (as most actors are prone to do), so I just ate a little Jell-O and sat with Stubby. After a few minutes I excused myself so I could go inside and look over the script, and that's where I was when the assistant director came over and said, "Gavin, Kerwin Coughlin wants to see you."

"The casting director? Okay." I noticed no one else had come back from lunch yet. "Where is everybody?"

"Oh, they're coming in. They're going to a different setup," he said. I started to go and he added, "Why don't you take your script and your sweater with you?"

Why would the casting director want to see me? I wondered. I didn't ask. I just grabbed my things and walked to his office. It had a screen door on the back, I remember, and as I put my hand on the door handle I thought, *You know, Hal March wasn't all that friendly to me. Could I be getting fired?*

All that glorious excitement I had felt suddenly wrenched into a knot in my stomach. I stepped into the office and asked the secretary right away, "Is something happening to me that I think is happening to me?" She said, "Yeah. They let you go."

It was like a dagger to my heart. I'd never been fired. From *anything*.

Coughlin called me in and said he was sorry. He explained that Hal had someone else in mind and that I was still going to get paid. "I don't care about that!" I said. *Acting is the only thing I know how to do. How can I be getting fired?* The explanations were all a bunch of baloney. *This is Hollywood?* I thought. *I didn't even get to show them what I can do! How can they fire me?*

I was destroyed. I held that sweater in my hand and cried all the way back to my rented car. I didn't know what to do, so I drove to my agent's office.

"What are you doing here?" he said.

"Hal March fired me." My agent couldn't believe it either. He called over to the production office and they assured me I was going to get paid, which my agent thought would appease me, but it didn't. I was crushed.

My happiness was so tied to my work back then that I thought it was all over. I honestly wondered if I would ever act again. *I've barely begun, and my career is already finished.* I'd never even entertained the possibility of getting fired, so I let that news destroy me. *And now,* I thought, *I have to go home and tell my wife?*

Harry Guardino, another great actor, lived right across the way from me in those days. I ran into him as I got home. He and I had gone on the road together in *A Hatful of Rain*, but he had come to Hollywood much earlier and had done *Houseboat* with Cary Grant and Sophia Loren by then. I really looked up to the guy. He knew I had a big show that day and he was surprised to see me. "What are you doing home?" he said.

"Hal March fired me."

"That no-talent . . ." Harry picked up an ashtray and threw it. He was a real Italian guy and on the volatile side. "That show's not gonna work," he said. "This is gonna come back to him, you watch. You gonna get paid?"

"Yeah," I said.

"Well, that's all right," he said. "I never liked Hal March anyway."

It was nice to have the support. I thanked him for saying it. But it didn't help. I walked in as my wife came out of the kitchen.

"What are you doing home?"

I was so ashamed I just looked at the floor. "They fired me."

"Oh no."

"Oh yes!" It felt like my whole life was over. I'd let her down. I'd moved us all the way to California from Manhattan, and now I'd let her down. "I don't know," I said. "I don't know if I'm ever going to do this again." My mind started racing, wondering what I did wrong. *I didn't even have a chance to show them anything!* I sat there lost in the fear that I'd made a mistake, that everything I'd done in my life had led to this failure. I'd blown it somehow, and I didn't even know how. Thank God I didn't have kids then and have to tell *them*. I don't think I could have faced it.

I sat there wallowing in that horrible feeling of failure for the better part of the afternoon. And then the phone rang. It was my agent: "Gavin, do you know Blake Edwards?"

"I've heard of him," I said. *In fact, I think I sent him a flyer with my picture on it, trying to promote myself.*

"Well, he's doing a new pilot called *Peter Gunn*. Can you go over to see him at four o'clock?"

"I guess so," I said unenthusiastically. *Why would anyone want to hire a guy who's just been fired?*

"Should I bring my hair?" I asked.

"Yeah," he said, "bring your hair."

I had been bald since college. There wasn't much work for a young bald actor, so I kept my hairpiece in a box, ready to go. (I'll tell you a funny story about that hairpiece a little later on.)

It was almost four, so I got up, kissed my wife good-bye, and hurried over to Blake Edwards's office. I tried to be cheerful after what had just happened to me, but I felt defeated again as I walked in. There was another actor there waiting to be seen, a very handsome actor (whom I would later recognize as Carl Betz, the guy who played the husband on

The Donna Reed Show). I thought, *What am I here for? I can't be here for his part!*

They finally called me in, and I met Blake Edwards and another guy with a bald head—his friend, Dick Crocket—and we started talking. I didn't mention that I had just been fired. Instead, I mentioned that I had recently done a small part in a film called *I Want to Live!* Blake perked right up. He told me his stepfather was the production manager on that, a guy named Jack McEdward. "I remember him!" I said. Suddenly the conversation seemed energized. We started talking about my other credits. He was aware of my performance in *A Hatful of Rain*, which had picked up some really good reviews.

I said, "I've been acting since I was a kid, but I'm new out here." We talked and laughed about a bunch of stuff. Then all of a sudden, he stopped. "You know what?" he said. "The lead heavy in this pilot was gonna be Italian." (The "heavy," for those who don't know, is an old Hollywood term that refers to the bad guy in a film.) "But I want you to play him," he said. "I'm gonna make him Irish. His name's gonna be Fallon."

I could hardly believe it. Blake Edwards was re-envisioning and rewriting a part right there in his office, just for me. "Thank you so much, Mr. Edwards," I said.

What I wanted to do was drop to my knees and say, "Thank you, God!" I was floored. *Gee whiz*, I thought. *What a day! To go from being fired and thinking I was finished to a thing like this, where a director is going to change and rewrite a part just for me? Wow.*

My agent told me *Peter Gunn* was the fastest-selling pilot ever made up to that time, and as fate would have it, that meeting would mark the beginning of a long and fruitful working relationship with the great Blake Edwards. A couple of weeks later I was invited to go to the show's first screening, and I brought my wife to mingle with all those big stars. Oh, and by the way: Hal March's pilot never sold! If I hadn't been fired, I would have been tied up for months and I never would have had the chance to work with Blake.

A couple of months later, Blake hired me again—this time for a role in a film called *Operation Petticoat*, starring Tony Curtis and Cary Grant. A film that would be nominated for an Oscar for Best Screenplay. He'd bring me back for roles in three more films after that, too, including *The Party* with Peter Sellers and *High Time* with Bing Crosby. (I've got a picture from that set where Bing's in drag and I'm dancing with him! How many actors have *that*?) It was all those great parts that eventually helped me land *The Mary Tyler Moore Show* and *The Love Boat*.

So I'm here to tell you: even on what you think is the bleakest day of your life, don't give up. In the acting business, you learn that lesson pretty quickly. You work, you don't work, you work, you don't work, you work. Life is like that too. One door closes; another one opens. It all works out eventually. For a lot of years I wondered, *Why is that?* Only now I know: even if you don't believe it, even if you're not fully appreciative of it, God is there watching over you. Always.

I wish I had that kind of faith back then. Sure, I believed in God, but a God I should fear—not the God of love and mercy I've come to understand and give thanks to every day for almost thirty years. If I knew then what I know now, maybe I wouldn't have worried so much. Maybe I wouldn't have been so upset when things didn't go my way. There are a lot of maybes and coulda-beens in life. I don't spend time second-guessing any of them now. After all, they've all been a part of my journey.

My life has taken one incredible turn after another. I've gotten to do what I wanted to do. I've been a captain! I've traveled the world. I've been helped by a lot of great people, and I've been blessed to have touched a lot of lives myself. I'm thankful for that, and oh so grateful. I've been given this incredible gift of a life, and now I want to use it to give back. That's why I'm sharing my story here, the fun parts and even some not-so-fun parts, in the hopes that maybe someone will take a nice walk down memory lane with me—hopefully a very entertaining walk!

My greatest wish, though, is that whoever reads my story will walk away at the end with a smile. And maybe, just maybe, there's something to be found in my journey—especially in my journey of faith—that will help give someone a little bit of hope. Maybe even change someone's life for the better.

Wouldn't that be something?

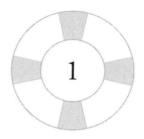

PLEASANTVILLE

I KNEW IT WHEN I WAS FOUR YEARS OLD.

I don't think I had ever *seen* a play, let alone been in one. I'm not sure I knew what a play really was. Yet somehow, when my preschool teacher cast me as the lead boy in our Mother's Day show, it felt as if my whole short life had been leading to that very moment. I knew what to do. I gave it my all. I hammed it up as I went around and asked all the little animals in the forest, "What should I give to my mother for Mother's Day?" When the largest boy in class, who was of course playing a bear, told me I should give my mom a "bear hug" for a present, I went back and gave the girl who played my mom a big ol' bear hug on that humble stage, and the real moms and dads all went, "Awwww."

All of us kids took a bow at the end and, lucky me, I was the last one to go out there. That's when I *felt* that sound for the very first time: applause.

I think a lot of actors understand that sound—a sound that resonates from your ears to your heart, right down to your toes. That sound says, *Somebody likes me.* It's full of a sort of love that many actors don't experience anywhere else.

The first time I heard that applause, man, that was it. I was hooked! Whenever I had to write a composition about what I wanted to do with my life, all through school, I wrote that I wanted to be an actor. Whenever there was any sort of community theater happening, or any opportunity to get on stage at Sunday school or anywhere else, I was there: this chubby kid who wanted to act.

My mother supported all my artistic endeavors as a child. I think she liked getting credit for making such a cute kid. In fact, one time she entered my photo in the *New York Daily Mirror*'s "Charming Child Contest"—a picture of me with round cheeks, blue eyes, and curly blond hair—and I won! My little brother was mad. Ronnie ripped up that photo when he saw it. But my mom taped it back together and kept it for the rest of her life. A mom's gotta be pretty proud of her son to do something like that.

My dad? Well, let's just say he had other ideas about what any son of his ought to be doing with his life.

I was born Allan George See on February 28, 1931, in a hospital in Mount Kisco, New York. (I realize "Allan See" isn't the name you see on the front of this book, so I'll tell you about my name change in a little while.)

My mother, Margaret, and my father, George See, raised my younger brother, Ronnie, and me in the nearby town of Pleasantville, which is situated about thirty miles north of New York City. Among other things, Pleasantville was the home of *Readers' Digest.* My mother worked for Mr. Wallace, the founder, before I was born. There were only four or five girls in the office back then. None of them had cars—they all had to walk to work. For some reason, Mr. Wallace would always pick my mother up and drive her in—something she would speak of proudly for the rest of her life. It's incredible to me to think of the potential career she gave up in order to stay home and raise her two boys.

Not only were my younger years spent in the depths of the Great

Depression, which of course were followed by the trying times of World War II, but we lived on what most people would consider the "other side" of the railroad tracks that split Pleasantville in half. By the time the war came around, my father ran a gas station that he owned with another guy. He had worked his way up from being an attendant, and I'd go over there on my scooter just to get a chance to see him. He worked all the time, and he'd put me to work, too, which I loved. I'd get to help clean up the joint, or he'd hand me a little whisk-broom and send me out to sweep the interiors of the customers' cars—including the back of the local funeral parlor's hearse when it pulled up to the pumps. I'd climb right up inside the back of that big, cool-looking car and get it clean as a whistle. It was great! I felt like a little man.

Ronnie, who is two years younger than me, used to come along too. I remember one time he got his hand stuck in the nickel candy machine. He was so eager to get his candy bar, he couldn't wait and reached his whole arm up into the slot. Boy, was my dad mad. He couldn't get the machine open, so he had to call the distributor, who lived all the way down in Yonkers. We each took turns holding up Ronnie's arm for an hour until the guy arrived. The man was nice enough to give him the candy bar once the ordeal was over, though, so it had a happy ending.

My dad did a lot of side jobs too. He was always trying to make some money. Especially since so many of his customers would fill up their tanks, promise to "pay him next week," and then never make a payment. I have memories of going around to some of their houses with my father, knocking on doors as he humbly asked them to pay up. Sometimes they did. Many times they didn't. Those were hard times for everybody.

I remember putting cardboard in my shoes because they had holes in the bottom. That's how broke we were. I had to share a bed with my brother while my mom's brother, my uncle Jimmy, crashed on a bed on the other side of the room in order to help my parents with the rent on our cramped railroad-style apartment. Uncle Jimmy would live there for a few years, until he got married and moved into his own place. Our bedroom was all the way at one end, and we had to walk through my parents' bedroom to get to the bathroom and out to the kitchen and the living room and the front door. But we were rich with love. My grandparents on my mother's side always bought new clothes for us at Easter, and my uncle Al—the world traveler—would sometimes come and whisk Ronnie and me off for a day in Manhattan. So I didn't feel sorry for myself. Not at all. I think we had it better than a lot of people.

Given my physique in those days, it's clear that I wasn't lacking for food. My mom showed her love through cooking, and all the old ladies in the neighborhood thought I was just so cute, they'd stuff me full of cookies and pastries every chance they got. I developed the nickname "Tubber." (Ronnie would follow the same fate and become "Tubber-Two!") I looked nothing like my dad, who was tall and fit. He towered over my five-foot-tall Irish mother, even when she stood on a step in photographs so she wouldn't seem so tiny next to him. He also had a ruddy complexion from working outside all the time.

I didn't really like working outside. I didn't really like hanging out at the gas station, to be honest, other than to see my dad. My friends' parents were doctors and lawyers and other professional people who lived in the nice houses across the tracks. I found those people more interesting and comfortable to hang around than a lot of my dad's gruff friends. In a way, I think he thought of me as the black sheep of the family. Almost as if he never really understood me.

The thing is, in addition to being an incredibly hard worker, my dad was an incredibly popular guy. Everyone loved him. Everywhere we went people said hello. He had friends all over town. I think he inherited some of that likability from his father, my grandfather See, who at one point had a big, beautiful house. Lots of people told me that my grandfather could've been mayor at one time, which I thought was just spectacular. Unfortunately, it didn't turn out that way. I think my father inherited something besides charm from my grandfather too— something much less pleasant.

The day I'd get to see the most of my dad was on Sundays, after church and Sunday school were over. Our mom raised us Catholic, and she took us to mass at Holy Innocence Church, followed by Sunday school with the nuns, which was fun because they had a bowling alley and a stage where we'd get to watch minstrel shows. Dad was raised Episcopalian, so he wouldn't come with us. He would go to his own church. Or not. "Some of those people who go to church every Sunday, what do you think they were doing the night before?" he'd say. He had that attitude toward church. (The ironic thing is that his brother, Al, was just the opposite. He was a lay minister at my dad's church. He would go out in robes and assist the priests. Eventually Al even had his own church upstate. Two brothers. How different they were!)

Out of my mother's five siblings, she was the only one who went to church. We sat in the wooden pews, sometimes upstairs, listening to Father O'Toole, a big man with white hair who was so godly looking, and Father O'Dwyer, who used to play ball with us boys in the fields. Like most kids, I only went to church because my mother made me go. But there were parts of it that I got into, because it was so significant. Learning about the stations of the cross, for example. The God they spoke of in that church, in those days, was a God we should fear. I wasn't a bad kid, but I remember how much I always wanted to do the right thing, in part because God was watching over me and I didn't want to make him mad! In fact, I wanted to do the right thing so badly I'd wind up fibbing when I went to confession. The priests and nuns told us we had to confess our sins, and what did I know? I was a little kid! I was so scared about the whole thing, I'd make something up. "Father, bless me, for I have sinned. I disobeyed my parents six times this week." I hadn't disobeyed my parents at all, but I was actually sinning by fibbing about confessing to sinning! And then I'd feel guilty about *that*!

Finally, after it was all done, the four of us would come together as a family. Sometimes we would gather at my great-grandmother's house, where I'd sit on the floor and draw pictures while the adults had their conversations. Or I'd go down to the room where they kept their big

Victrola and listen to records or the radio. There was always entertainment there, and I could lose myself in those sounds for hours.

The best days, though, were the days when the four of us would pile into the car and take a long Sunday drive.

With all the fights about money and the stress my dad was under, those Sunday drives were the moments when I saw the love that existed between my parents. I can still smell the fresh spring air and picture my dad leaning over and singing to my mom as he drove: "When your hair has turned to silver, I will love you just the same." It was my mother's favorite song. "Peg of my heart, I love you," he'd say. He was the only one my mother ever allowed to call her "Peg."

Eventually my parents would stop the car at a little place up in Chappaqua and treat my brother and me to a hot dog. *Wow.* Ron will tell you the same thing: to this day, there's something about eating a hot dog that brings back such happy memories. Somehow the smell and the flavor and the sensation of biting into a hot dog bring a feeling of those childhood Sunday drives. I knew that hot dog was all my parents could afford, and it was such a treat.

I longed for that peaceful Sunday feeling all the time as a kid. I liked things simple. Pleasant. But life wasn't like that, even in a place called Pleasantville.

Being poor is no picnic. Even the car at one point—for all of its great memories—became a source of shame for me. It was a rickety old hunk of junk that my dad got from his older brother and barely kept running. I remember one day I was sitting up front while my dad drove, and I saw one of my friends from school, a boy named Richie, coming toward us down the side of the road. I was so embarrassed to be seen in this car, I slid down below the window. "What are you doing?" my dad asked. I made up an excuse about playing a game, saying Richie and I were hiding from each other, but my father must have known.

I disappointed my father for sure when I quit the football team. It was the very beginning of what should have been many years of playing football. I was just becoming a teenager. One day the coach told two of us kids to really take down the other team's quarterback. So we did—and we broke the kid's leg. I didn't like that. I didn't like it one bit. I was really upset and said I wanted to quit, and a lady who was there on the sidelines said, "Hey, Allan, why don't you join the school play instead? They need another boy." I jumped at the chance.

My father couldn't understand it. Just like he couldn't understand when my mother wanted to send me to art camp when I was nine. I showed enough talent that I applied, got accepted, and even won a partial scholarship to a summer program at a school in Chicago. "It's stupid," he said. He just couldn't see the point in spending *any* of his hard-earned money so his son could draw pictures. He wouldn't let me go.

He couldn't understand when I joined the school marching band, either, or how I could practice my drums—*flam-a-diddle, flam-a-diddle, flam-a-diddle*—on the table while simultaneously doing homework and listening to the radio. It drove him nuts! The older I got, the more of a black sheep I became to him.

Sometimes in the afternoons I would walk up the hill by the railroad tracks to watch all the folks on the commuter train make their way home from Manhattan. Other times I'd walk up and see the train coming in from Chicago, headed through our town on the way to Grand Central Station, with its dining car and the red roses on the tables just peeking over the edges of the windows. And I'd dream, *Someday I'm gonna take that train. Someday I'm gonna go places!*

In many ways, living on the other side of the tracks; not having any money; not having the fine things that I saw in the parlors, yards, and driveways of all of my friends' houses on the other side of town—that was the easy part. It was other stuff that left me longing for a real escape.

Once I was old enough, I spent my Saturday afternoons at the movies, where the great stars of that golden era of the silver screen could take me to faraway places as I munched on candy in the darkened theater. I would lose myself on the stage, too, even as a youngster, simply because I could pretend to be someone else for a while. Play rehearsals allowed me to break away, to go somewhere different for as long as I could.

As difficult as this is for me to admit, I needed those escapes—because there were times when I was scared of my father. Not all the time. Certainly not on those Sunday drives. But at other times. Like when he sat around the gas station with his longshoremen pals, smoking and carrying on. Or when he and those buddies went out fishing. Or in the dark of night as I lay awake in bed, wondering where he'd gone off to, hoping he would come home safely but terrified of the things I'd hear when he finally walked through the front door.

In case you haven't caught on yet, I was scared of my dad when he drank.

I don't like to say negative things about people. It pains me to include these memories in my book, but I think it's important not to gloss over it. We all have struggles to overcome. We all have challenges. I don't think there's anyone, no matter how successful he may be or how happy he may seem, who hasn't overcome some adversity in life.

Alcohol was something that would cause a lot of adversity for me.

People didn't talk about alcoholism running in families back then. There wasn't as much awareness as there is today. Drinking was just what people did—men, especially, to take the edge off, to find their own escape, I think, from the stress and awfulness that life could sometimes bring. Grandfather See was a drinker, too, and he lost everything to that bottle. The big house he once had. The chance to be mayor. Everything went out the window because of his drinking and gambling. One day on the way home from school a friend of mine said, "Hey, Allan, isn't that your grandfather?" I looked over and there was a man lying in the gutter, right out in the street, passed out drunk in the middle of the afternoon. Sure enough, it was my grandpa See.

"No," I said. "That's not him." I turned away and walked back home.

My mother's father, Jimmy Shea, was an alcoholic too. He was a little Irishman, a master carpenter with a bald head (like mine would be someday), married to my Swedish grandmother—the best chef in the world. He had so much going for him. Yet he would always get drunk on payday. I remember it well because whenever he got out of control they'd call my mom: "We found him in the gutter" or "These guys tried to beat him up" or "He's coming after your grandmother." My five-foot-tall mother would trudge out and rescue him, time after time, because for some reason she was the only one he would listen to.

In the early days, I was afraid of Grandpa Shea. He was gruff and seemed to be in a bad mood all the time. Then something changed.

The Second World War came on, and his youngest son, John, went off to fight in Europe. Later, when my uncle John came home from Europe, my grandfather stopped drinking. Just like that. He became one of the greatest guys I ever knew. When I was a little older, I asked him, "Grandpa, how did you change?" He said, "Well, sonny, I made a deal with God. I told God if he would bring Johnny home safe, I would never drink again. And I never have. And I won't."

"I wasted forty-eight years of my life," he told me. "All because of the bottle."

My father would never get a chance to make that same change. He was heading much closer to the path his own father took, and as I neared my teens, it kept getting worse. One night he came home drunk and he and my mom got into a big, big fight. Uncle Jimmy was asleep, and my brother was probably pretending to be asleep, and the fight got so heated I couldn't take it anymore. I got up and ran through their bedroom and into the kitchen just as my father picked up a knife. He was gonna go after my mother! I ran over and took it away from him. I just snatched it from his hand. He seemed shocked, and they both calmed down after that. Nothing like that ever happened again. *Thank God!* I didn't know what gave me the strength to do it. He was drinking, and I was the oldest son, and *somebody* had to do something. *Why is he like this?* I kept asking myself even though I knew the answer. *It's the alcohol.* Without the alcohol he was the greatest guy in the world.

He was my father. I loved him. He loved me, and he loved Ronnie too. I know he did. He never said it out loud. I never heard those three words from him. But I saw it in the way he smiled at us over those

9

Sunday hot dogs, and in the fact that he worked so hard to do all he could to support us. When I was ten or eleven, he moved us into a small rental house, which was a step up from that railroad apartment. When the booze wasn't in him, he was the sweetest man. I kept hoping that things would change.

Then, one day, they did.

My dad had been feeling sick, and on this particular morning my mom finally convinced him to go to the doctor. He *hated* going to doctors, but this had "gone on long enough," she said. I went off to school, and when I got home that day, my mom wasn't there. My dad wasn't there, either, but that was expected. I assumed he was still at work.

Four o'clock rolled around and the phone rang.

"Hello?"

"Allan?" It was my mother. "I'm at the hospital with your father." She instructed me to run over to my uncle Jimmy's house right away. "I need you to go over and tell your uncle that your father has cancer. They've given him six months to live."

Alone in that house, I started weeping. It was unimaginable. I didn't know what else to do, so I heeded my mother's instructions. I ran out the back door as fast as I could, over a brook and across the highway and the train tracks, up to my uncle's third-floor apartment, just weeping and weeping as I repeated what my mother had said.

The only time I ever saw my father cry in my whole life was about two years earlier. He came into the house, sat down, and wept. I can still see him on that sofabed in the living room. The reason? His best friend had gone to the doctor and found out he had cancer. His friend was so distraught that he got in his car, drove to a remote area, took out a shotgun, and killed himself. It broke my father's heart. I don't think he ever got over it. And now my father had cancer himself.

At some point they brought him home from the hospital. They didn't have shots for pain and things like that back then, and as the days dragged on my brother and I used to hear him wailing. I prayed that God would take him so he wouldn't have to be in such agony. I watched this vibrant human being, my strong father, reduced to walking on a cane. He was only thirty-nine years old. *How could this happen?*

After a few months, even the cane didn't help. He couldn't walk at all. So they took him to the hospital for the last time. Hospitals were restrictive in those days. They wouldn't allow Ronnie and me in to see him. We both have memories of standing outside that hospital room window, looking in at our father lying helpless in that bed.

We prayed that he would get better, even though the doctors said it was impossible. We prayed for our mother. We prayed for ourselves. *I'm only thirteen, God. Please don't take my father!*

We prayed to God for a miracle.

A miracle that never came.

LIFE GOES ON

I'LL NEVER FORGET SEEING MY FATHER'S BODY IN
the casket in our living room.

It was the Irish way, they told me. We held the wake in our
house, and all these people showed up. I couldn't understand why they
would want to have a party when my father was dead.

We had a little white dog named Suzy then. At the end of the wake,
after everyone was out of the house—including my father—we finally let
her up from the basement, and that dog went right over and lay on the
very spot on the floor where my father's casket had been resting. *She knew.*

The hearse that carried my father's body was the same one I used to
sweep out with a whisk-broom when I helped him down at the gas station. I kept thinking about what it felt like to crawl on that floor in the
back—what it looked like from the inside.

Everyone kept telling me that my father "was so well liked." It was
"the biggest funeral Pleasantville had ever seen!" Somehow, that wasn't
a comfort.

I remember walking with my mother from the Episcopal church when the service was over and all the people coming up to me: "Well, Allan, you're the head of the family now." *I guess so*, I thought. That is quite a responsibility to throw on a little kid, especially when he's grieving. But I listened. And a big, big part of me wanted to live up to that responsibility—for my mother, if no one else.

My mother was only thirty-nine. She would never get married again. She never even dated. There were plenty of men interested in her. She was still so young and beautiful, and the sweetest person you could ever meet, always going out of her way to help everyone around her. But she was never interested in anyone besides my father.

My dad's death changed everything. My mother had to get a job. She went to work for a bank over in Croton-on-Hudson, which meant a long drive back and forth every day. She couldn't be home after school to take Ronnie and me to practice or rehearsals or anything anymore. I had to go to work, too, and thankfully people were glad to help us out. The ladies in town would hire me to clean their kitchen floors or bathrooms. I had a set of clippers and I had certain people who would hire me to do their hedges. I mowed lawns for a dollar apiece. I even mowed at the Masonic temple and some of the other big places in town.

The summer after my dad died I took a job mowing lawns and landscaping at a cemetery two towns up. I had to walk all that way just to get there. We needed the money but, boy, that was a strange job. I remember this one person used to come every day and sit over one grave and read the newspaper to the deceased person. I had never seen anything like that in my life. I used to wonder, *Why doesn't she read the funny parts? She's reading the bad news to this dead person?* It was the weirdest thing. We were all young people working in that cemetery except for this one old Italian guy. He used to go into the mausoleums to eat his lunch because it was cool inside. Imagine eating surrounded by a whole family of dead people! Like I said: strange.

One day, during the long walk home, a dog bit me on the leg. (I've got thick legs. There's a lot of meat there!) A lady came out and helped me, and it turned out she owned a restaurant that was opening nearby. She offered me a job as a waiter, so I quit the cemetery job and started at this restaurant. The first person I waited on was a boxer, with his nose flattened to the side from one too many punches. He ordered soup and something else. It was my first day, so I wasn't too sure of myself and, well, you can probably tell where this is going: I dropped the soup all over him. I apologized profusely. I was worried the guy might stand up and punch me! He might have if I wasn't such a little kid. And I was so upset. *My father dies and I leave the cemetery job and now I'm going to lose this job!*

The owner came over and said, "Will you come with me?" She took me in the back and said, "Let me tell you something. What you just did is a sign that you're gonna be a great waiter."

I was shocked. "No kidding?" I said. "You're not mad?"

"No. I'm not mad," she said.

We cleaned the whole thing up, the rest of the meal went fine, and the guy left me a $1.25 tip. That was more than I made in the cemetery for a whole day's work!

That moment taught me how important it is what you say to people. She could have dressed me down to a point where for the rest of my life I would've been too scared to pick up a fork. But she didn't. And guess what? She was right. I became a very good waiter after that. Right from the beginning I loved serving people. And having that higher-paying job turned out to be more important than I could have imagined.

When someone dies, everybody seems to talk about how "So-and-so left this or that to so-and-so in the will." All my dad left us were bills.

The finances were the least of my worries, though. Nothing compared to the heartache of losing my father to cancer when I was just thirteen years old. I've often reflected on what he would have done with his life had he lived. He missed out, and so did I.

I could have closed up into a ball right there. Could have turned into a "bad kid." Could have given up. But instead, I did the opposite. I set myself on a trajectory to do something else. To go somewhere else.

I wanted to get out of Pleasantville and to do something with my life. A lot of that attitude, I think, was thanks to my dad's older brother, my uncle Al.

Uncle Al was a merchant marine—and he loved the theater. He took my brother and me to our first Broadway musical, *Helen Goes to Troy*. It was glorious. I wanted to be on that stage so badly, and I admired every one of those actors for getting up there and performing like that. It was amazing to me that people could be so talented (including Donald Buka, a star I would meet fifty years later on Cape Cod).

My uncle didn't have any kids of his own, and he really took to Ronnie and me. He was always coming back from some faraway place. My grandmother kept a stack of postcards from Al next to her chair— postcards from all over the world. I remember one time he came to my class, I think in the sixth grade, and talked about his recent trip to Alaska. He showed us all sorts of artifacts, and he wore his uniform, and I was so proud to be his nephew. Then at Christmastime, in the town of White Plains, which is as close as we have to a big city in that part of the state, he would put on the red suit and play Santa Claus in Woolworth's. I thought that was the greatest thing! But my mom and dad didn't appreciate it very much. They didn't appreciate much at all about Al. They thought he was nuts or something, which made it a little uncomfortable for me one day when they looked at me walking down the sidewalk and said, "You walk just like your uncle Al!"

I just loved the guy. He took Ronnie and me to Madison Square Garden; he took us downtown Manhattan to the merchant marine headquarters; he took us to see Ethel Merman in *Annie Get Your Gun* on Broadway; he bought us our first take-out Chinese food. He wasn't like most people in the family, who just settled in Pleasantville forever. He was an adventurer. My family would say all this negative stuff about him when he was off in India or somewhere, but I thought it was great! I'm not putting my family down; they just weren't educated enough and their view was very, very small. My mother often told me that my father would've been "so happy" if I'd been an accountant. But I couldn't do that. After a while, you wonder what's really important. You look at all the possibilities of what you want to do with your life and ask yourself, "Can I do *anything*?"

I knew one thing I could do for certain: I could act.

Shortly before my father died, when I gave up the football team to focus on acting and music, it made me happy. I remember getting my first real laugh in a high school play, and it was almost as significant as that first applause I heard way back in preschool. Now that my father was gone, I had even more reason to throw myself into the areas I loved and to work as hard as anyone ever could. I became an all-state timpanist. I entered one-act play competitions and won the best actor award three years in a row. No one had ever done that before! I don't know how I did it. I just did it! I'm certainly not an overachiever. I'm just a happy guy. That's who I am in my heart. I loved this stuff, and I wanted to be happy, so I set goals for myself that I thought would continue to make me happy—little things I'd try to achieve—and then I'd achieve them.

If there's one thing life had taught me it's that life can *end*. At any moment it can all go away. So what choice do you really have? You've gotta live!

Again, I attribute a lot of that outlook to my uncle Al. He inspired me to march to the beat of my own drummer, and that's exactly what I would do.

I shot up in height during my high school years. Maybe it was all the odd jobs I worked or just a change that came after puberty, but I lost all my "Tubber" weight too. My first girlfriend of significance was Martha Lois Meyer. She was a cheerleader. I was crazy about her. Acting, singing, music, and Martha—those were the things that mattered to me most, all through high school. To this day I still have great Martha memories.

As graduation drew closer, the pressure to think about the future started to build. *What am I going to do with my life?*

I had opportunities. A friend of mine was gonna get me a roofing job. There was good money in roofing! My family supported that choice wholeheartedly. I didn't really like heights, but no one seemed to take that into account. I had also been playing in a dance band on the side and making pretty good money doing that, but it didn't seem like steady enough work that I could make a career out of it. I never thought about going to college. No one in my family had gone to college, and I didn't take any college preparatory courses. It just didn't seem possible.

There was really only one thing I *wanted* to do, but no one I knew made a living as an actor. Judson Laire, an actor who played in one of the very first television series, *Mama*, lived in Pleasantville. I knew where he lived. I used to walk by his house wondering what he was up to, having no idea how he broke into the business or managed to get himself on TV. I had won all of those competitions. People told me I had talent. But I certainly didn't have movie-star looks. In many ways, acting didn't seem like a real career choice for me, either, even though it was the only thing I felt I knew how to do.

It was a daunting and frustrating time—especially when my girl-friend started asking what I was going to do with my life. Martha wanted me to get out of showbiz when I wasn't even in it yet. I wanted to act! She knew that. So what if I didn't know how to start? I didn't need discouragement. And her asking me about what I was going to do after graduation made it seem like she didn't understand me. I know she was thinking about marriage. In those days, getting married out of high school is what a lot of people did. But as our senior year progressed, I knew in my heart it wasn't going to happen.

But what *was* going to happen? For a while there, I was full of questions with absolutely no answers.

I should've had more faith. Wouldn't you know it? Before my senior year was up, God sent an angel my way—in the form of a college girl carrying flaming batons.

Shirley Ballard was her name. I was busy performing with my high school choir, doing some sort of big show at the White Plains County

Center, and Shirley was one of the other performers on the bill—a baton twirler who yelled, "Turn out the lights!" halfway through her act, as she lit her batons on fire and got the audience oohing and aahing. She was fabulous!

I didn't know Shirley, but she apparently knew me. She walked right up to me backstage at one point and introduced herself. "Allan? I go to Ithaca College, and I'm going with a guy from Pleasantville. Lou Gallo," she said.

I remembered Lou Gallo. He was a couple of years ahead of me in school. He was an actor too!

"He thinks you're a really great actor and that you should try to get a scholarship to go to Ithaca."

I had never even heard of Ithaca College. I never thought about going to school for acting. I dreamed about going to New York and getting in with Lee Strasberg and that whole crowd, but it all seemed so far away.

"A scholarship to college? For acting? For real?"

"Why not?" Shirley said. "Tell your counselor and see if they'll set up an audition."

Wow, I thought. *God sure works in mysterious ways.* Back at school, I did just what that flaming-baton-twirling young lady said to do. My guidance counselor wrote a letter to Ithaca College on my behalf, and they soon wrote back asking to see my transcripts. I thought that would be the end of it. I was pretty sure my transcripts would do me in, since I was a B student at best. But somehow word of my ambition got around to Walter Roberts, the head of a well-known children's theater company in Pleasantville. Walter had seen me perform in a play called *Captain Applejack,* and he liked me. Turns out he was a former professor at Ithaca. "I'll write them a letter," he said, and that's what he did! Next thing I knew, Ithaca wrote back and set up an appointment for me to come up and audition.

My good friend Jimmy Downey drove me up that day in his '33 Chevy. Because of those one-act competitions I'd done, I had a knack for putting stuff together that would pull at the heartstrings and show off my range—from slapstick comedy to tear-jerking drama. So I worked up the drunken porter scene from Shakespeare's *Macbeth*, and juxtaposed that with a bit from *Balcony Scene*, a new one-act play from Yale University about a guy sitting in a balcony and looking down at his own funeral. I had a lot of emotion to draw on for that one.

I did my best, I met some people, and I shook some hands. Some weeks later I was sitting on a swing in the woods with Martha when I saw my brother come running up the hill with a letter in his hand. "Allan! Allan!" he yelled.

"What? What is it?"

"The mail just came!" he said. "I couldn't wait! I opened the envelope. You got a scholarship!"

I could hardly believe it. I must've read that letter a dozen times. *I won the scholarship.* I actually did it! I was about to become the very first person in my family to go to college—and it happened because of my acting.

Just as I lost my "Tubber" weight in high school, I lost my boyish blond locks at college. It was incredible how fast that hair disappeared from my head. Luckily, on the college stage, it didn't matter. There were young guys playing senior men in lots of those plays. If anything, my early baldness was an asset! Ithaca College was fertile ground for me. I blossomed quickly and was given the chance to play all kinds of delicious, varied roles under the tutelage of some fabulous professors.

My favorite was a woman by the name of Beatrice MacLeod. (Now, there's a name you can't forget!) As a drama teacher, she knew how to bring out the best in me. I learned so much from her in my years there. But more than that, I think she was one of the smartest and most creative women I ever met. She was trained at Yale University, and her husband was the head of the psychology department at Cornell. I admired the way she gave of herself, as a teacher and as a human being. In fact, she gave me a leg up financially: she noticed me working as a server in the dining hall and knew I was a scholarship student who was struggling to find money to pay for books and living expenses, so she hired me to mow her lawns and trim hedges at her home. She was a very special lady.

The head of the drama department was named Eugene R. Wood, and he was quite a fellow too—directing us in plays by Chekov and Moliere, some real heavy stuff. He said of our class, "This is the best acting group we've ever had." And I don't think he was exaggerating. But the really fun thing is that whatever we were doing as a group, whatever my peers and I brought to the table, it got his juices churning again to get back on the stage himself. After we all moved on, so did he. He left the school to pursue his acting career anew. A couple of friends and I went to see him on stage in New York City a few years later, when he played a small role in *The Pajama Game* at City Center.

I don't believe in that awful saying, "Those who can, do; those who can't, teach." I don't think that's true at all. I think sometimes those who *can* do it very well, but they also want to pass it on and to help maneuver other people into being better. That's a talent in and of itself. I was fortunate to encounter many gifted teachers at Ithaca College.

I also made some great friends, and together we started writing and producing our own material. One year Ted Mack came up with *The Original Amateur Hour*, a television show that was like the *Star Search* or *America's Got Talent* of its day. My friend John Bartholomew Tucker and I put together a vaudeville act with Barbara Randall—a beautiful, smart, talented performer who had been named Miss Subways in New York City one time—and we called ourselves "The Sophisticates of Comedy." (We were teenagers! What did we know about sophistication?)

Anyway, I can't recall if we lost to a bird act or a dog act, but we came in second place. That was pretty encouraging stuff, and John and I would never forget it. In fact, with John's talents as a writer—he could write all kinds of songs and lyrics, almost anything, really—combined with my talent for interpretation, the two of us were convinced we could make it on our own. Sometime during our junior year we told ourselves, "Who needs college? Let's put together a vaudeville act and go hit the big time!"

So we did. We quit school. I spent some time in John's hometown in Pennsylvania and we started writing. We came up with this incredible vaudeville act. We were so excited! There was just one problem. As we went looking for theaters to put up our act, it suddenly hit us: vaudeville was dead. Nobody wanted to see it anymore, and none of the theaters were interested in hiring us.

Dejected, I decided to head back to school. The University Club of Pleasantville arranged to give me a loan, since I had (rather naively) given up my scholarship. But my friend John was instrumental in convincing me to do something very important when I went back. He convinced me to change my major from a bachelor of science degree in drama education to a straight-up performance degree—a bachelor of fine arts in drama.

He said, "Look. Everybody else is going for teaching. I know when you start out, if things don't go the way you want, you're going to teach. You'll have that to fall back on. Now, suppose you *don't* have that to fall back on. Then you'd be forced to stay in the game. To stay *in* there!"

It was very idealistic—but isn't that how you're supposed to be when you're young?

I thought about what John said and I went to my mother to ask if she would mind if I switched majors. "If that's what you want to do," she said, "do it." So I did.

I would think about that decision many times over the next few years, whenever I hit a rough patch. And believe me, there were plenty of rough patches. If I could have gone to teach, to make some steady income, would I have done it? I'll never know, because I didn't have the option. I had no choice but to stick it out.

I think that made a difference, and I'm thankful to John for that.

After all, I wasn't looking for a fallback career. I wanted to act. I wanted to be onstage. And I wanted it bad enough that I was not only willing but eager to do that crazy thing actors do—to go off into the great unknown, to the big city where actors either find their footing or get their hats handed to them on their way out the door. After donning my cap and gown and picking up that diploma, it was time to leave behind Ithaca and Pleasantville and everything I'd ever known.

Time to put myself to the test—to see if I could make it after all.

3

THE BIG APPLE

MANHATTAN WAS ONLY THIRTY MILES SOUTH of Pleasantville, but it might as well have been a million miles away. How do you find a job with all those millions of people? How do you find an apartment? I only had one "in" that I knew of, so I gave it a shot.

Vince Klemmer, a friend of mine who was a very good actor and looked a little like a young Kirk Douglas, had quit college in his second year to move to New York City. I heard he had landed a job as an electrician at Radio City Music Hall, so I gave him a call and said, "Vince, think you can help me out?" He said, "Yeah! Maybe I can get you a job as an usher."

Lo and behold, just like that, he did.

The only time I had been to Radio City was when I was young and my mom took Ronnie and me to see the *Christmas Spectacular*. We had lunch at the Horn and Hardart Automat. I had an egg salad sandwich. Then in high school, I cut school one day—the first and only time I ever did that—to see the *The Al Jolson Story* on that gorgeous big screen. Wow, was that something. Now I was going to work there, making a salary of thirty-four dollars a week! That sounded like a lot to me, but I had no idea how expensive New York City really was. I sure found out fast.

Vince needed a roommate, so I moved in with him and another guy, a pianist, way up on 71st and Central Park West. With three of us splitting the rent, we could almost afford it. Radio City is on 50th Street and Sixth Avenue, which runs up the middle of Manhattan. I couldn't afford to take the subway every day or I wouldn't have any money left at the end of the week. So I walked. Let me tell you, that's a *long* walk every day. So long that I'd have to stop to catch my breath every once in a while. For some reason, I always seemed to stop in front of this one particular men's shop on Sixth Avenue. It had a display in its window for Fruit of the Loom underwear: sixty-nine cents a pair—and I couldn't afford it.

I would stop and look at that underwear and think... *Someday.* (Now I go in and buy a six-pack, just like that! I've really made it, I tell you!)

It didn't take long before they promoted me to elevator operator at Radio City and raised my salary to thirty-seven dollars a week. And one day, who should step into my elevator but Lucille Ball and Desi Arnaz! I was speechless. I had to be speechless; I was working. I wasn't supposed to talk to people like that. But wow, what a thrill to be the guy to take them up in my elevator for their big movie premiere. To be standing inches away from two of the most famous people in the world was breathtaking.

I lived for those sorts of thrills, because let's face it, on that kind of salary, New York was a struggle. All I could afford to eat some days was a roll. The delis would let you take as much butter as you wanted, so I'd pile on the butter and make it a meal. I couldn't afford to get a sandwich from the Horn and Hardart Automat in Times Square, but the ketchup there was free. So like some of the other struggling actors, I learned to take some ketchup and mix it with hot water, which was also free, and to savor that tasty "ketchup soup." Other days, when I just couldn't take it anymore, I'd buy myself a hot dog. I'd pile on the mustard and relish and onions and sauerkraut, whatever they had to offer on the side of the hot dog cart, as much as I could, knowing it would be my meal for the whole day. Man, if hot dogs made me happy before, you should have seen how happy they made me *then*. The hot dog vendors must've thought I was a crazy person the way I oohed and aahed and mmmed!

It really didn't feel like that big of a struggle at the time. I was young. I was happy to get to work in that magnificent building. I was thrilled to go to work each day and be near so much talent, including those beautiful Rockettes—even if they hardly ever took a second glance at the bald kid working the elevator.

The problem was that agents weren't giving me a second glance either. I went all over town looking for an agent, but no one was interested in representing a young man with a bald head. I had no idea what a problem it would be. Back at Ithaca, I played older guys all the time. But here, in the real world? Older guys played older guys, and no one wrote parts for a twenty-two-year-old who looked like me.

I knew what I needed to do. I needed to buy myself a hairpiece.

Hairpieces were something special. A good one cost a lot of money. I knew that. I kept putting money aside, but after saving for what felt like forever, I could only come up with a measly twenty-five dollars. My roommate Vince, who was such a great guy and was doing pretty well for himself as an electrician, saw me struggling. He knew how badly I needed that hairpiece, and would you believe he gave me a hundred dollars out of his own pocket to go get some hair? "I can't have a roommate with no hair anymore. I'm sick of it!" he told me. Ha! Combined with my own savings, I was sure I could afford any hairpiece I wanted. I was so grateful and excited.

I ran right down to a place called Senz Brothers, somewhere between 50th and 60th Streets, and climbed the narrow wooden staircase to the second floor. I was greeted by a man with a shaved head, which was startling. You didn't see many fully shaved heads in those days.

"Hello there," he said. "I'm Ziggy. Can I help you with something?"

I swear, for the rest of my life, anytime I've gone into a hair place there's a guy name Ziggy. Anyway, I said, "You sell hair. I need hair!" So Ziggy walked around and looked at my head and said, "Well, I tell you, it'll cost between five hundred and six hundred dollars."

I was shocked. "All I have is a hundred and twenty-five dollars," I told him, and he basically replied, "Tough. Come back when you have five hundred!"

I explained that I worked at Radio City making thirty-seven dollars a week, and that I couldn't get an agent because of my bald head, and that it would take me forever to save that kind of money. But he wouldn't budge. So I left, dejected.

As I was walking down the stairs, I heard, "Hey, kid. Come back up here."

I turned around and followed Ziggy to the back of the shop where he pulled open a curtain to a room with a long table, and on that table was a block with a hairpiece. He said, "Sit down there." He was very bossy. I sat down and he put it on my head. "What do you think about that?"

I swear it was like looking into a magic mirror. *Are you kidding?* "It looks fantastic!" I said. (To tell you the truth, if it had looked like a bird's nest it wouldn't have mattered to me. It was *hair!*)

"If you want it," he said, "you can have it for a hundred twenty-five."

"How come?" I said. "You told me five hundred."

"The truth is, somebody came in this morning to get a new one. He didn't have any use for this. He left it here. So I'll let you have it for a hundred twenty-five."

I pulled that money out so fast. I thought, *Oh boy! Wait 'til the Rockettes see me now!*

I was curious about something, though. Before I left I said, "Ziggy, if you don't mind me asking, who did this hair belong to?"

"I can't tell you that!" he said. "That's private information." I shrugged my shoulders and started to leave, and two seconds later he said, "You really want to know? It belonged to Andre Baruch."

"No kidding!" I said. Andre Baruch was a famous radio personality in New York who was known for his deep, booming voice. I swear to you, from that moment forward, I spoke with a deeper voice whenever I wore that hairpiece.

Decades later, I told the story of my secondhand hair on *The Tonight Show*. A week later, I got a call on the set of *The Love Boat*. "Gavin, there's a phone call for you." I asked who it was. "Somebody named Baruch?" I thought, *Wow!* I picked up the phone and there was that big, booming voice: "Gavin, this is Andre Baruch!" I said, "Oh, what an honor for you to call me." And he said, "Bea and I are in town now, and I'm wondering: Would you be interested in another hairpiece?" We laughed and chatted, and he invited me down to Florida. He and his wife, Bea Wain, who was a major singer during the big band era, had a radio show down in Florida, all those years later. The whole thing was just a hoot.

Anyway, that was that. I now had hair.

Coincidence or not, life changed pretty quickly for me after that. For one thing, I caught the eye of one of those Rockettes!

St. Patrick's Cathedral sponsored an Easter breakfast at the Waldorf Astoria in those days. I had been to mass many times at St. Patrick's since moving to New York, but for some reason my mother thought it was important for me to go to that Easter breakfast. "I don't know, Mom. I don't really have money to spend on something like that," I told her.

"Well, I'll loan you the money," she said, and she did. She insisted that I go. To this day I'm not sure why, but I took that $1.25 and bought a ticket. I went to mass by myself, received holy Communion, and then walked over to the Waldorf. My ticket put me up on the third-level balcony in the Waldorf's grand ballroom, but there weren't any reserved seats. The place was packed! Finally I saw a couple of empty chairs at the end of one table, and I recognized some of the girls who were sitting there. They were dancers at Radio City.

The Rockettes did a number in those days where they all came out in a big circle, and the announcer said their names and where they were from. Lo and behold, I recognized this one beautiful brunette from that show. I could hear the announcer's voice in my head: ". . . and now, Joan Rootvik . . . Rootie! From Seattle, Washington!" There was a seat open right next to her, and for a moment, I hesitated. I honestly thought she was far too beautiful for me to sit next to. She was wearing this Grecian goddess sort of dress, and it was purple—one of my favorite colors. She was stunning. But I finally got up the courage and asked if that seat was open. She smiled and said it was.

She was kind. She was gracious. If I hadn't already been taken by her looks, I would've been taken by her personality alone. I was just *taken* by her. Best of all? She laughed at my stories.

The two of us started going together. We couldn't really go to the movies or anything like that. There wasn't enough money between us to do very much at all. But we would see each other, and walk together, and sometimes we'd save up enough money to go to a little restaurant nearby where some of the other dancers would go.

I fell in love, and the more I learned about her, the more perfect it all seemed. Her father's name was George; my father's name was George. Her mother's name was Rose Margaret; my mother's name was Margaret. They were all Catholics. It was just perfect.

She didn't seem to care that I was an elevator operator. She saw something in me. She believed in me. I made her laugh! I was thrilled.

As the months stretched on, I tried not to let the lack of food or the lack of agent bother me. I fed myself in other ways. Nourishing the soul, as it were. I took acting classes. I landed a couple of small parts off-Broadway, performing in front of tiny audiences, but audiences nonetheless. Rootie came to see me and was a big supporter of everything I did. I fell more in love with her by the day. And I wanted to be able to do right by her.

I realized I needed to make more money in order for us to have a future together. So even though it would take me away from the New York stage, I auditioned for a road company. I wound up getting cast on a tour of *Androcles and the Lion*. I don't remember what the salary was, but it was significantly more money than I was making at Radio City. So I quit that job, kissed Rootie good-bye for a short while, and hit the road. It was a children's show that toured to schools. We had to set up and perform at seven in the morning. We had six actors all crushed into a station wagon with a trailer off the back to hold our gear. I remember at one point the trailer broke loose, and the head of the lion costume wound up smack in the middle of the highway. Can you imagine what people must have thought?

Coincidentally, I played the part of a captain in that show—only this captain wasn't a likable character. Kids hated him! They threw stuff at me. They booed when I came onstage. I heard more booing during that road trip than I heard for the entire rest of my career.

I pinched my pennies along every inch of the road during that *Androcles and the Lion* tour—washing my shirts in the sink instead of taking them to the laundry, staying in rather than going out carousing, splitting the cost of hotel rooms by only paying for one of us and then sneaking in when the manager wasn't looking. By the time it was over, I was able to pay back all of my student loan debt and put some money aside for Rootie and me to start a life together.

I was glad to get back to Rootie and to my beloved New York City when that tour was over. But as I jumped back into the grind of auditions and agent-seeking, things still weren't working for me. Getting the hairpiece had given me the confidence and ability to at least get seen. But there was something more: I felt as if my name was getting in the way of my success. "Allan" just wasn't strong enough. It wasn't memorable. It didn't have a nice ring to it. And "See" was always confusing to people, especially in the multicultural city of New York. I had always been told that "See" was a Chippewa Indian name and that my dad had Chippewa blood. But later in life my mother said that wasn't true. So even *I* didn't know where that name really came from. I went through life getting responses like, "See what? See this?" I'd go to pick up something I ordered at a store and the cashier would say,

"Oh, with a name like See, I thought you'd be Chinese." So I finally said, "Enough."

I was hanging out with a friend, Jan Peters, and his wife, Rita, one night, and we started bouncing names around. (Jan had changed his name too. He was born Irwin Padolsky.) I was really determined to do this. I was pretty sure I knew what I wanted my last name to be: MacLeod. I loved it. I thought so fondly of my Ithaca drama teacher, Beatrice MacLeod, and all that she did for me and so many other students. It just felt right to me. Coming up with a first name was a little more difficult, though. For a moment I considered taking Jan's old name, to honor him, but "Irwin MacLeod" didn't sound quite right. We tossed a few names around, but nothing sounded right with "MacLeod"—until I mentioned an old TV show I'd seen in college, an episode of a series called *Climax*. It was a powerful show, starring Jean-Pierre Aumont as a father who bragged about his son named Gavin. There was a twist at the end, where it became clear that every brag the father had uttered had been made up! It was moving and dramatic, and there was something strong about that kid's name, which also happened to be the name of the episode: "Gavin."

I spoke it out loud. "Gavin MacLeod." My friends said it, too, in deep, Andre Baruch–like radio announcer voices: "And now, the star of the show . . . Gavin MacLeod!" It sounded great! So that was that.

In those days, you had to post proposed name changes in the newspaper and then wait a couple of months to make sure there were no objectors before you could make it legal. I had no objectors—except for one. When I told my mother, she said, "Your father will turn over in his grave." At that point in my life, I said to myself, "I'm not gonna feel guilty about that."

My new name gave me a new start. I felt refreshed. Reborn, almost. At least in my career. I felt like I was ready to take on the world. "Hello, world. Meet Gavin MacLeod!"

I also started a brand-new job at a place that would put me closer to all the action on Broadway: Jim Downey's Steak House on Forty-Fourth and Eighth—a theater district hot spot that was so famous in its day, they brought it back to life sixty years later on an episode of *Mad Men*. I worked as a cashier there, where many of the big producers and directors and even stars would pop in for a drink, a bite, and maybe some deal making. How did I get that job over hundreds of other starving actors looking for work? As they say, it's all about who you know. The owner, Mr. Downey, was Jimmy Downey's father! Jimmy, my high school buddy who drove me to my scholarship audition at Ithaca College in his '33 Chevy, was living in New York now and working for his dad. When we were growing up, Mr. Downey owned a couple of restaurants upstate, but this was the big time. I mean, *big*! His place was a West Side version of Sardi's. *Everyone* went to Downey's.

I wound up moving into Jimmy's apartment, just a block and a half from the restaurant. Now I was living and working right in the thick of it, walking past all the theaters every day, surrounded by the hustle and bustle of Broadway—everything I wanted to be a part of. Life was great!

Rootie and I were head over heels for each other. I was twenty-five years old, and I felt in my heart that we were meant to be together. So I popped the question, and she said yes. We married in 1955 in a nuptial mass at St. Malachy's, The Actors Chapel, right in the heart of the theater district. I'll never forget looking down at my grandfather, Jimmy Shea, in the front row. He was crying and crying. He had quit drinking by then, but he had always been a real emotional guy. Maybe that's where I get the tears from. I cry at the drop of a hat! Always have. I remember in one of my first nightclub acts, I sang that famous Stephen Sondheim song "Anyone Can Whistle." When I sang the line, ". . . whistle for me," I heard a whistle from a little boy in the audience and I just lost it. Right there onstage! I cry at movies too. *An Affair to Remember* with Cary Grant and Deborah Kerr—I cried like a baby when I first saw that. When that movie plays nowadays, I cry at the opening credits just knowing what's gonna happen.

The wedding was spectacular. I wore my hairpiece and looked handsome as could be, and Rootie was gorgeous. She always was, but on that day—*wow*!

In addition to both of our families, the church was filled with my buddies from college, friends from my acting classes, and our pals from Radio City Music Hall. The wedding made all the New York papers, too, with a photo and everything, because Rootie was a Rockette. (Certainly not because I was an ex-usher and elevator operator. That wouldn't have made the news.) They even put the wedding announcement in the *New York Times*. I was moving up!

My college buddy Ron Pedrone was my best man, and Jimmy Downey was my head usher. Our friend Marta Curro, who was a big, tall dancer, caught the bouquet. She wound up marrying the song-and-dance man Jerry Orbach (who would be known later in life for his long run as a detective on *Law & Order*).

Rootie and I planned a honeymoon trip to New England, but we weren't sure we were going to make it. I didn't have a driver's license! I was living in Manhattan. I never needed to drive. But my mother agreed to loan me her car so we could take a proper honeymoon. Weeks before the wedding, one of my brother's friends took me out for driving lessons. Then I went and took the test—and I passed. But they mailed your license to you in those days. Two days before the wedding we thought we'd have to change plans and just take the train out to Long Island to start our life together. But luckily, with just a day to spare, my license arrived. We were good to go!

As Rootie and I drove out of Manhattan, the whole group in front of the church cheered. Secretly, I think they were praying, "Lord Jesus, protect them!" It was the first time I had ever driven on my own.

We wound our way northeast to a place called the White Turkey Inn, in Connecticut, where I spent my wedding night picking rice out of my hairpiece. Well, part of my wedding night anyway. (*Wink, wink.*)

We wound up driving all the way up through Vermont and New Hampshire in the days that followed—some of the most beautiful countryside either of us had ever seen. We were two kids in love and on top of the world.

Rootie and I moved into an apartment on Ninth Avenue at 54th

Street—across from a bus depot, where they fixed the buses. There was a lot of noise at night, but we didn't mind because we were in love, living in the city of our dreams, surrounded by everything we wanted to be a part of.

It was around that same time when I landed my first part on a TV show. It wasn't much of a part, but it was on TV and in a show I had heard of! I played one of a group of people picketing on the street, protesting something or other in a scene for the show *Lamp unto My Feet*, a spiritual program that aired on Sundays on CBS. (Kind of interesting that my first TV show was something of a spiritual nature. Foretelling, perhaps?) It was a union part, and I remember how good it felt to sign up for the union under my new name: Gavin MacLeod.

The union categorized how you got paid by the number of lines you had, and I think I had a "five and under" part, which meant I had fewer than five lines. Well, guess who else was there in that same group of fictional protestors, playing the very same kind of part? Billy Dee Williams. He and I have had a few laughs about that whenever we've run into each other through the years. There we were, two young actors trying to catch a break, taking whatever gig came along.

An actor's life is tough. You get a gig like that on a TV show, and you think you've got it made. You're flying high! And then nothing else comes of it. I did some other theater work during that time, and every bit of it was a great learning experience, but it wasn't really leading anywhere. I came to New York because I wanted to be on Broadway, like all of those amazing actors I saw when my uncle Al used to take Ronnie and me down to the city. I tried everything I could think of to get noticed.

With some of the money I made at Downey's I enrolled in more acting classes, including one class led by Frank Corsaro, a disciple of Lee Strasberg himself (who of course was one of the greatest acting coaches who ever lived). Frank was only a few years older than I was, but he was already causing quite a stir in New York, and he gave me a huge boost of confidence on the first day of class. We worked on a scene from *Death of a Salesman*, and as we were walking out of the building he said to me, "I really like the stuff you're doing." He liked it so much, he said he would consider using me as an understudy in a new play he was directing—a play called *Johnny Had a Yo-Yo* that was on a fast-track for Broadway.

"Wow!" I said. "Thank you!"

After the class was through, though, I never heard from him about that role. I'd see him at Downey's now and then, but I didn't want to ask him about it. I was honored just to have that compliment in my back pocket. *Maybe at some point he'll remember he said it*, I thought. In the meantime, I just kept doing what I was doing.

After all my days of living on buttered rolls and ketchup soup, Mr. Downey made sure I ate at least one square meal a day at his restaurant—even though I only ate Jell-O on Fridays. I wanted to stay slim. I needed to be in shape. I had heard that Jell-O was made from ground-up horse hooves and was good for you! That's what I'd been told, anyway.

I filled myself up just by being around those talented producers and directors, and even some of the biggest names in the world who walked through those doors. In fact, who should walk into Downey's one afternoon but Marilyn Monroe.

Marilyn had come to town to study with Lee Strasberg at the Actors Studio. Eli Wallach, the great character actor, was a regular at Downey's, and he and his wife, Ann Jackson, had taken Marilyn under their wing. I was standing at the register, and I looked up and saw this lovely creature standing at the door with Eli, with a sweater on her shoulders, and a blouse cut down to there—she was wearing no makeup, just a little powder, and I said, "Whoa! That's Marilyn Monroe." They came in and sat at the booth right across from me. I kept looking and looking until finally Eli said, "Come on over, Gavin! Meet Marilyn Monroe." I said, "Oh, what a pleasure to meet you. Are you enjoying yourself in the city?" She replied, softly, "It's different. Everybody's been such a help to me."

I was flummoxed, of course. I said, "You're so sweet!" And then I didn't know what else to say. "Well, I've got to get to work. But can I tell you something?"

She said, "Sure."

I said, "I'm gonna call all my friends tonight and tell them I met Marilyn Monroe!" She laughed at that.

To think: I made Marilyn Monroe laugh.

Sometimes I had to pinch myself. *How in the world did this chubby kid from Pleasantville wind up living and working in the heart of Broadway, in a job where he gets to talk to Marilyn Monroe?* It was mind-boggling.

As fun as it was, though, I started to wonder, *When am I gonna get my big break?*

It was 1956 and I still didn't have an agent. Even with the hair! I went to auditions. I paid my dues. Almost four years had gone by since I moved to the city. That was as long as I'd spent in high school. As long as I'd spent in college. Wasn't it time to graduate from a cashier job and bit parts?

Twenty years later, Kander and Ebb would write a song about the showbiz-dreamer experience, which a lot of young actors and performers like me went through: "New York, New York," with that powerful line: "If I can make it there, I'll make it anywhere."

As optimistic and happy as I was, there was a little part of me that wasn't sure: *Am I gonna make it here?*

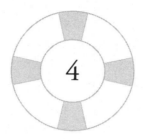

4

BROADWAY, BABY!

WHENEVER WE COULD SAVE UP ENOUGH MONEY, Rootie and I would go to the theater. We wanted to see *everything*! And it was a glorious time on Broadway, with so much new ground being broken on the stage. One of the most unforgettable shows of the era was *A Hatful of Rain*, in 1956, starring Ben Gazzara, Anthony Franciosa, and Shelley Winters. As I recall, Walter Winchell called it the best-acted play in New York in ten years. It was astounding, and quite an emotional experience. It was a play that dealt with morphine addiction, and it was really quite dark. I had never seen a play about junkies before. It was eye-opening, to say the least.

Well, guess what? That play was the very same play that was originally called *Johnny Had a Yo-Yo*, directed by Frank Corsaro. The same play he had mentioned I might be good for as an understudy many months earlier. *I sure wish he would remember what he said to me*, I thought as we exited that theater.

That was a magnificent time in New York for my wife and me. She got pregnant. We were so excited about starting a family.

I also knew it wasn't going to cut it for me to keep working as a cashier. I needed to make something happen in my career, pronto.

Seeing the shows, going to acting classes, working at Downey's—I was in the thick of it, man, and I heard things. I knew things. I had my ear to the ground. I think that's important no matter what industry you're trying to break into. The thing was, *A Hatful of Rain* was getting so much acclaim, and its actors were winning over so many fans and critics, the cast wound up getting raided by Hollywood. Anthony Franciosa was picked up for the movies, which meant Harry Guardino—another talented actor, who was his understudy—was moving up into Anthony's role. I knew that meant they would have to find another young actor to fill Harry's spot, and I wanted that part badly. The character was called Man in Hallway, and he only had one line: "Back up, Johnny! Back up like a mule!" At that point I had never been around drugs, never tried a drug in my life. But I knew I could play that junkie character. I just knew it.

Frank Corsaro walked into Downey's one day, and I decided to speak up. "God, give me strength!" I prayed. It was a big risk. He could have dismissed me entirely. He could have forgotten all about what he said. Maybe he didn't really mean it and was just being nice to me all those months ago. By speaking up, there was a chance that I could have been put down, humiliated even. But I didn't let those feelings stop me. "Frank, can I talk to you?" I said. "I understand that Tony is leaving, Harry is moving up, and you need someone for the show. Remember you told me—"

"Oh, yes, yes!" he said. "I'll talk to Jay Julien, the producer, and arrange a reading for you."

That was all it took. Lo and behold, he set up a reading for me that Saturday, at the theater where my wife and I had seen the show. It was the first backstage experience I ever had on Broadway. I was about to step out on the very same set where I had seen Shelley Winters and Tony Franciosa do their stuff—*wow!*

The amazing thing was that stepping out onto that stage felt as natural as could be. I was nervous, sure. But I had worked hard enough to feel like that stage was where I belonged.

My audition was strong. I could feel it in my bones. I was standing downstage, in the part of the set that looked like a kitchen. It was a lower level, and then the living room was up on a bit of a platform, which unfortunately I didn't notice until it was too late. Right after I got up under those lights and did my thing, I turned around to walk backstage and tripped and fell over that step. I bounced right up and brushed myself off, but I was embarrassed. I thought for sure I had blown the audition. There were so many people from the Actors Studio auditioning opposite me. I was still such a newcomer, and now I looked like a klutz. *And with a hairpiece, no less.* I tried not to be too hard on myself. But I was. As I left the theater, I shrugged my shoulders and told myself I was glad that I gave it a shot.

I went to work that night and was standing behind the cash register when the producer, Jay Julien, walked over and said, "Gavin? Kid, you've got your first Broadway show." At Downey's restaurant! Behind the register! That's how I found out I got my first Broadway play—and a salary of ninety dollars a week!

I could hardly believe my good fortune.

I ran over to Radio City to tell my wife as soon as I could. The doctors said it was okay for her to keep working even though she was pregnant, so there she was, night after night, kicking those legs sky-high. On my way in, I bumped into my friend Vince, my old roommate who gave me the money to get the hairpiece. Without that hairpiece, I couldn't have gotten the part! I was so excited to tell him. "You're not gonna guess what happened. I'm going on Broadway in *A Hatful of Rain*!" I said. He replied, "Eh, they're gonna close soon, anyway."

I said, "What's wrong with you?!" I wasn't gonna let anyone rain on my parade. I went and found Rootie, and she was thrilled. She was so excited for me. For *us*! This felt like the start of everything. Like the big time.

The fact was, all I wanted to do was land a Broadway play. I told myself a hundred times, "If I can just land one Broadway play, I'll be happy. That's all I want."

Of course, God had a lot more in store for me than I could have known at that time. There was a whole journey ahead of me, bigger than anything I could even dream about.

In the last few months of *A Hatful of Rain*'s run on Broadway, just before they took it out on the road, the cast went through a few more changes— including the addition of one soft-spoken guy who would make quite an impact in the world.

They read a lot of people to replace Ben Gazzara when he left to do his first film, *The Strange One*. Ben was the toast of New York at that time, the new sensational young actor, and the producers wanted some- one with enough presence to fill his shoes. Wouldn't you know it? Of all the people who read for the part of Johnny Pope, the one who got it was a newcomer—a guy named Steven McQueen. (That's how he was billed in the show too: "Steven." He wouldn't change it to "Steve" until he, too, got drafted out to Hollywood.)

Frank Corsaro really saw something in McQueen, and I was lucky enough to have all of my rehearsals with him as he was getting ready. My wife asked, "What's he like?" I said, "Well, he drives a motorcycle. He parks it right in the back of the stage door. He's kind of friendly. But I tell you, when we're playing a scene and I'm down left and he's down right, I can't hear him! When we get close, though, he's fascinating. Just fascinating. He's got something going on." Little did I know, close-ups were where he was really going to shine—on the big screen.

McQueen didn't last that long in the play, and he'd be the first one to tell you that live theater wasn't his strong suit. But my mother, whom I got tickets for whenever I could, saw three people play that leading role: Ben Gazzara, Steve McQueen, and Peter Mark Richman (who replaced

Steve after he left). I asked her, "Mom, who did you like the best of those boys?" And she said, "That McQueen boy." I was surprised. I said, "Could you even hear him?" She said, "A little." I asked, "Well, what was it you liked about him?"

Her response said it all: "I don't know. I just wanted to put my arms around him." Steve McQueen had a vulnerability that makes certain actors shine.

Broadway's a funny place. As I learned the ropes, I found out that the curtain puller made more money than some of us actors on the stage—including me. He worked two theaters that were right near each other, running back and forth between them on the same nights, so he got paid by both shows! That blew me away. Here I was putting in all this work and practice, and the guy who opened and closed the curtains made more dough. I wasn't in this for the money, though. The reward was bigger than money. Standing there, hearing that applause on Broadway? It's like taking a shot of B12. There's nothing like it.

I basked in the warmth of that applause for a good couple of months before tragedy struck. My wife lost the baby. She was pretty far along. But one day, she started having pains. Rootie was never one to complain, so I called the doctor, and they told us to get to the hospital. They put her in a ward with a few other people, with nothing but thin curtains between the beds. At one point, Rootie asked me if I could close the window. She said she felt cold. I looked around, and the window wasn't open. It wasn't cold in that room at all. Something was wrong. Suddenly she felt pains again, and I ran to get the nurse. She called in another nurse, and then another, and suddenly they pulled the curtain closed so I couldn't see anything.

There weren't any screams. I didn't know what was happening. But when they opened the curtain I saw a metal pan—and blood. I couldn't believe it. The doctor had heard a heartbeat. We thought everything was okay. They didn't have ultrasounds and all the technology they have today. I felt lost. So did Rootie, of course. We were crushed, and we cried in each other's arms.

The doctor recommended that she have a hysterectomy at that point, but Rootie refused. We wanted kids. We had to try again. I had dreamed of having four kids, ever since I was in high school. I don't know why, but I just envisioned myself as the father of four children. No matter how painful that loss had been, we both insisted that we would try again.

It was the second time in my life that I'd been affected so deeply and closely by death. Finding the strength to go on isn't easy. I spent a lot of time in church. It was the only place I knew to find some solace. I guess being dragged along by my mother as a kid had instilled something important in me.

By the grace of God, we both got through it. We were young and idealistic, and Rootie was so brave. We weren't going to give up. Rather than let myself fall into a depression, or to think that life as I knew it was over, or to give up on my dreams, I found a new strength. A strength that once again fired me up to *live*. To go after my dreams even more than before. To not let anything stop me.

My friend Vince was right about *A Hatful of Rain*: they were getting ready to close it. I got to enjoy that Broadway run for about six months before they closed up shop and took that show on the road. They asked me to go on the road, too, but I turned them down. I didn't want to leave my wife for so long. They understood, and they found another actor to take my place. It was just a few performances in, though, when Frank Corsaro himself called me from the road: "Gavin, this guy can't cut it. I'm pleading with you to please go on the road. Do me a favor."

I said, "Well, you certainly did me a favor giving me my first show." I talked to Rootie about it. She had gone back to dancing after she recovered, and she said I should do it. She knew it would be good for my career and ultimately good for both of us—even if it meant sacrificing our being together in the short term.

So off I went. I took the train out of Grand Central Station, headed for Chicago. At dinnertime I found myself sitting in the dining car with Harry Guardino. There was a red rose on our table, and when I looked at that rose, it struck me like a bolt of lightning. It happened just as the train approached Pleasantville. I could hardly believe it! I looked out the window and looked and looked, until finally I saw it: that little hill behind our old apartment where I used to stand and watch the train go by when I was just a kid.

Holy smokes! I thought. *I'm actually starting to achieve some of my dreams!*

We were on the road for about seven months in *A Hatful of Rain.* A young actress named Diane Ladd joined the cast at one point. And when Peter Mark Richmond left with his wife, Helen, Ben Gazzara came back to the show and toured with us. The rotation of actors and the nature of a road tour allowed me to understudy different parts and to wind up playing some of the bigger parts in different cities. Because I had the hairpiece, I could get away with playing the Man in Hallway role, and then step into one of the bigger junkie roles too. The audience didn't recognize me at all. It was fabulous! And there was something about being a young bald guy that made me believable in those junkie roles. I don't know why audiences think junkies should be bald, but I was a hit everywhere we went.

For me, traveling to all of those different cities gave me a chance to see some beautiful sights too—including some stunning churches. I loved feeling the presence of God in those magnificent buildings. Some of the other guys in the show patronized other sorts of establishments in each city on the tour. There was a lot of carousing going on, and the fact that they would bring different women back to the hotel rooms we shared made for some awkward moments. I learned how to pretend to be fast asleep pretty quickly! I called home to my wife whenever I could and made the most of every moment I had on that stage.

One of the biggest thrills was getting the chance to play in Los Angeles. We had a lot of directors and producers come to see us, and the energy you receive as an actor in Hollywood is something else. In fact, during our run at a theater called the Huntington Hartford, I received an offer to go play the part of another junkie in a movie directed by

André de Toth—the director of *House of Wax*, *The Bounty Hunter*, and more. I was astonished. There was just one problem: I couldn't get out of the play. I had a contract. Not to mention I'm a loyal guy. I wasn't going to abandon Frank Corsaro after all he'd done for me. I simply wouldn't do that. As badly as I wanted to take that part, the timing just wasn't right.

When the road tour finally closed in Boston, I couldn't get that movie offer out of my mind, though. I got home to New York and I told my wife, "I think I have some action on the West Coast."

5

HURRY FOR
HOLLYWOOD

AFTER ALL THAT TIME, AFTER ALL OF THAT EFFORT, after getting my big break, I still couldn't get an agent in New York—all because of my bald head. A lot of people don't understand what a struggle showbiz can be, even after it seems like you've "made it." At first it made me sick to my stomach. I thought, *What kind of a business is this? I'm on Broadway, and I still can't get an agent?*

It was time to try something new. With California dreams rattling around my head, I started asking around to see if anyone I knew had any good contacts on the West Coast. Rosemary, a dancer who had been a roommate with my wife, was going with a guy named George, who said, "I know an agent in California named Lou Irwin. I'll call him. He handles the Ritz Brothers and people like that. I'll call him!" So he did. I flew out there, and I rented a car, and I was sitting in the waiting area at Lou Irwin's office when I first met an actor named Ted Knight—yes, the very same Ted Knight I wound up working with on *The Mary Tyler Moore Show* in the 1970s. This was way back in 1957! He was just another actor trying to get work, just like me. He had already been in Hollywood for a while, though. We started talking, and he insisted that I needed to get a business manager. "Business manager? I don't have any money!" I said. "Neither do I!" he said. "But I've got a business manager . . ."

Ted was like my big brother, right from the start. It marked the beginning of a lifelong friendship.

Oh, and guess what? After all those agents dismissed me in New York City, Lou Irwin, the very first agent I saw in LA, took me on as a client right away. He liked my credentials, he said. You know what else he liked? The fact that I carried my hairpiece in a box when I went to see him. To him, the fact that I could play two very different looks, either with my hairpiece or without, could potentially get me in the door for some interesting character work.

"Great!" I said. I could hardly believe it. He saw my bald head as an asset. After all the rejection I'd faced, that was quite a turnaround for me.

While I was out there on that trip, inching closer and closer to thinking that Hollywood might be the town for me after all, I went to see a friend who knew a lot about the business. "Gavin," he said, "the most important thing when you're out here is that people have got to see you. They're about to open *A Hatful of Rain* at the Players' Ring Gallery Theater in West Hollywood, and I know that they're not satisfied with the guy playing Mother. Why don't you go see 'em?"

I had understudied for the part of the junkie named Mother on Broadway, and then taken that show out on the road for months. I could do that role, piece of cake. Still, I said to him, "I've been in that play for a year and a half. I don't know." He insisted it was worth it, so I called the producers and went down there. To my delight, they had actually seen me play the role at The Hartford, when I was on tour. They were excited to have me come by even before I got there. So I did a couple of lines and they said, "Okay. We open Tuesday night. Can you do it?"

It was almost too easy. Almost too good to be true. I said yes, and we talked about rehearsal times, and suddenly I found myself onstage with Robert Blake, Brian Hutton, Jocelyn Brando, Lee Farr, and Al Lettieri—all of these brilliant actors who would go on to do big, big things.

So that was that. My wife and I moved to Hollywood.

It's funny how people in your hometown, your family, like to stay where they are, and they want you to stay too. My mother was so nervous about me moving to California. She didn't think anyone could be an actor full-time. As if it weren't a real job. Or maybe it just wasn't possible for someone from our family. A lot of people have that self-doubt: "No one from our family could ever do that." Well, why not? I could never understand what holds someone back. Why can't someone go after his dreams? At least give it a shot, you know? There's no one type of person or one type of family that gets to have all the success in life. There's no rule that says you can't be a successful actor because of your background, whatever that background might be. I assured her I had an agent and everything was gonna be all right.

Moms worry. It's just in their nature, I suppose. But I thought back to that chance I had to get a job as a roofer after high school. I remember thinking, *So I'm gonna put things on the roof?* I would jump off the roof from boredom! I *had* to go to New York. I *had* to chase my dream. Some people are happy being roofers. People are happy being a lot of things. My instinct told me roofing wasn't for me, and look where following that instinct took me: Hollywood. After only a few short years of trying.

I tell you, I was so grateful for the opportunities. Right from the start.

I suppose that sense of gratitude is why I've never been competitive with other actors. Whenever I walked into an audition, I was determined to do the best I could do, and that's all, knowing, *Hey, if somebody else gets the part, that's okay. I'm gonna get my thing someday.* And I did. More than I ever imagined.

In fact, my friend was right: acting in that Players' Ring production of *A Hatful of Rain* gave me just the visibility I needed. My agent could send people down to see me. It made a big difference. Fortuitously enough, a lot of television shows that had been shot in New York were relocating to Hollywood in those days, and it wasn't long after Rootie and I settled in California when I got my first steady TV gig. You'll never guess where? At Desilu Productions—Lucille Ball and Desi Arnaz's production company. Five years after I'd been so thrilled to give them a ride in my elevator at Radio City, here I was, an actor on their ever-evolving slate of TV shows. I didn't get to work with Lucy or Desi directly, but to think I was now working for their company? *Wow.* And I worked a lot. Want to know why? Because of my bald head.

They produced *The Sheriff of Cochese, Whirlybirds,* and *U.S. Marshalls*—I did all those shows. Because I didn't have hair, *and* I had hair in a box, I could play a young guy in one show, and then take off the hairpiece, change my clothes, and play a totally different guy in another show. The audience never caught on, because I looked so different with and without hair.

We shot all those half-hour shows in two and a half days each. It was a workout as an actor, I'll tell you, jumping from one completely different role to another from day to day.

It was also there that I met and worked with a talented young actress who would become a lifelong friend: Marion Ross—who would eventually be known far and wide as "Mrs. C" from *Happy Days.*

Desilu was doing *The Walter Winchell File,* which was a hot show at that time, based on crime stories that famed gossip columnist Walter Winchell had covered while working as a journalist in New York City. I went in and picked up the script—there was the part of a bartender, and then there was the part of a young guy picking up women in a bar and taking them back, molesting them, stealing from them, and killing them. I figured I was going in to read for the bartender. So I went in and met Desi's "henchman," the guy who did all of Desi's dirty work. He said, "You want to read?" I said, "Yeah!" So I started to read the bartender. And he said, "No, no. You're here for the lead. I know all the other things you've done for us, so this is a courtesy thing." I said, "Oh! So with my hair!" I put on my hair and got that part. Even though I was playing what's referred to as a "heavy," this criminal who did terrible things, I couldn't help but infuse that character with a little bit of me. It's a strange thing, and I say this not to be boastful but because I've never understood exactly what it is about me that makes audiences react this way: even when I'm playing a really terrible character, there's something about me that audiences still like. It's the strangest thing. But it worked for me in Hollywood, and this was one of the first instances where it really took off.

The studio got so much mail from that one show that they brought me back for another one. And in the other one, I played a John Garfield kind of character—also with the hair. They told me, "You're going to be working with Marion Ross in this one." I didn't know who she was. "She's a brilliant actress," they said. "She's doing a play in Santa Monica now and we're so happy to have her."

Marion played a Dinah Shore–like character, and we played opposite each other. The very first scene we had to do was at six forty-five in the morning. They introduced us. We shook hands. Then the director said, "This is the scene where you start to seduce her." He placed Marion lying down on the divan. He put me on the floor and said, "Open your shirt and pull up your sleeves. Now, you're going to con her into saying that if she opens the club for you, it can get a lot of attention."

So just as the script suggested, I took her hand and started kissing her arm, and said, "You know, of all the singers around today, nobody comes close to you. And besides that, you're beautiful. We could make great music together. All you've gotta do"—and I was kissing her—"is say yes." I kissed her arm higher and higher. "Will you say yes?" By the time I worked up the arm and got to her neck, we were in love! I mean, imagine doing that sort of thing with someone you only just met.

Marion and I laugh about it to this day. We were in our twenties, and we had so much fun together on that shoot, just as we did on the many, many shoots and shows we did together in the decades to come.

Marion and I have always been just friends, but I started to notice other actors and actresses would film a "love scene" like that and then continue their lovemaking off the set. There were a lot of guys in Hollywood who were fooling around behind their wives' backs. I wasn't one of them. Maybe it was my Catholic upbringing that kept me on the straight and narrow. There were times when I looked around and definitely felt like some kind of "square," but in the end, I'm a lot happier with myself for making the right decisions.

All this incredible stuff, all this work, all this excitement happened in 1957 alone. It's hard to imagine, even now, as I look back on it. I've tried to think about what it was that worked for me, and why I started to get work when other actors didn't. A lot of young people just starting out in the business want to know the secret. And you know what the secret is? I think it's simply that I didn't give up. Remember, I had been on Broadway making less money than the curtain puller, and no matter how hard I tried, I couldn't get an agent. A lot of guys might have called it quits right there. A lot of wives might have pushed their husbands to hang up their hats and go get regular jobs at that point. But Rootie didn't. And I couldn't. I loved acting too much. I kept going, and I was fortunate enough to have a wife who supported me in that.

Another part of my early success? I finally found a way to turn my bald head into a positive rather than a negative. For some reason, having that bald head at such a young age gave me the edge I needed to play heavies, drug dealers, bad guys—even though there was something about my personality or my presence that made people like me, even when I was playing a bad character. And having the diversity of ages and character types with the hairpiece gave me that extra leg up when I needed it.

Come to think of it, even four or five years later, that bald noggin of mine was directly responsible for my first guest role on *The Dick*

Van Dyke Show, in an episode called "Emperor Carlotta's Necklace"—which would mark the first time I'd work with Mary Tyler Moore. I got the part of Mel's cousin (Mel was Dick's producer on the show), simply because I had a bald head just like actor Richard Deacon's! That's what got me the part.

It's funny, but in music, they say sometimes a player's flaws become his "style" once he hits it big. It's kind of the same thing in acting, or in comedy, or in lots of jobs. That thing that makes you different from everyone else just might be the thing that sets you apart in the best way possible. But you've gotta embrace it.

The fact that my career was buzzing along in 1957 was great, but I would never forget that it came after *years* of hardship and struggle. It was a valuable lesson, actually. I'd have to call on that success-after-struggle memory again and again in order to keep my head on straight and to keep a positive outlook on my life and career. Especially once I settled into the sometimes-awful business behind the glittery facade the rest of the world sees as "Hollywood."

6

THE ELEVATOR
GOES UP . . .

A S I MENTIONED IN THE PREFACE, IN THEATER, you work, you don't work, you work, you don't work. It's a cycle you learn to live with and make the best of. It's no different in Hollywood. And like lots of actors in my generation will tell you, the key to survival in those days was the unemployment office. If you were out of work for even a couple of weeks, you'd go and they'd help you. Everybody went.

I was at the unemployment office in Hollywood one time and I saw Adolphe Menjou, one of the best character actors of all time, whose career went all the way back to the silent era. A guy you'd recognize from *The Sheik, A Farewell to Arms,* or *A Star Is Born*! His chauffeur drove him up. He got out of the car and went inside to get in line for unemployment. Why? Because he was out of work, and unemployment was a part of the gig in those days. I saw Herbert Marshall there one day.

Herbert Marshall, who played opposite Bette Davis in *The Little Foxes* and everything else! (He had a wooden leg. Nobody knew.) I used to love to go to unemployment because I'd see these people I wanted to be like, and I'd say to myself, "Gee, they're really human! They're just like the rest of us!"

Although I was working quite a bit, none of those little roles I picked up paid very much. Not even the really exciting ones. So unemployment was the saving grace between the highs of getting gigs and the lows when the phone wasn't ringing.

As I rolled into 1958, I would come to experience those ups and downs in ever-widening swings.

On the upside, I landed a part in my first major motion picture: *I Want to Live!*, starring the gorgeous and talented Susan Hayward— from *The Snows of Kilimanjaro* and *I'll Cry Tomorrow* and so many other great films. I almost got to play her husband, except I had the hairpiece on when I read for it. She thought I looked too young for her!

Robert Wise was the director. He had already established himself as one of Hollywood's most talented and prolific artists, with *The Day the Earth Stood Still*, and the just-completed *Run Silent Run Deep*. He would go on to direct *West Side Story* and *The Sound of Music* and so many classic films. What an honor to get to read for a guy like that! And he liked my reading, so even though I didn't get the part I was after, he said there was a small part he wanted me to do instead. He cast me as a police lieutenant, and I geared myself up for a big interrogation scene where I'd have to pull Susan Hayward's hair.

I had a friend back then who claimed to know a lot about things, even though he never worked as an actor. He read all the gossip columns and knew people and heard things. When I told him about the part, he said, "You gotta pull her hair? Oh, man. I heard she can be a pain in the you-know-what. You'd better be *careful* pulling her hair."

When the shoot started, we spent all day on that one scene. When we got to the part where I had to pull her hair, I couldn't get that friend's advice out of my head. I pulled Susan's hair very gently—as gently as I could while trying to look like a tough guy trying to get answers about a murder. Bob Wise did a lot of takes then, so we did it over and over again. I probably wouldn't have pulled her hair hard even if I wasn't spooked by my friend's advice. I didn't want to hurt her. *It's Susan Hayward!*

At one point, Susan said, "Can I talk to you?" She pulled me aside and said, "You know, there's a rumor that I could get an Oscar for this. It would really help me if you would really yank my hair." I respected women too much. I had never yanked on anyone's hair before—even my own, which I didn't have. "I'll do the best I can!" I said.

So we did the scene again, and this time I yanked it. Hard. She threw coffee on me in a spontaneous reaction. Bob loved it! We printed the scene.

Nine months later: "The best actress award goes to . . . Susan Hayward!" I was thrilled as I sat at home with my wife watching the Oscars on TV. *I helped her get that award!* I still hated doing it to her, but what an honor!

What people forget is that after shooting my little part for a day on that film, I would go back home. I might not get a call for a while. I'd be back in the unemployment line. It was up and down, up and down, all the time. And the wildest up-and-down ride of them all came for me on that one day in 1958, when I rented a car and bought a new sweater to wear for my big first day on a brand-new pilot for a sitcom with Hal March.

I already described that day in the preface to this book, so I won't repeat it here. I'll just say that going from thinking you're on a television pilot as a regular character—I was set to play Hal's director pal, like a John Frankenheimer character who was always trying to get him to do this or that—with one of the biggest television stars of the era, to getting fired within an hour of my arrival, rattled me to my core. Acting was all I knew how to do. To get fired from an acting job shook the very foundation of who I thought I was as a human being.

I thank God it turned around so quickly. I thank God my agent called me that very afternoon and sent me over to see Blake Edwards.

I based so much of my self-worth and happiness on my work in those days, who knows what would have happened to me had I been left to my own devices and wound up in the unemployment line again after being *fired*? I really can't stand to think about it.

What I didn't realize at the time was how much the casting director for the Hal March pilot really liked me. He would wind up casting me later in *Perry Mason* and all kinds of other TV parts. I couldn't see the potential for any of that in the darkness of that moment.

At the time, I never could have imagined that Blake Edwards would rewrite a part, just for me, in his pilot for *Peter Gunn*. I never could have imagined that *Peter Gunn* would get picked up and that a few weeks later I'd have my wife on my arm as we attended the screening with Craig Stevens, who played Peter Gunn; his wife, Alexis Smith; and Lola Albright, who played his love interest; and everybody in the show.

I couldn't see the positive in all the negativity of getting fired. I wish I could have. I wish I could have known! I didn't have a true faith in God then. I didn't trust in anything other than my ability to act. Without faith, the darkness sure seems a lot darker.

Cut to just a month or so later, when I was at Universal Studios to pick up a script for another TV series called *Steve Canyon*. As I was walking on the lot, a car stopped—it was Blake Edwards! I said, "How are you!?" He said, "I was just talking about you this morning. I'm doing a new movie and I want you to be in it." He told me to come over to the producer's office right then and there, so I walked across the lot and met the producer, and Blake started telling him all about me, doing a big sell. Finally he turned to me and said, "I want you to play this character Hunkle; he's the yeoman."

I said, "What's he like?"

"Well, he's kind of a schlub."

I said, "That's nothing like my character in *Peter Gunn*."

And Blake said, "No, but you can do this. I see you doing this." How and why he took a shine to me, and saw things in me, I will never know.

So we made a deal, and suddenly I was off on a plane to Key West,

Florida, to start work on my second feature film: *Operation Petticoat,* starring Cary Grant and Tony Curtis. I mean, come on! Cary Grant! Oh, to look like him for ten minutes. Tony was brilliant and funny. But Cary Grant was a real movie star, in the biggest sense. And here I was in a film with him!

We all worked together in Key West for a couple of months, and then we came back and finished the rest of the movie on the Universal lot. And guess who else worked on that film? Marion Ross. She had a small part as a nurse. If you really watch her, you can see that she played that whole part seasick. She's truly a brilliant actress.

Anyway, for all of the wonderful memories, and the big deal about getting to work with Cary Grant, the thing I probably remember most vividly about that film was filming the scene where we had to steal a pig.

It was nighttime (we were shooting night for night, which wasn't always the case in those days), and I've never been good with wild animals. Tony wasn't exactly comfortable either, and we were supposed to jump into a pig pen, steal a pig, and somehow get it up into the front seat of the truck we were driving, where it would sit right between us. The two of us had the worst time trying to grab one of those beasts!

Blake said, "Oh, we're going to be here until one o'clock in the morning!"

Some of that stuff gets improvised, of course, because you just don't know how it's gonna go. So we got into the pig pen you see in the movie, and Tony said, "You get him, Hunkle. You get him!" I said, "You're the star. You get him!"

Well, Tony Curtis finally got ahold of one of 'em by the back legs, and he walked him like a wheelbarrow. Then he said, "Put him in the truck!" And I had to wrap my arms around the pig and lift it up into the truck—and that pig was so scared it started defecating all over everything. Oh, the stench!

I haven't eaten pork since.

That's the unvarnished truth, folks. That's the "glamour" of Hollywood in a nutshell.

Operation Petticoat would go on to be nominated for an Oscar for Best Screenplay, and Blake Edwards would bring me back again to work on his projects repeatedly over the next decade. As I've already mentioned, I did another episode of *Peter Gunn* for him. In the 1960s, he brought me back for *High Time*, *The Party*, and *Mr. Lucky* for TV. And I tell you, Mr. Lucky is how I felt. Blake and I just grooved, man. We had fun. We had a fantastic professional relationship that I cherished. I loved him.

7

CONNECTIONS

H OT ON THE HEELS OF MY SECOND FEATURE film, I went in to read for another major motion picture: *Pork Chop Hill*, starring Gregory Peck, and directed by the legendary Lewis Milestone—the director of *All Quiet on the Western Front*.

The part I auditioned for was that of a young soldier. I knew that if I went in bald I wouldn't get the part. So I wore my hairpiece. Think about that: what soldier in real life wears a hairpiece? It doesn't make any sense! So I did the only thing I could: I never let them know. I wore my trusty secondhand hairpiece when I first went to see them, and I got the part, and I wore it every day on set—no one ever saw me without it. So Mr. Peck didn't know, Mr. Milestone didn't know, and it's there on film for all eternity now—me in my hairpiece as a young soldier on the battlefields of the Korean War.

All the big parts in that film went to actors who were represented by the William Morris Agency. But to get a chance to work with Lewis

Milestone—just to be in the presence of that man—I would have taken *any* part. Turns out there were three parts to choose from. Milestone had storyboards in his office, and in one I could see there was a soldier character who got his foot blown off. The drawing showed the soldier's foot in the foreground while the rest of him was still moving around in agony in the background. I said to myself, "He's the only one who loses his foot in the movie? That's the part I want to play." My thinking was, *People will remember me for that! This is a black-and-white war movie. The audience might not remember a soldier who gets hurt or killed under normal circumstances . . . but this?*

I always wanted my characters to leave a memorable impression.

So I got the role, and when we were shooting the part where my foot gets blown off, I did one more thing to try to get myself noticed: I added a line. I had my character cry out, "Mama!" As an actor, I tried to put myself into that position, to imagine what it would feel like. I thought back to when you're a little kid and things happen, and you instinctively call for your mama. It was just one word, but Mr. Milestone liked it, and it stayed in the film.

There was another scene in that film where I got to work side by side with Mr. Peck. We were shooting somewhere in Thousand Oaks, and the two of us were positioned under a truck, waiting for the scene to start. There was a fire burning, and we were wearing fatigues, and I told Mr. Peck that I had heard a story about him back when I worked as an usher at Radio City Music Hall. "The story is that you were a tour guide next door at NBC, and one day you were fed up, so you took a whole group of tourists down to the basement, to the boiler room under the building. You then told them, 'The next tour guide will be along any moment to continue your tour,' and you left them there. The legend is that you then went to your locker, changed your clothes, flew to California, and became a big movie star!"

He laughed and laughed. "Well," he said, "that's a good story, but there's no truth in it." Then he said, "But I'll tell you something. You know what I did do when I went to New York to get started? I modeled men's underwear in the Sears and Roebuck catalog." Gregory Peck, an underwear model. I could hardly believe it! But I heard it with my own ears.

I'm sure there are stories like that tour-guide story floating around about me out there. When you make it big, people always want to spread stories. The key is to laugh at them. And if a star as big as Gregory Peck could laugh at them, I certainly knew I could too. Stardom certainly has a strange set of downsides and pressures. Laughter and levity are so important. And what a gentleman he was to listen to my story and to share that kind of truth and camaraderie on a set when, comparatively speaking, I was a nobody! I would never forget that.

As the 1950s came to a close and we headed into the 1960s, my career seemed to be on an upward trajectory that couldn't be stopped. From the bit parts I'd started out with, I quickly settled into costarring film roles and top-billed guest appearances on TV. My highs got higher, and my lows got higher too! Everything just picked up steam.

After working in those big motion pictures, I sort of graduated to the next level. I worked with legends such as Milton Berle—Uncle Miltie himself—on a *Dick Powell Theater* episode. (Mr. Berle would wind up doing a couple of episodes of *The Love Boat* many years later, and we reminisced about these days over lunch. He was in his nineties then. What a long, memorable career he had!)

Mr. Berle was nominated for awards for that *Dick Powell* episode, called "Doyle Against the House." I remember I was sitting there ready to go to work on the first day, and he came in the room and said, "Are you the doctor?" I said, "No, I'm just an actor." "Oh, I'm looking for the doctor." *Holy cow! Milton Berle just spoke to me!* I thought. I didn't care that he had no idea who I was. I wound up having all these scenes with him, playing Arnie the Geek, a guy who dealt against the house so they beat him up and crippled his hands so he could be a symbol of what happens when you deal against the house. Those were the sort of juicy roles I was getting! And there were so many stars I was fortunate to work with. I shot Blake Edwards's *High Time* during this period and had that moment where I got to dance with Bing Crosby.

In fact, I was on the set of *High Time* when I saw Marilyn Monroe again. It was such a thrill. We were shooting on the Twentieth Century Fox lot, and I knew Marilyn was doing *Let's Make Love*, with Yves Montand. I had just gotten my makeup done and started walking down to the soundstage—ironically, the same soundstage where we started *The Love Boat* years later—and a limousine went by with the windows down. And there was Marilyn Monroe. The *movie* Marilyn Monroe, with the beauty mark. My friend Whitey Snyder designed that look for her. He was a makeup artist who did a lot of Blake Edwards's films too. I remember watching her go by and thinking, *What a difference. I met the real Marilyn. She was humble and sweet. And this is "the star."*

I tell you, seeing someone like Marilyn Monroe on the lot—oh, and John Wayne, who I also saw coming out of makeup one day—sure makes you feel like you're onto something big. These weren't just stars; these were legends. And there I was in the thick of it, man. It was great!

My personal life was on the upswing too: Rootie got pregnant again. I was finally going to be a father. We were so happy.

There was just one thing missing in my life, and I was sure I knew what it was: applause. I had been so focused on doing television and film work, I had neglected my first love. As rewarding as it is to play those juicy roles in front of the camera, there is nothing like working in front of a live audience. I needed that. I needed to hear the sound that resonates from my heart to my head to my toes. And in 1960, a role came my way like no other. A role that would be remembered by many people in the industry for the rest of my career.

Our son Keith was born just before I got back onstage in an avant-garde play called *The Connection*. Finally I was a father, filled with this newfound joy that you just can't understand until you hold your child in your very own arms. I never heard the words "I love you" from my own father, and I think I overcompensated with Keith, and all of my kids, right out of the womb. I held them and told them I loved them and kissed them, and promised to always be there for them. I would never allow myself to become like my own father. I promised myself that.

How blessed I felt to be going back onstage at the very same time, returning to the roots of everything I felt I was meant to do in this life.

The Connection had already made a name for itself. It had been performed at The Living Theatre in New York City to much acclaim. It would be made into a movie that same year too. But for our performance at the Las Palmas Theatre, where the Stage Door Canteen had been during the Second World War, we were working from a brand-new script. There was a certain amount of improvisation and interaction with the audience, which I loved. It was a little like a nightclub act, and I love nightclub acts. But the script was fabulous, and my character was just awful! His name was Leach, an asexual drug dealer with a big boil on his neck. The production was so realistic, people in the theater would get up and leave. People thought we were really druggies, all strung out and everything. Oh! And the music! The legendary jazz saxophonist Dexter Gordon was the leader of our band. He was just out of prison, and he had a big following in those days, so he was a draw all his own. Dexter had dealt with some serious drug addictions in his own life, so he knew this material well. He would play this piece of music he wrote called "O.D." right when my character overdosed on heroin on the stage. I did my research and learned from a real drug user how to simulate shooting up. It was horrifying to watch.

The play was so accurate that a few people who saw it tracked down my unlisted number and tried to score drugs from me—because they thought I was a real drug dealer!

I reteamed with Robert Blake in this show, and the two of us developed a close friendship during this time. He played the guy who broke open my boil onstage. I squealed in a high-pitched voice as the audience squirmed in their seats. I remember saying to the director, Brian Hutton, "Let's make Leach as repulsive as possible." As I've mentioned, there was something about me that no matter how awful the character was, the audience, even though they hated him, still liked him a little. It's just an organic thing, nothing I do as an actor. But I wanted to see how far I could push it. I wanted to make him grating, annoying, irritating, and uncomfortable. I use a lot of memories and observations to put a character together. In this case, I remembered some girls in high school who used to wear loafers and white socks, and they had this lethargic walk, scuffing their feet along as though they had no energy. So I thought, *Let me try that!* My goal was to leave the audience thinking, *What is this person?* I put on a high-pitched, effeminate voice. I did strange things. I ate an entire pineapple during my thirty-five-minute monologue. It was so off-putting and bizarre. Such a delicious character to play.

Edwin Shallert, movie reviewer for the *Los Angeles Times*, did a review of *High Time*, which hit theaters when I was in *The Connection*, and he printed side-by-side pictures of me as the nutty professor character in that Blake Edwards film, and me onstage with a boil on my neck as Leach. He couldn't believe it was the same guy, and neither could anyone else!

I was making my mark. In a big way.

The irony of this is years later Dexter Gordon did a movie called *'Round Midnight*, and of all the brilliant actors in *The Connection*, Dexter was the only guy ever nominated for an Oscar for Best Actor in a movie. Not Robert Blake. Not Morris Erby or Jan Peters. None of them!

Awards didn't matter. The show did. The role did. The applause did.

Anyone who came to see it still talks about it to this day. That's how groundbreaking and original and disturbing and powerful it was. In fact, decades later, Carl Reiner introduced me one night at a big function and said, "I want you all to know, one of my top five male performances onstage of all time was Gavin MacLeod in *The Connection*."

I had a son. I was getting applause. I was doing work I wanted to be doing. Without putting any kind of a drug into my system, I was high as a kite on a windy day.

Those highs kept coming too. I got a job on a new film. There were a lot of war films happening in those days, and I got hired to do another one set in the Korean War. Only this was a very different sort of movie: *War Hunt*, starring John Saxon as a psychopath who covers his face in black and goes over enemy lines to kill Koreans single-handedly in the dark of night. In many ways, it was like an early "indie" film. Sydney Pollack was in it, too, and he was already preparing to become a director himself. If you've never seen it, you should see it. The National Board of Review named *War Hunt* one of the Ten Best Pictures of the Year.

The Sanders Brothers, who produced and directed it, came after me to do this movie just after winning an Academy Award for a college film they did called *A Timeout of War*. They had seen me in *The Connection*. Apparently they were looking for talent on stages all over. They hired a couple of newcomers you might have heard of for that film too: Tom Skerritt (of *Alien*, *Top Gun*, and many other great films), whom they discovered in a production of *The Rainmaker* at a small theater in the San Fernando Valley; and a guy by the name of Robert Redford, who had just made his debut on the live-theater TV show *Playhouse 90*.

War Hunt was the first film for both of them.

The entire film was made for $250,000. We shot in Topanga, where they'd had some fires. That scorched landscape was used for the Korean area. Then we shot in the very same soundstage where Charlie Chaplin had made his movies. (You know who bought that studio later on? Herb Alpert, the trumpet player who cofounded A&M Records! I love all that history.)

Redford and Skerritt and I used to hang out together. Redford invited us to a little house that he and his wife, Lola, were renting up in Laurel Canyon. I remember him showing us a papier-mâché ranch he had designed. He was an artist. And he said, "This is what I want to build up in Utah." I think now, *Was that the beginning of Sundance? Way back in 1960?*

When Redford came on that screen to the declaration, "Introducing Robert Redford," this all-American guy with big eyes, astonished at the horrors he sees happening on the battlefield, all of Hollywood noticed.

Everybody who saw that picture said, "Who *is* this?" It was like when you first laid eyes on Montgomery Clift or someone like that.

I remember Skerritt and I were up at Redford's house one time, and we were standing outside, and he said, "I don't know what I'm going to do. They want me to do a lead in this new TV show as a psychiatrist, and the money is *fantastic*—but I don't think the audience would believe me. I'm young. I don't think the audience would believe I would know more than these people who are coming to me for help."

Well, of course Redford turned that TV show down. He wanted to be true to the character. The greats are like that. It's not about the money. It's about something more. He turned it down and did some other TV work over the next few years, and then he became one of the most popular movie stars of all time.

Anyway, the three of us used to play football on the set. I visited with Redford and Lola in New York before I opened my last Broadway play, back when Redford was doing *Barefoot in the Park*. Skerritt and I became very good friends, and my kids would get to know him as "Uncle Tom" in the next couple of years. (In fact, they would always complain when he called on the phone, because he has that very . . . slow . . . deliberate . . . way of talking . . . It's perfect for the movies, but my kids would get impatient trying to listen to what "Uncle Tom" had to say on the phone!)

I tell you, the highs just kept coming, right on into 1962.

Rootie got pregnant again, and we had another son, David. I showered him with love too. We were a family of four now! I got offered a role in a new play that was bound for New York. I had saved up some money and I decided it was time to buy a house for my growing family. Rootie and I found a place we loved up in Granada Hills, and we made an offer.

Everything in my life seemed to be going just right.

That's when things got scary.

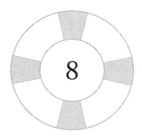

GLORIFIED

I WAS IN CALIFORNIA IN 1961, AND I READ THAT Steve McQueen was going to do a leading role on the TV hit *Wanted: Dead or Alive*. I thought, *He's going to play a cowboy! That's great for him.* And he *was* great. Then I read that he was doing a couple of big movies and that he had signed on for *The Great Escape*, with James Garner and Richard Attenborough. *This guy is moving up quick!* I thought. It was clear to everyone that he was about to become a major movie star. It was incredible. That quiet guy with the vulnerability who didn't quite fit in on the Broadway stage had found his niche, and I was so happy for him.

My career wasn't on that sort of "star" trajectory. I never even expected to play the leading man. That was okay with me, because unlike guys like McQueen, I truly did feel that my home was on the stage. With all of the TV and film credits I'd accumulated, my role in *The Connection* left me hungering for more. So I was thrilled to get back onstage in what I believed was set to be a big Broadway hit: *The Captains and the Kings*, a show about the first Jewish rear admiral in the navy, on the first nuclear submarine. The production starred Dana Andrews, Lee Grant, and Peter Graves, and it was directed by Joe Anthony. I was all fired up to play the part of a slimy lawyer in that show, a guy named Roy Cohen. He wasn't as slimy a character as Leach, but still—it was the type of part I enjoyed sinking my teeth into.

We opened in San Francisco to good notices and traveled to a few theaters across the United States, then up to Toronto, Canada, before finally landing in New York City.

"We're sold out for four weeks," the producer said, "so bring your families!" He assured us we were going to have a big Broadway run. It felt like something secure in this very unsecure business full of ups and downs. It felt great. Especially given the fact that I'd just signed a purchase agreement on a new home in Granada Hills for $24,750. That was a lotta dough in 1962. But a steady Broadway gig was just what I needed to help pay the mortgage.

Taking the producer's words to heart, I flew my wife and two kids to New York City for the opening. We had a big party—where else, but at Jim Downey's Steak House! We were all so excited. And then the show closed—in a week.

That's showbiz.

Devastated, we all flew home. I started scrambling to make some money. I did a Brinks robbery TV special and an *Untouchables* episode, pulling in a little bit of cash. I used the last of our savings for closing costs to move into the house. We didn't even have furniture. The monthly payment was $147, and with the ups and downs of TV guest roles and the sporadic film roles, I didn't know how I was going to pay it. I panicked. I prayed that something would happen. God has always been a part of my life, even when I wasn't living correctly—so I prayed, somewhat selfishly, for a solution.

One day my pal Robert Blake happened to be over for a visit when I got a telegram from Universal. They were starting a new television series called *McHale's Navy* and wanted to talk to me about playing a part.

Was this the answer to my prayers?

Robert was thrilled for me, and Rootie seemed relieved. I think the ups and downs of my career were really taking a toll on her, even though she never would have said so, and even though she still believed in me. It's a different story when you're the mother of two kids. It wasn't just about us anymore. The ups and downs were taking a toll on me too. Especially with that mortgage. There was something about it that piled the weight of the world on my shoulders. The idea of working on a TV show with regular hours and a good, steady paycheck seemed like a dream come true. So I went over to Universal.

The part they were offering me was a character called Seaman Joseph "Happy" Haines. There was just one problem: it was a small part. Very small compared to the costarring roles I had worked my way up to. Tiny for an actor who had earned the kind of acclaim I'd had in *The Connection*.

My wife said, "Don't do it." My agent said, "Don't do it." But I didn't see a choice. *I have a mortgage now. I have a family to take care of.* In my mind, I thought I *had* to do it.

So I dismissed the opinions of the people in my life who cared about me most, and who truly had my best interests at heart. Instead, I listened to my fear.

What a mistake.

I signed on and started shooting this series about a misfit crew on a PT boat in World War II. I got billing under two newcomers. *Two!* I only had one or two lines a week. There was nothing to sink my teeth into as an actor. There were moments when the director would position me in a shot just to block a building in the background, almost as if I were a prop.

Marilyn Monroe died on August 5 of that year—two months before *McHale's Navy* debuted on television. It was such a shocking and sad day for everyone, of course. I would cherish my brief memory of making her laugh that one time back at Jim Downey's Steak House the rest of my life. But I think the sadness I felt only made the time I spent on that set feel worse—as if I were wasting my life. Life is so precious, and we all feel it a little more when someone so well known dies, don't we? It's as if the whole country mourns together.

My hairpiece died on that show too. My trusty secondhand hairpiece that had given me my career and served me well started looking so ratty, I thought it would run right off my head. So one day on the *Navy* set, we threw it in the sand and shot it! (I bought a replacement later on. From another Ziggy.)

Not that there wasn't plenty to feel miserable about on that set already. We had this one director who was the meanest man I ever worked with. He would pick on actors—not me, in particular, but other actors coming on, and especially some of the older actors. It was awful. And it was really a shame, because the show was a hit, and the cast was a bunch of really talented guys, including Ernest Borgnine, Tim Conway, and Joe Flynn. Off the set and during downtime, we had a lot of fun together, including quite a few experiences I'll never forget.

Bob Crane, who would later become a big star in *Hogan's Heroes* (on which I would appear as a guest star more than once), had a radio show in those days, and I remember one morning hearing him report on his program that Ernie Borgnine had gotten engaged to Ethel Merman. Ernie came on set and I said, "Ernie, I heard you're engaged!" and he said, "We are! And you're going to be invited." In fact, they were planning a big engagement party and some people from Texas were going to pay for the whole evening. I could hardly believe that someone I knew was engaged to a woman I'd marveled at on the Broadway stage when I was a kid— back when Uncle Al took my brother and me into the city to see her.

Tim Conway and I were close at that time and I asked him, "Are you going to this engagement party?" He said, "I'm not going to go. Are *you* going?" I said, "Yeah! I want to meet Ethel!" So he changed his tune: "I'll go too."

I kept pinching myself that whole day. I was going to meet *Ethel Merman*. The very same magnificent star I had seen in *Annie Get Your Gun* all those years ago.

I walked up to her the night of the engagement party, and I'll never forget she had this old-fashioned kind of thing they used to do in the theater, beading on the eye. On the end of the eyelash there was a big black dab of something, and her eyes were so big.

Ernie saw me and said, "Oh, Ethel! This is Gavin! He's going to be our ring bearer!" I said, "I am?" She said, "Oh isn't that great? It's so nice to see you!" She was so happy.

I was sitting with Conway at dinner, and he's so funny. When the strolling musicians in this restaurant came around, with all the violins and things, Conway looked at Ethel and said, "Sing, Ethel! Sing!" And she did! She stood up by her fiancé, put her hands on his shoulders, and sang, "They say that falling in love is wonderful . . ."

When she finished a verse, everybody cheered and stood up, and we all sat down—except for Conway. He stayed on his feet and kept clapping, saying, "More! More!" So Ethel got up again and continued the song!

Years later, Ethel wrote an autobiography. You know what she wrote in the chapter about her marriage to the great Ernest Borgnine? Nothing. The chapter was just the title and three blank pages.

I tell you, that blank-page feeling is exactly what *McHale's Navy* gave to me. As I said, I had graduated to costarring parts before that show. Now I barely had two lines a week. A *week!* My friend Ted Knight came on as a guest star one day, and he looked at me and said, "How can you do this, man? You're a glorified extra!"

I told him the reasons. "It's for the kids," I said. "I need to pay the mortgage."

Eventually that excuse didn't seem like a reasonable one anymore, and that thing he said started to eat at me: *You're a glorified extra.* I was on my way up! I was working with big stars, getting positive reviews, getting hired by some of the most magnificent directors in the world. What had I done?

That worthlessness stayed with me and started eating me up, until finally I started drinking to ease the pain.

That's where I started drinking. On *McHale's Navy*.

There's a bar across the street from the Universal lot. Universal wasn't that big at that time, and we would all go to the bar at the end of the day. I remember Clark Gable saying, "If you want to keep your marriage together, go home after work. Don't stop and have a drink." A lot of guys do that and they start BS-ing with each other, and one thing leads to another, and suddenly there's a rift in the marriage.

Well, guess what? That's exactly what happened. My marriage began to suffer. Sometimes I wasn't sure which came first, the drinking or the unhappiness, but either way it wasn't pretty. I got ugly when I drank. I said some rotten things. I was irritable.

"I am *not* drinking too much!" I would yell at my wife. The fighting was miserable, and very much my fault.

I remember we were up at Ted Knight's house for a barbecue one afternoon, and Ted's wife, Dottie, implored me to stop drinking. She said I was throwing away my life! I couldn't believe someone *else* was laying into me like that. I wasn't drinking too much, I kept telling myself. I was just doing it to ease the burden, to have some fun, to let off steam.

On the way into work some days I'd pick up a six-pack of beer. It wasn't all for me. I was sharing it with the guys! We'd drink between takes, or during breaks. Though I tried it, I never got into hard liquor, and I truly didn't drink a whole lot, in terms of volume. I was just an Irish slop, I suppose—a little bit was all it took to get me going.

Looking back today, it seems clear to me: I was missing something in my life. There was a huge hole that needed to be filled, and I was filling it with all the wrong things.

I was on that show for two years. Two *years*. That may not seem like a long time. A lot of people stay at jobs they hate for decades. But given how quickly my career had been trucking along ever since Rootie and I moved to California, two years felt like a lifetime. I wasn't able to do the kind of work I loved. I wasn't able to do anything outside of this show, where I sat around and occasionally got propped up in front of the cameras.

One night I went back to Tom Skerritt's house after work, and I really had a lot to drink. I was pretty inebriated. Too inebriated to get behind the wheel, for sure. But I did. I climbed into my car feeling the weight of the world on my shoulders. Defeated. Terrible. I kept thinking, *This is it. My career is gone.* I'd destroyed it by signing my life over to this "glorified extra" role on a TV show.

I drove around for who knows how long, feeling awful about myself, awful about how I was destroying my marriage, about everything. I got all the way to the top of Mulholland Drive, which overlooks all of the sparkling lights of Los Angeles, and I thought, *It's just not worth it!* I turned the wheel toward the side of that winding road and sped straight toward the edge of a cliff.

With the city lights spread out before me and my eyes glazed over, I could see the trees disappear to each side of me and nothing but open sky ahead as the car got closer and closer to the edge until suddenly, *Pfft!* My right leg stomped on the brake and the car skidded to a stop in the dirt.

I slumped over the wheel. My heart was pounding. I took deep breaths, trying to regain my composure. *What am I doing?* All I could hear was the sound of the engine, and as I looked up all I could see were the lights and the stars. There was no road left in front of me at all. My tires were just inches from the edge of that cliff.

If my right foot hadn't hit the brake when it did, it would have been all over.

I can't begin to explain why I stopped, or how that happened. It's almost as if something else lifted my leg and stomped my foot on that brake for me. The only explanation I have after all these years is that God was looking after me. Even though I didn't know it, he was there. God is there 24/7, and clearly he had other plans for me that didn't include dying on that dark LA mountaintop!

I put the car into reverse and gently eased off the brake, backing up and turning around to get my bearings. I realized where I was. Robert Blake didn't live far from there, so I drove over to see him. I woke him up. He said, "What are you doing up here by yourself in the middle of the night?" And I just laid it all on him.

"I'm not worth anything!" I moaned.

Like a lot of men, especially men with young families, I was getting all of my identity through my work and not through who I really was. I didn't know that then. I didn't realize, as I would many years later, that my identity comes through my Lord and Savior and my relationship with God. That's the whole answer for me. But I was *decades* away from that realization.

On that particular night, the lowest point of my life, Robert Blake was the guy who set me right. "You've got to get to a shrink," he said. "You can't keep going on like this."

He called his guy, Dr. Joe Shore, and I started to see him once a week. You know what? It helped. And it wasn't too long before he gave me a plan of action—a plan I knew I had to take. "You know what you have to do?" he said. "You have to get out of that show. If your identity is coming from the size of your parts and your billing and the money, you *have* to get out of it."

I knew he was right.

The second season was over and the studio had sent me a stack of pictures of my character, "Happy" Haines, to sign—and I just couldn't sign them. Our producer Eddie Montagne was a great guy. But I said to myself, "I have to take the bull by the horns. I can't stay here and go down the tubes." We did the *McHale's Navy* movies. And finally they called one day wondering where those pictures were, and I said, "Can I come down and talk to Eddie?"

I went to see him and said, "I know I've got a signed contract, but you can save me and my whole family. I just feel as an actor that I'm almost a nonentity on this show." I told him about being used as a prop to hide buildings in the background. I told him what Ted Knight had said: *You're a glorified extra.* Eddie knew what I was capable of as an actor. He knew the acclaim I had received for *The Connection*. He

A highlight of the year: my brother, Ron, on the pony (I'm the wrangler)

My parents: George William See and Margaret Teresa Shea See

On a family trip—I wore knickers until high school

The last photo of my dad before he passed away in June, 1945

Brotherly love personified

Ron and me, getting rays at the beach

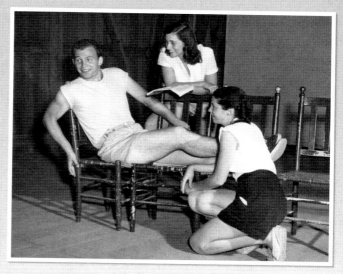

Keuka Park Playhouse with beauties Francine and Susan, 1950

Sophomore at Ithaca College, 1950

Uncle Vanya at Ithaca College— playing Vanya himself

Isn't this a lot of hair for $125?
Rootie sure is beautiful!

Rootie as a Rockette—even with
long ears, she's gorgeous!

Big night out with Mom
at Lawrence Welk's
dinner and dance show

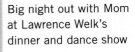

The most beautiful
baby in the world:
Keith George MacLeod, 1960

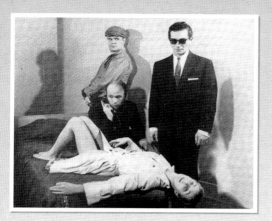

Four junkies from *A Hatful of Rain*.
The legs belong to Helen Richman,
my college sweetheart.

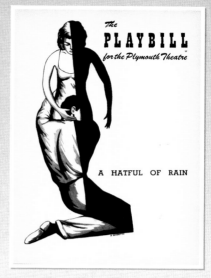

My first Broadway play, in which
I performed with several great
actors—including Stephen McQueen

An unbelievable experience!
I worked with one of my all-time
favorite directors, Brian Hutton,
and producer Al Ruddy.

Playing this
despicable character,
Leach, was a
breakthrough role

Susan Hayward's Oscar-winning performance in *I Want To Live!*

Bing Crosby in drag, from Blake Edwards's film *High Time*—a very special moment in my career

THE SWORD OF ALI BABA A Universal Picture

The Sword of Ali Baba— I played the evil Khan in a turban

A tense moment: Dick Crenna, Steve McQueen, Barney Phillips, and Charles Robinson— all terrific actors

The Sand Pebbles, filmed in Taiwan, Hong Kong, and at home on the 20th Century Fox Studios lot and ranch

Me, Donald Sutherland, Stuart Margolin, Clint Eastwood, Telly Savalas, and Perry Lopez in *Kelly's Heroes*

Kelly's Heroes—in Yugoslavia, playing Moriarty with his "negative waves"

My son Keith; his wife, Carolyn; and my youngest grandkids, Liam and Keilyn

My brother, Ron, Mom, and me at daughter Meg's wedding

My son David and me, Princess Alaskan cruise

My daughter Meghan; her husband, Shawn; and my grandsons, Peter and Andrew, in Cape Cod

My daughter Julie and her husband, Patrick, at a reunion

listened to me, and he said, "I had no idea. Of course you can get out." And that was that. No more "Happy" Haines.

The very next week I got a call from my director friend John Erman for a recurring role on *My Favorite Martian*. I put on the hairpiece and a suit, and I became a young guy all over again. It was a fresh start.

Our daughter Julia was born in January 1964. I asked Robert Blake to be her godfather, and he accepted. I have showered her with love and affection ever since the day she was born.

Of course, I also celebrated that day by going out drinking.

In spite of the therapy and in spite of the newfound joy I felt once I was free of that "glorified extra" role, I still felt miserable inside. The fights with Rootie were growing worse. I loved my kids, and I was involved with them, but I also felt the overwhelming need to provide a better life for them, and I was driven like never before. I needed more work. I wanted more work. I craved it, much more than I ever craved alcohol. But I couldn't stop drinking, nonetheless.

I took roles in all kinds of TV shows. I jumped at roles in a series of plays in Los Angeles. Work, work, work was all I wanted to do. In 1965 my wife gave birth to our fourth child, our daughter Meghan, and I filled up once again with that fatherly love, showering her with affection. Rootie and I saw a marriage counselor. We wanted to make things better between us. But the counseling didn't help. Something kept pulling me away from the marriage. I felt like I was the breadwinner, and I was responsible for taking care of her and the kids, yet at the same time I felt this pull to be somewhere else. I couldn't explain it.

One day, the great Robert Wise called. I hadn't worked with him since *I Want to Live!* in 1958, but he said he was thinking of me for a part in his next film. "I have one question to ask you," he said. "How tall are you?"

I said, "How tall do you want me to be?"

He said, "You can't be taller than Steve McQueen."

"I know Steve!" I told him. "He and I played brothers on Broadway, and Steve is definitely taller than me." He told me all about this new starring vehicle for Steve, which would be shooting in Taiwan. It would take us overseas for ten months, he said.

Without a moment's hesitation, without one thought about the effect that might have on my family, I said, "I'd love to do it!" He hired me over the phone.

The film was *The Sand Pebbles*, starring Steve, Candice Bergen, Richard Attenborough, and Richard Crenna. I kissed my wife and kids good-bye. I went from LA to Hawaii, then Hawaii to Tokyo, slept overnight, then Tokyo to Taiwan—first class. I had never done that kind of a trip before. I got off in Taiwan and the smell hit me. *Phew!* This was gonna be a long ten months!

The studio sent a car to pick me up and take me to the hotel, and standing in front of the hotel as I drove up was Steve McQueen. He recognized me right away and said, "Well, bro. You ever think I'd be a big movie star?" And I said, "To tell you the truth, I didn't! But I always thought you were really interesting close up." We talked for a couple more minutes, and I remember telling him, "You've really got a *home* now." He smiled and said, "I'm really glad you could do this." I said, "Me too."

That was the most substantial conversation I had with McQueen for those whole ten months. He was such a movie star! In fact, he'd get nominated for an Academy Award for that role. Years later, he had cancer and went all over the world trying to find a cure. What a sad ending he had.

I think of the ending I almost had, on that cliff on Mulholland Drive. It all could have ended right there. What would I have been? Another Hollywood story. A bald-headed character actor with a bit of acclaim whose life was cut too short.

I never could have imagined that someday I would be the captain of my own show, anchoring a TV series! Or that I would someday represent a cruise line, a huge company, as an ambassador who would travel all over the world! I never imagined that I would be an ambassador in a much more important way either.

All I needed to have was faith. Faith in myself. Faith in God. It seems so clear now looking back on it. But it wasn't clear then.

I wrote home to Rootie, telling her I was sorry. I promised to be a different man and a better father as soon as I returned. I always smiled at the thought of my children, and I knew they were in such capable hands. Rootie was, and always would be, a fantastic mother to them. I knew that. And I wanted to be a better father. Even as I kept drinking. Even as I gained weight to the point where some of the cast and crew on *The Sand Pebbles* started calling me "Moby Dick."

I spent long nights getting into deep, dark conversations, questioning what it all meant, questioning what it meant to be an actor, wondering aloud whether there really was a God. Candice Bergen would tell me to lighten up. Life's supposed to be fun! I agreed with her. I had always been a happy guy. I enjoyed life. I liked it when life was easy and light. I just couldn't understand why I felt the way I felt. I kept asking myself, *What's wrong with me?*

Then one day, I decided to find out. Word got around that there was a powerful Taiwanese fortune-teller in town. You had to make an appointment with this man, and he would tell you your future, they said. "If you bring your problems to him, he will help you." So my friend Joe Di Reda, who played "Red Dog" Shanahan in the movie, and I scheduled an appointment. We both walked in, and this guy was sitting at a table. He had a box filled with different objects and cards with colors, letters, numbers, and different things. First he looked at my hands, and he asked if I had a favorite number—I always used to say "seven" because it was my grandmother's favorite number—and then he shook this box and some cards with numbers came out, and he spoke. I don't really remember much about what he said during that portion of the reading. But when he touched my forehead, he said, "You know, your grandfather very spiritual."

He was talking about my mother's father, Jimmy—the one who had made a promise to God to stop drinking if he brought his son home safe from the war. I had never really thought about him as a "spiritual" man.

But he *was*. And it struck me as odd that this fortune-teller would say such a thing. It didn't answer my big question about what was wrong with me, but still, I thought it was interesting.

We paid him, and he said, "Next!"

Then, as I had my hand on the door, just as I was about to go, that fortune-teller shouted, "You!" I turned and looked at him, and he stared directly into my eyes. "You," he said. "Be like Jesus."

I didn't know what to make of it. I didn't know what to do with that order. I just walked out thinking, *What a strange thing for a Taiwanese fortune-teller to say.*

9

HALF-FULL . . .

A s soon as I came home from *The Sand Pebbles*, I was hired to do a new series called *The Rat Patrol*—a series they were shooting in Spain. So off I went. It was only a weeklong shoot, but the disappointment in Rootie's eyes was almost too much for me to bear.

I was only a guest star on *The Rat Patrol*, yet here is the irony of movie making: I had more lines on that show in one week than I had in ten months on *The Sand Pebbles*. That's just what the business is like. I had a death scene too. I love death scenes. Most of the shows that I died in, the first scene I shot was my death scene. I remember in the black-and-white days, they used Karo syrup and had it coming out of your mouth to simulate blood. Then we got color and they had to use the red stuff. (I've been in this business a long time, haven't I?)

For a guy who liked doing death scenes, I shudder to think how close I came to the real thing. I couldn't stop thinking about it. I think a lot of people hit those moments before they really know who they are.

It doesn't matter how successful you are in your work. And it certainly doesn't matter how successful you are in other people's eyes. I was on TV and in the movies! People would say, "You're a big success!" And I was, I suppose. But people don't know what you go through. We all go through struggles. We're all on this journey, trying to find out who we really are and what really matters.

Interestingly enough, I did some of my best character work in the latter half of the 1960s, at the very same time I was going through this struggle.

One of the most memorable characters I ever played was on the first season of *Hawaii Five-O*, with Jack Lord. The guy's name was Big Chicken and he was this fat, slimy, condescending guy who would get kids hooked on drugs and then get them to steal for him. The reviews were incredible! With my bald head and my ballooning weight, I just went for it. I made him as despicable as I possibly could. The papers said they had never seen a character like this on television before. Ever. There are still references to Big Chicken found all over the Internet to this day. It was quite a thing. In fact, the response was so overwhelming, they wrote me into another episode later on, after Big Chicken had gone to jail. Jack went in to see him to try to get some information to help with another case he was working on. I loved getting another shot to bring that awful character to life.

Jack Lord asked me to have lunch with him in his trailer during that shoot. "You're the most courageous actor I've ever seen. You take such chances!" he said. It was incredibly flattering. "Where do you get the nerve to do this?"

"It's the character. It's not me," I told him. "When I'm playing it, that's who that guy is."

Ed Asner did a guest role on *Hawaii Five-O* when he was younger, too, playing a jewelry thief. In the new version of the show that debuted in 2010, they brought back that character (and Ed). The detectives went to see him to ask about something years later, when he was out of prison. My brother, Ronnie, says we should start a petition to get them to bring back Big Chicken! The only way I would do it now, I think, is if that slime ball were rehabilitated and helping kids instead of hurting them. But I'd sure love to get another shot at it!

It's odd to think about how many times I've played pushers or druggies or some heavy who's involved in something related to drugs. In real life, I only tried drugs twice in my life, and both times were during my late 1960s run of great roles.

The first was during the filming of Blake Edwards's brilliant 1968 comedy *The Party*, with Peter Sellers. Several people on the set would take a little lunchtime smoke break, if you know what I mean. That sort of thing was par for the course in those days. It seemed as if everyone was smoking something!

The Party was improvised, start to finish, with nothing but an outline for a script, which was so much fun. In fact, there's a hilarious bit in the movie involving my hairpiece that we improvised on the spot. My character's last name was Divot, which is another name for a hairpiece. I normally wouldn't like people to see me wearing it and then not wearing it, but I would do anything for Blake Edwards.

We shot on the Sam Goldwyn lot (where I would shoot some of *The Love Boat* a decade later), and a bunch of us had heard that if you smoke some banana leaves, you could get something going. So we tried it! And we got nothing. Afterward, a girl in the film said, "Why don't you follow me home tonight, and you can see what it's really like?" I have to admit, I was curious. So I went to her apartment, and I looked over and there was a couple sitting motionless, just staring at the television set with no sound on. *What's going on here?* I wondered. Anyway, she handed me a brownie and I ate it. And I waited around a little bit, and I said, "Nothing's going on here!" She asked me if I wanted to smoke, and I did, and that didn't really do anything for me either. So that was that. I went home.

The Party was such a fun shoot. I remember on our closing night, Blake said, "I'm gonna bring somebody to the party tonight. You're gonna be surprised." He brought Julie Andrews! Julie was at absolutely the top of her game at that time, and that night was the first time people saw them together—the first time they went out in public as a couple. They would later get married and stay together through thick and thin. They were still together when Blake passed away in 2010. A beautiful Hollywood love story if there ever was one.

Funny enough, Julie Andrews used to come into Downey's restaurant now and then when she was in New York doing *The Boyfriend*, back when I was a cashier. I used to see her in those days, and I reminded her that we spoke a couple of times at the register. It was so great to meet her properly, and especially to see her and Blake together.

If you've never seen *The Party*, go rent it. It's such a treat of a film, and a snapshot of the excess of that era. It has survived pretty well as a cult hit all these years, still getting just as many uproarious laughs as it did back then.

Getting back to my illicit activities. Skipping ahead to 1969, I got cast with a fantastic group of actors in a film called *Kelly's Heroes*. It was another overseas shoot that would once again pull me away from my family, this time to Yugoslavia (which no longer exists), with Carroll O'Connor, Donald Sutherland, Clint Eastwood, Don Rickles, and Telly Savalas. *What a cast!* I didn't hang around Telly very much, because he headed the infantry in the film. The rest of us worked together in the tanks in the movie. So we shot on different schedules. We were back at my friend Shep Sanders's place one night, and he had some hashish in a pipe. We had worked together on *The Sand Pebbles*, too, so I knew him well and trusted him. I was curious. Everybody kept talking about doing drugs like it was the best thing ever, you know? Here I was, a character actor known for playing druggies, and I had no idea what it really felt like to be high. So I gave it another shot. I took a few hits (as they say) and said, "Oh, man . . . I feel so mellow!"

I fell asleep for about two hours.

That was it. That was my whole experience in the drug world. (By the way, Shep Sanders became a drug counselor later in life and helped people get *off* drugs and rehabilitate. I still see him around sometimes, and he's such a great guy.)

When it came right down to it, I had no interest in doing drugs. I was only curious because if it wasn't for drugs and the junkies I played in *A Hatful of Rain* and *The Connection*, who knows when I would have gotten another play? Who knows if I would've had a career? I might never have made a dollar if it wasn't for the existence of drugs in the world. It's so strange how it all fits together.

Speaking of how it all fits together, it's a small world in Hollywood, and the twists and turns are something else. It was during this same period that Steve McQueen turned down a role in *Butch Cassidy and the Sundance Kid*, and guess who filled his shoes? Robert Redford. That movie set Redford's career on fire. Somebody should do a study someday of who wound up with certain parts versus who the producers and directors originally wanted, and how many careers were propelled because of those twists of fate. I'm fascinated by this stuff!

Redford became the biggest star around. If not for a billing thing— the Sundance Kid coming under Butch Cassidy as the "star" of that film—McQueen might have done that picture, and Redford might still be making papier-mâché ranches. Or maybe he would have given it all up to live as a rancher in Utah somewhere. I don't know. He's a terrific guy, and I think he would have found success no matter what he chose to do.

For me, the further I got into my career, the more I wanted to choose theater. Obviously, theater doesn't pay nearly as well as film or TV. So I did both. And with the popular upswing in great musicals in the 1960s, I decided it was time to put more of my talents to good use. I did a series of plays on the West Coast—including a few for a fabulous casting supervisor by the name of Ethel Winant (who would soon play a very important role in my career)—and along the way I started training to do musical theater. I could picture myself as the star of one of those big musicals, like the ones I used to love seeing with Uncle Al on Broadway. It was a dream of mine, so I decided to put in the work I needed in order to make that dream come true, brushing up on my singing and dancing. Dancing also happens to be a great way to get back into shape, and that helped me drop some of the "Moby Dick" weight I had put on in the middle of that decade.

As for the acting? I was getting plenty of practice in the TV world.

I never stopped working in those days. I did a couple of episodes of *Perry Mason*. I did one-off appearances in *Ben Casey*, *Run for Your Life*, *Combat*, *The Road West*, *Iron Horse*, *Garrison's Gorillas*, *Death Valley Days*, *A Man Called Gannon*, *Ironside*, *The Flying Nun*, and more. I still made a habit of coming back to the same shows as different characters, too, either wearing the hairpiece or not, including turns playing four separate characters on *Hogan's Heroes*, and three turns on *It Takes a Thief*. It's amazing how much work I got with a little help from that hair in the box.

I got to work with Barbara Stanwyck three times on *The Big Valley*, too, and I had so much fun with that gifted, fabulous human being. We laughed our tushes off! The first *Big Valley* episode was called "Brother Love," with Robert Goulet and Strother Martin, and I did it with the hairpiece on. For the other two I came back as a heavy, with no hair. I remember in the last one, she and I were in a boat together. I was about 255 pounds then and playing a guy who was trying to throw her in jail or something. A lot of my friends laughed when they saw me being so mean to Barbara Stanwyck. She's so tiny!

But it was the second *Big Valley* I did, in 1968, that I'll never forget. First of all, I played a bad guy alongside Lew Ayres. Lew Ayres was one of my favorite actors of all time, and we would eventually get him to play my father on *The Mary Tyler Moore Show*. But here we were playing two heavies in the Old West, which meant working with horses. (Remember the story with the pig from *Operation Petticoat*? Right. I'm just not good with animals.) Well, because of my short legs, it's hard for me to get up on a horse. They had to lower the stirrups so I could get on, and then they called "cut" and somebody had to come in and shorten the stirrups so my feet could reach them to ride. Only *after* my feet were back in the stirrups could we start shooting again.

One day we were working in the rocky desert known as Vasquez Rocks, way up high, and they had just gotten me on the horse when somebody on the set yelled, "Okay!"—and man, that horse took off. I didn't have my feet in the stirrups! What do you hold on to? I was bouncing back and forth and back and forth, and I couldn't hold on. I fell off and landed, hard. My body went bouncing and skidding over that rocky terrain. I looked like the Phantom of the Opera when I finally got home from the hospital. (Interestingly enough, my stuntman was sitting on the sidelines watching this whole thing unfold.)

They took me off the set on an aluminum ladder, because they didn't have a stretcher. Missy Stanwyck (as we all called her) was coming into work just as it happened, and she looked at me lying on that ladder all bloody and said, "Look at you. I can't leave you alone for a minute, can I?" She was such a dear. She sent something to my house. They took me to the hospital. They took me home and the kids took one look at me and started crying. The whole right side of my face was bloodied and open.

In the meantime, I was missing my job. I got a call from the production office: "We need to finish the show!" I told them I couldn't walk. They said, "We'll carry you." They couldn't finish the show without me. They were too far into it to cast another actor. "We'll turn your hat so you can hide your face. We'll make it so you can lean on a railing," they pleaded. So I did it. I didn't want to let them down. Looking at the episode on TV, nobody would know I was so badly injured. Except for me and Missy Stanwyck, of course.

Things always seem to happen all at once in life, don't they? While I was recuperating from that accident, I got a call from my agent: "Norman Lear's doing a new show. They want to see you in New York."

"I'm on a cane!" I reminded him.

It didn't matter. This was a big, big deal, he said, and they'd overlook my injuries. Norman Lear had seen me in *The Connection*, and he had wanted me for an earlier series back in 1960 that didn't work out. So we had a connection.

I told him I needed to find out a little more about it before I would agree to travel all the way to New York in my condition.

Fortunately I knew Norman Lear's secretary, Marian Rees, from that early series encounter, so I went to see her to talk about it. She said, "Gavin, this show is called *Till Death Do Us Part*. It was an English series, and it was a big hit over there. Norman wants Carroll O'Connor for the lead, but I think you are perfect for this—because this character has to be *likable* before he becomes this bigot." Playing a heavy who's likable was sort of my specialty, after all. "So we want to send you to New York to see Norman and all the producers there."

She offered to put me up in the Algonquin, and I had never stayed in that beautiful hotel. "Can I stay an extra day to go see my mother and brother?" I asked. I hadn't been back to New York in a few years.

"Sure," she said.

So I said I'd do it. They made the arrangements, and I went to New York with a cane. I went to the Algonquin and studied the script. Immediately I thought, *This is not the script for me. The character is too much of a bigot. I can't say these things. If I say these lines, they're going to think it's me, Gavin MacLeod, who's saying them!*

Needless to say, I wasn't too excited about doing the reading—but I was glad to be back in New York. On my first day in town I stopped by Jim Downey's restaurant. It was the same place, but everybody had changed. The bartender was new. The staff was all different. Nobody knew me anymore. So I turned around and left.

Norman Lear's office was right up the street. I got there early and went to the men's room. Who should walk in right after me, but Norman Lear! He said, "Gavin, I'm glad you could make it!"

It was an odd place to share our first hello in nine years.

"You know," I said, "I always liked you. You don't have any hair, I don't have any hair—but I never thought we would be in a men's room together. This is kind of interesting."

To this day, people still mistake me for Norman Lear because of our bald heads. In fact, I once signed an autograph in his name, because I didn't want to disappoint a woman who was so excited to meet him—even though it was me!

I eventually went into the audition room and did some reading for him. I read for a couple of other people too. They said, "Can you come back later?" I said, "I've got a train I've gotta make to go up to my brother's house upstate." But they really wanted me back, so I squeezed it in and read again, and then again. I was getting laughs like I couldn't believe, even though my heart wasn't in it. I really wasn't right for this character. *Just keep at it, Gavin. It's an experience. It gave you a chance to come home.* That's all I kept thinking.

For some reason, even though I wasn't giving it my all, they really liked me. I finally had to leave or I was going to miss my train. So Norman said, "Where are you going to be?"

"I'm going to be at my brother's house in Lake Mahopac. This is the phone number," I said. He promised to call me the next day.

I made the train, just in the nick of time. I got to my brother's house and my mom was there, and my grandmother was there. We had a wonderful visit. I told them all about what I was doing in Manhattan, but later that night I told my brother, "Secretly, I hope I don't get this part. The things this character says!" It had only been three or four years since the Watts Riots. I couldn't imagine anyone putting a bigoted character on television. "And they're going to have a live audience? Whoever gets it will have to wear a disguise to get out of the theater or somebody will shoot him!"

Ronnie and I talked about something a little more serious that night too: our dad. As adults, we hadn't really talked much about what it meant to lose him when we were so young. As I've mentioned, Ronnie is two years younger than I am. He had even less time together with our dad than I did. His death was devastating to both of us.

After our dad's friend got his cancer diagnosis and killed himself,

Dad would talk about how he himself wasn't going to live to see forty. And then he didn't. He died at age thirty-nine.

"Do you ever wonder if you're gonna live past thirty-nine?" Ronnie asked me.

I couldn't believe those words came out of his mouth.

"Yes!" I said. "I worry about it all the time."

Here I was, just a year or so shy of that landmark birthday. *What if I am running out of time?* Looking back, I wonder if that's why I was always working, trying to squeeze so much in. Whatever it was, it was a relief to talk about it. Just to know that my brother had been thinking some of the same thoughts lifted a weight off my shoulders. I'm so grateful to him for that.

All in all, we had a really nice time that night. It was so good to see my family. And then the next day I got the call. My whole family was right there, sitting around the room, watching to see my reaction, but the phone call wasn't from Norman Lear; it was from one of the other producers. "Gavin," he said, "we've thought long and hard about this and we really liked you, but we're gonna go with Carroll."

"Oh!" I said. "Thank you! This is the way it was supposed to be. I wish you the best with the series and I'm so glad I got to come and see my family."

I was so relieved. I wouldn't have been happy doing that show. Of course, that show would get renamed and become *All in the Family*—one of the most successful, controversial, and influential series in the history of television. It would take a couple of different pilots and a couple more years before it would get made, and it wouldn't go on air until January 1971. A lot would happen to me both personally and professionally by then. But Carroll was brilliant in it. Jean Stapleton was brilliant in it. The whole cast was phenomenal. It turned out exactly right. Just the way it was supposed to. It was one of the most incredible shows ever. I wasn't right for that show, and that was okay. I knew that someday, at some point, the right thing would come along for me if it was going to happen.

When it came to my work, I really was a glass-half-full kind of guy. I always tried to keep that positive attitude. I was always excited to see what would come next.

Little did I know, my glass was about to get very, very full.

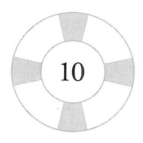

YOU'RE GONNA
MAKE IT AFTER ALL

TALK ABOUT A SMALL WORLD. I WOUND UP WORK-
ing on *Kelly's Heroes*, the very last film I would shoot in the
1960s, with none other than Carroll O'Connor. This was after
I went in for that audition, and a year and a half before *All in the Family*
would make it on air. The two of us, along with a lot of other really great
actors, worked together in an LA theater group called Theater West as
well. Hollywood was a very small world back then.

We all had fun on that *Kelly's Heroes* shoot, and Carroll and I became
good friends—and drinking buddies. We would stay up all night drinking and writing together. In fact, we came up with a project that we were
sure could be the next great American musical: *Guilt!* We worked on a
script, complete with songs with lyrics and everything!

It was months and months we shot—and months and months, once
again, that I was away from my family, drinking, and then fighting with

Rootie almost the moment I got home. While *Guilt* the musical never went anywhere, the guilt and shame I felt over the state of my marriage was eating me up. So I kept my mind on my work just about all the time.

All of us actors left Yugoslavia thinking we had done something really spectacular on that film. You never *really* know until the editing is done and they put the music in and everything, but I came home from *Kelly's Heroes* ready to tackle the world!

I belonged to another theater group at the time as well, called Words and Music. They were doing a production of *Carousel*, and the first thing I did when I got back to Hollywood was to play the part of Jigger in that fabulous musical. Jigger's kind of the heavy in it, which I loved, but the best part of that experience was that all four of my kids were in the cast. They played the Snow Children. They were all so young, and we enjoyed working together on that show, rehearsing in a space over a bowling alley. I loved being around my children. I would never stop loving being around them. Ever. No matter what happened between Rootie and me.

We were in the middle of rehearsing that stage musical when my agent called: "Mary Tyler Moore is doing a pilot called *The Mary Tyler Moore Show*, and it's CBS, and they want to see you."

I said, "Great! Where do I go?"

They sent me two scripts, and written on the front was: "Gavin— The part of Lou Grant." I read the pilot before going to sleep that night and thought, *This is funny stuff.* The writing was superb. As I read it, I told my wife, "This is written so well. But I worked with Mary on *Dick Van Dyke* twice, and I wouldn't believe myself as her boss. I'm more of a contemporary. I just don't see myself as being her boss. But there's a part of Murray, this guy, the writer Murray—maybe I could do something with him. That would be fun."

My agent set up the appointment and I was really excited. I thought this series had the potential to be something really special. Sometimes you just know these things. After all the not-so-good scripts you read, and especially given the breadth of experience I'd had in the thirteen years since I first moved out to California, you really know it when you read something great. So I went over to CBS Television City, praying, "God, let me say the right things!"

The first person I saw when I walked into the room was Ethel Winant, the casting executive I had worked for in a number of plays on the West Coast. She was now the first female vice president of CBS and was directly responsible for getting *The Mary Tyler Moore Show* on air. Seeing her was a good start, and seeing the other writer-producer talents in that room was astounding: James L. Brooks and Allan Burns. They asked what I had been up to, and I told them about *Kelly's Heroes*, and who was in it, and how the shoot went. Small talk, basically. And then I read for the part of Lou Grant.

I tell you, I got every laugh I could get—every laugh that was in that script. But I still didn't think it was right for me. The people in the room all seemed very pleased and said, "Thank you very much. You were so good!" But as I had my hand on the door handle to leave I decided to speak my mind. I stopped and turned back to them.

"Listen, you guys. The script is great. Lou Grant is a fantastic character. But the truth is, I wouldn't believe myself as him. I feel I'm more of a contemporary of Mary's. Maybe that's my problem; I always think I'm younger than I am! I don't know. But I really like the character Murray."

"You like Murray?" they said. They seemed surprised.

"Yeah! I like him."

"You want to read?"

"I sure do!" So I read a couple of lines, and the producers responded. Jim Brooks started laughing that big guffaw of his—"Oh, oh, oh!"— and Allan Burns kept saying, "Mmm, mmm . . ."

I thought, *Wow. Something just happened here.* So that's when I stopped. I stopped when they were all mid-laughter, enjoying my performance, and said, "That's all I want to do. Good luck!" And I walked out the door.

I went out into the lobby, and there was Ed Asner pacing back and forth, getting ready to go in and read for the part of Lou Grant—the very same part they had originally called me in for. We were back-to-back on our auditions. Can you believe that?

I went to a rehearsal for *Carousel*, and my agent showed up out of the blue. In person. (I had a new agent by this time, and I never expected to see him in person outside of his office, let alone walking into a rehearsal space above a bowling alley!) I said, "What's up?"

"I got a call from *The Mary Tyler Moore Show*," he said. "They want you to do her pilot."

"Wow! That's great," I said. "What part?"

He said, "I dunno. Is there a guy in there called . . . *Murray*?"

And that's how it all began—landing that fantastic role of Murray Slaughter on the hit TV show that would change my life forever, with a cast that would soon be filled with people who would become my friends for life. In fact, I came aboard early enough in the process that I got to play a small part in the casting process itself.

The writers and producers were unsure about who to cast for the neighbor, and they mentioned Cloris Leachman. "Oh, wow!" I told them. "I played opposite her. She's a gifted actress." Cloris is so gifted, she could turn "Hello" into a monologue. I saw her on Broadway and she lit up the stage. I never dreamed I'd get a chance to work with her, and then we wound up doing a Western together, *The Road West*, at Universal, during my nonstop work period in the late 1960s. I knew she'd make a fantastic Phyllis on this show.

I also loved the character named Rhoda, but I couldn't picture anyone I knew to play her. They mentioned someone named Valerie Harper, and I prayed she'd be gifted enough to handle that very important role of Mary's best friend.

We were talking about the second script even before we shot the pilot, and that second script involved Rhoda and her mother. "Who are you thinking of for the mother?" I asked. They said, "Maureen Stapleton." "Oh, what a good idea," I said, "but you know who Nancy Walker is, don't you?" They didn't. "Nancy Walker is one of the best comediennes who ever walked. She's directing a Noel Coward play, *Fallen Angels*, in

New York right now. As soon as I read your script, her first two lines, I said, 'That's *Nancy!*'"

I didn't know Nancy personally. I had just seen her on the stage.

When they finally got around to shooting that episode, guess who showed up? Nancy Walker. That show changed her whole career. She eventually found out that I was the one who recommended her, and we became very good friends.

Interestingly, CBS didn't want to include Rhoda's mother in the series. The censor department thought Rhoda was too Jewish as it was, and the mother was just *way* over the top. They didn't want them to shoot that episode or any other that included the mother. Grant Tinker, Mary's real-life husband and business partner in MTM Enterprises, said, "We're going to do it anyway." So we did it. Of course, that episode and that character went through the roof. The show won an Emmy. It started a whole new career for Nancy Walker. In addition to a series of Emmy-nominated roles in the coming years, everyone would get to know her as Rosie the waitress in twenty years' worth of TV commercial for Bounty paper towels ("the quicker picker-upper")! Hal Gould played Rhoda's father, and he was brilliant too. Those were the kind of results this show wound up getting, even when we went against the wishes of the network. It was just magic.

The final character they were missing before we shot the pilot was Ted Baxter. It took them forever to find just the right fit. Wouldn't you know it? They hired my old friend Ted Knight! We were going to be working together for the first time since he came in and did that guest role on *McHale's Navy* in the early '60s—when he told me, "You're a glorified extra." It's funny how such little moments become giant catalysts in your life. Ted and I were the best of friends, but that line made me do something. Without that harsh line he laid on me, I might never have quit *McHale's Navy* and might never have made it all the way to *The Mary Tyler Moore Show*. I'm glad he spoke up!

I could say the same thing about my decision to speak up about Murray at the *MTM* audition. I liked Murray. I didn't care that he wasn't the lead. He wasn't as big of a part as Lou Grant, and he wasn't as flashy a character as Ted—which really meant Murray was the *third* guy on the show. It didn't matter to me. I liked him. I thought I'd like to play him. It's about being honest to yourself and to others. That's all I know. I tell that to young actors all the time. I have a feeling it holds true in other professions as well.

Sometimes you don't feel that you should speak up. Perhaps it seems impolite. Perhaps you think the respectful thing to do is to let others speak first or to hold their own opinions. You keep quiet because you want to be accepted. But sometimes, speaking up gets you noticed. Sometimes speaking up is actually *more* of a show of respect to the person in charge than just sitting quietly and being respectful—because it sparks something in them. Maybe it shows them something they might not have thought of themselves. In the end, maybe that's the only way to get what you want: To speak up. To tell the truth. To say what you feel. To be honest. My own experience has proven time and time again that speaking up will get you accepted more than those times when you keep quiet in the hopes of *being* accepted. Funny, right? There's a life lesson in there about not being afraid.

Speaking of afraid, that's one thing I wasn't when we headed in for our first table read. I was excited, man! It's like opening on Broadway, where you're filled with anticipation for those curtains to open and the show to start and you just can't wait!

Walking in that first day, the writers were there, including co-creators James Brooks and Allan Burns, who introduced me to a guy named Lorenzo Music. I didn't realize Lorenzo was a writer. I thought his first name was Lorenzo and they meant that he was in charge of "music." *Wow, we've got a music supervisor for a sitcom? This is fantastic! Maybe we'll get to do a musical number,* I thought. I was embarrassed later when I realized that was the guy's name! What a fabulous, talented writer he was. He would go on to play Carlton the Doorman on *Rhoda*, and he and his wife, Henrietta, had their own song-and-dance show. They were wonderful people whom I'd get to know well over the years.

I saw Mary Tyler Moore right when I walked in, of course. We already knew each other a bit—not only from my two guest appearances on *The Dick Van Dyke Show*, but because she had come to see me in a couple of musical theater parts over the years. So it was nice to have that familiarity with the woman who was, as far as us actors were concerned, the boss.

I was looking forward to working with Ed, and it was a pleasure to shake his hand and have a laugh over the fact that we'd both been considered for the Lou Grant role. And I couldn't wait for Ted to come walking through that door. What good fortune to be working with a pal I'd known since the 1950s!

Grant Tinker was there. Some CBS people were there. I met Valerie Harper for the first time that day. Boy, oh boy! If I had any doubts that a new actress could pull off that important role of Rhoda, they went flying out the window like a hairpiece in a hurricane. She was *amazing* in her reading. She had that character *down*.

I felt as though I had my character down too. Murray was originally conceived to be an emotionally erratic person who would throw his notes in the air. But when I took over, he evolved into being an "average Joe." He represented the brown-bagger writers who work in newsrooms all over the United States of America. In fact, when the series became a hit and I went to different cities promoting it, every television station I went to had a real-life Ted Baxter (the comically egotistical, far-too-tanned, perfectly coiffed newsman), and at least one guy who would come up to me and say, "I'm Murray."

In LA, at the ABC affiliate, their newswriter's name actually *was* Murray. I met him one day and he said, "You want to see my brown bag? You're playing *me*!"

But enough about me! I can't say enough about this fantastic cast.

Mary Tyler Moore is fabulous. Intelligent. Funny. I pinched myself every day. It was such a treat to sit next to her. Everyone should be so lucky. She made going to work not only a great professional experience but a gift. She is a leader in the true sense of the word. She led our group without being condescending, without being bossy, but by example. She was on time, conscientious, never losing her sense of humor even on the most stressful, long days.

She was the first one on the set, and she never exhibited one iota of the sort of diva behavior an actress in her position might have on another show. Not one bit! And to think that she was giving herself two shots a day because of her diabetes. (She would become a powerful voice in the search for a cure for juvenile diabetes in the coming years.) She never complained. She spent her lunchtimes three days a week dancing in front of the mirror, staying in shape and at the top of her game.

I learned by watching her, and I would do my best during my *Love Boat* years, as the captain of that show's cast and crew, to emulate her professionalism. She is the best of the best.

Later on, the writers would hand us a script titled "Murray in Love," a show written especially for my character, and I have to say it was easy to play—because who wasn't in love with Mary Tyler Moore?

Then there was Valerie, a sensational person. The character of Rhoda took the country by storm. Her character gave hope to so many women who watched every Saturday night. After she won her first Emmy, she asked Mary if it would be okay to start losing weight. Mary said yes, and Valerie and I did Weight Watchers together. On some Friday nights after shooting the show, we'd frequent a well-known four-star restaurant that wasn't far from the studio—a place called Tail o' the Cock, on Ventura Boulevard. (By the way, that's the same restaurant where Ernie Borgnine held his engagement party, the first time I met Ethel Merman!) Valerie and I would get there, place our orders, and then take out our scales at the table to weigh our food. It wasn't very kosher to do a thing like that, but it sure helped us. Her weight loss was inspiring to many young women. Then she went on to star in her own spinoff, *Rhoda*. Her show was a winner, and so is she.

Lou Grant, the newsroom boss, would get his own spinoff years later, too, and that character was a breakthrough for the gifted actor and fabulous human being, Ed Asner. He was so caring, and his wife, Nancy, was one of my favorite people. Years later he became the president of the Screen Actors Guild, and he really was for the rank and file. He's a special guy and deserving of all those Emmys he won, which I think were more Emmys than just about any other actor on TV.

And Ted? What can I say about one of my best friends? He was seven years older and in so many ways was like a big brother to me. He had a tough life. I'm not sure a lot of people know about that side of him. He was a Polish kid from Rhode Island, and he lost his father at a young age. I suppose having lost our fathers was one of the things that helped create a bond between us. As funny as he was, Ted was an extremely gifted dramatic actor—and unfortunately that's not something a lot of people know about him either. Playing Ted Baxter would make it tough for him to get away with playing just about any other character for the rest of his life. That's not easy, especially for a guy as gifted as Ted. But again, I'll get into that more a little later on. For now, I'll just reiterate what a joy it was to work with that man every day, and what a joy it was to have him as a friend.

Then there were the four supporting women.

I've already mentioned Cloris Leachman, who was and is such a talent, and was quite a looker in her day too. Paul Henreid, one of my favorite actors from *Casablanca* and other things, directed us in *The Road West*. He had a crush on Cloris. Her Phyllis was a pain in the tush, but you saw a brilliant actress at work.

Joyce Bulifant played Murray's wife, Marie. She was the cutest, most lovable, giving actress I had ever worked with. Her voice was so unique—and who could forget the sass she showed off during her appearances on the hit '70s game show, *Match Game*. My wish was simply for her to have had more episodes to shine in.

Georgia Engel became one of my favorite people in the world. She is an amazing, talented actress. She's so unique and lovable. We could hardly believe her honesty and her take on Georgette. Talk about comedic timing! She was one of the best I've ever encountered, in all my years in show business. Georgie, as I call her, is also so honorable a person I would trust her with my life. That's the truth. She's never out of work on TV or in theater, and she's a gift to the world.

Georgie and I almost had the chance to do a musical together on Broadway many years later. I blew my audition, though. I got onstage and instead of doing a well-known musical number from some fabulous show, I performed a song I cowrote with my friend John Bartholomew Tucker back in college. The song was called "Bath, New York." And it went, "I like to take a bath in Bath, New York—cleanest city in the state." Ridiculous, funny lyrics that would've gone over well in the days of vaudeville! Oh, well. I blew my audition, but I had so much fun calling John to tell him, "Our song made it to Broadway!"

Finally there was Betty White. What can you say? Her Sue Ann Nivens was classic. Do you remember the episode when she was ill, and you weren't supposed to see her, so Ted, Lou, and Murray went into her bedroom and looked up and her whole ceiling was a mirror? The ceiling was only upstaged by her vibrating bed. The audience roared with laughter. Our characters didn't even have to say anything. Betty had done so much with that man-crazy character, just that visual image made your imagination run wild! She breathed so much life into that character of the Happy Homemaker. Betty made every moment count. She still does. I've declared her an American treasure, because she is just that.

Out of everyone, it was the three guys who hung out the most with each other off the set: Ed, Ted, and me. We'd always find something fun to do. Our kids all knew each other. We got together for family barbecues, and hung out at each other's houses.

Ted and I were as close as could be. He would call me after every showing on Saturday night and dish the show. Every single Saturday night for the first few years we were on: "What do you think? If we did it this other way, would we have got a bigger laugh?" He was very analytical. He would analyze the whole episode, start to finish. He cared about the work that much—as did all of us.

Because he was the last man cast, the rest of us had nice dressing rooms and Ted had a lean-to—one of these canvas things they prop up, like they had for me way back on that fateful day when I went to shoot the pilot for Hal March. This was just for the first year. Ted would say, "Well, you go to your dressing rooms. I'll go to my pizza oven." Oh my, he was funny. The fact is, they only had so many dressing rooms to work with. MTM Enterprises didn't have a lot of dough in those early days.

Our first year we shot at General Services, smack in the middle of Hollywood. The lot had its upside. They were shooting *Green Acres* there, and we'd see Eva Gabor on the lot; Shelley Winters and Debbie Reynolds were doing a movie on that lot, as were George Burns and Gracie Allen; I think Coppola started one of his major films there too. But it left much to be desired. One night, during a Friday shoot in front of our live audience, the rain started coming through the roof, all over our set! Mary's husband said, "We have to get out of here!" So we went to CBS Radford the next season.

CBS Radford is located in the Valley, closer to where everybody lived, so it was more convenient and a big step up. Years later they put a plaque on that stage: "On this site a group of friends produced *The Mary Tyler Moore Show* between 1970 and 1977." That's all it says. I've always thought that was a nice thing for them to do—and a wonderful way for them to put it: "a group of friends." That's exactly what we were. They were friends who in some ways were very much like family to me—at a time when my marriage was falling apart.

You know what show shot on that very same stage years later? *Roseanne.* Another hit show that broke through a whole new set of cultural barriers. Then a few years after that, the studio broke through two soundstages, and *That '70s Show* shot there. Mary and I did one of those shows, all those years later. And I did another with Dick Van Patten— right there on my old soundstage. I went down and saw my old dressing room, just for kicks. That was cool! As I've mentioned, I love all that Hollywood history, and feel so privileged to be a part of it.

The thing that really showed me how little money MTM had at the beginning, though, wasn't the location, or Ted's "pizza oven" dressing room. It was how little we were paid. I think it's off-putting to talk about money, but I met a very sweet woman, an actress and dancer over at Words and Music, who had a daughter who happened to be on TV that same year. Her daughter was just a kid with a small part on a much smaller show—but she told me her little girl was making more money per episode than I was!

Our salaries would change pretty significantly once *The Mary Tyler Moore Show* started pulling in big ratings every Saturday night, once it became a cultural phenomenon that television critics and women's rights advocates alike viewed as important, and once it earned its first slew of Emmy nominations in 1971. But the real reward for playing Murray wasn't the money. It was something much more important to me—a wonderful side effect that would brighten my life by the time our first summer hiatus came around.

Oh! And that little girl's mom that I mentioned? That sweet actress and dancer I met over at Words and Music? She would become a dear, dear friend to me.

In fact, she would soon become my new wife.

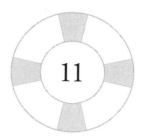

11

LOVE IS ALL AROUND

I MET PATTI IN 1970. ROOTIE AND I WENT TO SEE A
performance of *The Chocolate Soldier*, put on by the theater group
I belonged to called Words and Music. The leading lady was from
the New York City opera that night, a very high-level performer. She
was extraordinary. One of the things I find so wonderful about theater
is that actors (and singers and dancers) want to *work*, and it doesn't
have to be on Broadway. So the best of the best can be found on stages
all over this country on any given night of the week.

But my attention was pulled away from that grand dame and my
eyes were drawn to a little soubrette on stage that night—that's the
old-fashioned term for the ingénues, the younger ones in opera and
theater—this blonde in pigtails, cute as can be, dancing up a storm. I
hadn't seen her before, and I thought, *Who is that?*

I knew the choreographer, so when everyone was coming out
through the stage door I asked, "Who was that little blonde?" She said,

"Oh, that was Patti Steele." (Kendig was her maiden name, I would learn a little later. Not a name you hear very often.)

A few minutes later, Patti walked out and the choreographer introduced us. "Oh, I know you!" Patti said to me. "I love your show." So we talked for a bit.

There was something special about her. I don't want to say I met my soul mate, because part of my soul was with Rootie. We had been in and out of marriage counseling for nearly eight years. We had tried. We really had. But I felt a pull to be somewhere else so often.

And I felt something for Patti right away. There was a connection there.

I asked her what she did at Words and Music, and she told me she was a dance teacher. She was about to start a new tap-dancing class, and I had always wanted to learn tap, so I enrolled in the program.

I wasn't much of a tap dancer, so I would always be in the back of the class. "You ruined every class you ever attended!" she likes to tell me. Still, we got to know each other.

I did a show there, *A Funny Thing Happened on the Way to the Forum*. She played one of the dancing twins in that show, together with a talented singer and dancer named Albeth Paris. So we got to know each other a little bit more. Loretta Swit (from *M*A*S*H*) was in that show, too, as one of the dancing girls. It was a really great group! Everybody from *The Mary Tyler Moore Show* came to see it, and they went crazy for it. I was flattered because the lyricist who wrote "Somewhere Over the Rainbow," Yip Harburg, came to see it. He also wrote, "Buddy Can You Spare a Dime" and "Ten Cents a Dance." He's one of the great lyricists of all time! Anyway, he came to see us and he said I did well. That really meant a lot to me. Onna White, the famous choreographer who did *The Music Man* in New York and so many other things, also came to see us. She enjoyed my musical theater work too. To be acting by day on a hit TV show and moonlighting in theater was so fulfilling and gratifying, I can hardly contain myself when I write about it!

There was nothing romantic between Patti and me in the beginning.

I want to make that clear. But we became friends, and the feelings that were bubbling underneath were very real and very strong. People in Words and Music used to say we were like two peas in a pod.

Before anything romantic started, I thought Patti was such a great person that I tried to set her up on dates. Jim Brooks had gotten a divorce, and I tried to set him up with her. I said, "Jim, wait 'til you meet the girl who's coming to see the show tonight."

Jim was a young guy then. He said, "Gavin, she's too old for me!" Ha!

Patti is two weeks younger than I am. We're the same astrological sign. Not that it matters to me now, but we're both Pisces. (Patti was getting into astrology and New Age thought during that period—an attempt at finding some peace in life that we would explore together, and which I'll discuss later on.) She used to say, "Once a Pisces makes up his mind, *anyone* can change it."

She was working at an advertising agency by day back then. She had been divorced and was earning a living as a secretary. She and her three beautiful children, Thomas, Stephanie (the actress, who was fourteen when we met), and Andrew lived in a house over in Santa Monica. I used to go to voice lessons over in that seaside town, and I'd drive past her house on the way. She had rosebushes out front, and she would be out trimming the roses when I would drive past. I would always look for her.

I still lived in Granada Hills, so I'd go home afterward. But I started to think about her. A lot.

When the Primetime Emmy nominations were announced in 1971, *The Mary Tyler Moore Show* was the big story of the day. Mary was nominated. Ed was nominated. The writers were nominated. The show itself was nominated. Valerie was nominated.

I wasn't.

I'll admit I was feeling melancholy about it, even though I was happy for everybody else. I was glad for all of us to get the recognition for the work our whole crew had done. We had all worked so hard!

But that morning, as she read the paper, Rootie commented on the number of nominations. "Everybody got one but you," she said. She didn't say it in a mean way. She was just pointing it out. The thing is, I didn't need it to be pointed out. It stung enough as it was.

On that very same morning, Patti called and left me a friendly message. She said, "I just read the paper and I'm so sorry. If you want to talk about anything, give me a call." It was like somebody understood. Without me saying a word, she understood that I might be hurting, and understood that perhaps I was feeling a little left behind, or not "in the same league" as the rest of the actors on my show.

Actors are a funny bunch. We can be hard on ourselves. Our self-esteem can be pummeled pretty easily. As a dancer, Rootie understood those feelings. She just handled them in a very different way. A tougher, more pragmatic way. Looking back, I can see that we were just a little different, Rootie and me.

I called Patti back. We talked. I felt like she understood me. I made her laugh, but more importantly, I think, she made *me* laugh. Uncontrollably, at times. I just felt happy whenever I was around her. I wanted her to be in my life every day.

It wasn't long afterward that Rootie took the kids and drove up to visit her parents in Seattle. My mother, who was visiting us at the time, went to Seattle with them.

I suddenly had the chance to spend some time alone with Patti for a couple of days—and that's when I knew.

When Rootie came back, I selfishly told her, "I want a divorce."

It was, I think, the most heartbreaking thing I've ever had to do. But there was no turning back. My marriage to Rootie was over—and I had fallen in love with Patti.

I told my mother and the first thing she said was, "What are they gonna think?"

I said, "Who's *they*, Mom?"

"The family back home."

I said, "I don't care about that."

My mother was so hurt. She said she wanted to go home, so I arranged a flight and drove her to the airport. I said, "Mom, please don't think ill of me. It's just what's happened."

She was getting ready to get on the plane when she looked at me—my beautiful mother—and said, "You know? I've never understood you. But I love you anyway." I was crushed. For all the work I'd done, I hadn't made enough money to take care of her quite the way I wanted to. Thankfully, that would soon change. But in that moment, all I felt was that I had let my mother down.

I let my kids down too. I remember going into the backyard with them, to tell them that their mom and I were getting a divorce. Our dog had recently died, and David was so upset about the divorce, as if those two things were related: first the dog, and now this. He kicked a table and stormed away while my daughters bawled their little eyes out. Keith, our oldest, was just sullen.

If Patti hadn't come into my life, would I have stuck it out in my marriage to Rootie? I don't know. Maybe. Even if I had, it would have fallen apart in a matter of months. My daughters had bunk beds in the bedroom next to ours, and Julie would tell me much later, "Daddy, we used to cry just listening to you two fight in there." It's sad. It's terrible.

I think immaturity might be a word that describes it, as I reflect on it now. Getting married at twenty-four years old, back then I think I hadn't lived enough. I hadn't experienced enough to get married. It doesn't mean you don't love somebody. I loved Rootie. I always will.

I regret so much. You can't go home again, but I regret not being with my kids every single day. I moved in with Patti in Santa Monica. Being twenty miles away from my kids was miserable. I would see them every weekend, but it wasn't the same. We all used to go to church together, and bring the kids up for Communion, and I was doing every-thing with the children up until the split. I helped with their homework, and their school projects. We had just been in that glorious musical together. Only now? I barely saw them, and when I did they were often upset with me.

Their mother was so good. She was there. She was there to discipline them, and to be their friend, and she was their rock. She was a wonderful mother. That was a gift from God. I've asked for forgiveness from all of my kids, and I believe they've all forgiven me. But it took a long time. They didn't accept Patti in the beginning. Who could blame them? It was a difficult time for all of us—Rootie as much as anyone.

The marriage had been strained for so long. In reflecting back, those were my drinking days, and I know that hurt my marriage. But I tell you, she's a fabulous person. Many years later, I asked Rootie for forgiveness, and she forgave me. I'm thankful for that. But I'll always be sad about what I did to her.

The strange thing is, what I had learned in my career was now happening in my personal life too: one door closes; another one opens.

As painful as it was, the ending of my first marriage marked a new beginning in my life. To me, Patti was, and is, a miracle. She would change my life in so many positive ways, I can hardly begin to count them. I never expected to have more than four children in my life, yet I grew to love her three children. Suddenly there were seven kids in my life who all meant the world to me.

My divorce from Rootie was finalized in 1973, and Patti I got married on February 22, 1974—George Washington's birthday. The wedding had a red-white-and-blue theme to mark the day. There's a photograph from just after the ceremony. It's us and all the kids, and only one kid is smiling. Acceptance would take time, on both sides. But it would come. As would a whole lot of happiness.

I was starting a whole new life, smack-dab in the middle of that fabulous moment in my blossoming career.

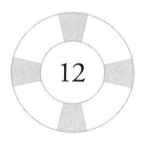

CHUCKLES

To say *The Mary Tyler Moore Show* was a hit is an understatement. It was *huge*. And I'm proud to say that every one of us who worked on it—the writers, the actors, the directors, the crew—played a part in that show's success.

During rehearsals, we sat around a big worktable, with fruit in the center. The smokers sat at one end and the nonsmokers sat at the other end, and we would work on the script and our delivery and our ideas. We would go back and forth and work around this table, the same way they did on the old *Dick Van Dyke Show*. Five days a week we were around that table. Even on shooting days, on Fridays, when a live audience would come in for our tapings, that morning we'd gather around the table and run lines or whatever we had to do.

We had a fabulous blessing in Marge Mullen. She was our script girl, keeping track of all the changes and everything, but she did much more than that. She had worked on *Dick Van Dyke*, too, and she was always full of ideas. She'd throw something out there, and we'd try it, and the writers would put it in. Week after week this would happen.

We all contributed ideas during rehearsals. It was like a committee—and let me tell you, that is not the norm! Jackie Cooper came to direct one time. He was the head of Screen Gems, and he wasn't used to that sort of collaborative atmosphere. He wanted to be one director, that's it. But we'd do a scene, and he'd get it all set up just the way he wanted, and then all of a sudden Jim and Allan would pipe up, "Why don't we try this, instead?" We were all used to that. He wasn't. He only directed one episode.

It really was a committee, and everybody participated. You have to have a lot of respect for one another to do that. And we did. I used to go out and watch Mary and Val do their scenes, when it was just the girls. It was such a treat to get to see them all work. I could have stayed in my dressing room or gone home at times, but I didn't want to miss seeing the other actors do their thing. We were that kind of a cast.

The writers would take cues from our lives too. They were so inventive. One day on the way home from rehearsal, I stopped into a store called The May Company to pick up something, and out in the lobby they had a new display of hairpieces. I went right over there, naturally, and the sales guy tried something on me. (I'm pretty sure his name was Ziggy.) He thought it looked great. *I* thought it looked great! So I bought it. I wore it home, and the kids screamed. No one was used to seeing me with a hairpiece at this point. Everyone was used to me as bald-headed Murray! So I thought, *I'm gonna wear it to work tomorrow.*

I walked in with my Hawaiian shirt and the hairpiece on, and the cast didn't know who I was for a minute. Once they recognized me, they screamed! Mary said, "Show it to the boys!" So I went and showed it to the writers, and they all cracked up. A couple of weeks later we got a new script, and it was a story about how Ted is unable to do the news one night, so Murray jumps in and does it for him—with his hairpiece on. Turns out, he's worse than Ted! After all of his criticizing Ted for blowing his lines, Murray couldn't read the news on-air to save his life. And the hairpiece was ridiculous on the head of this humble brown-bagger of a character.

I still have that hairpiece. I bring it with me sometimes and wear it when I give talks. I say, "You may remember this from *The Mary Tyler Moore Show* that we did waaaaaay back when."

That's how adaptable and creative and quick the writers were with ideas.

I've mentioned already how Murray was really the third guy on that show. Even so, the writers turned their attention to him a few times and centered whole episodes on Murray's life. Those were wonderful to play.

One of my favorites was an episode called "Strangers in the Night." Lou Grant had broken up with his wife. Mary threw a party, and Barbara Barrie was there, playing a widow or divorcée, an attractive older woman, a piano teacher or something, and they tried to fix Lou up with her. But Barbara's character had eyes for Murray. She invited Murray over to her house. Before he went to her house, he stopped and talked to Mary about it. He was nervous! I loved the friendship Mary and Murray had. He said to her, "I don't know what to do. She's going to have me at that house!" And Mary told him to be cool.

So Murray went over, and they talked, and they sat at the piano together—and I remember the song they played was, "Strangers in the night, drifting and dreaming . . ." Fans of *The Mary Tyler Moore Show* still bring up "Strangers in the Night" when they see me! Anyway, Barbara's character made a play for Murray, and just before he left, she looked at him and said, "Give me a kiss before you go." We had been doing the show three years at that point, and the live audience knew these characters inside and out, so when she said that line, and my (married) character looked at her, considering it for a moment, the live audience gasped. They started saying, "No, no, no!" They were saying it out loud! They didn't want Murray to be a cheat!

Thankfully he left. He didn't kiss her. *Whew!*

On the way home Murray stopped to see Mary. He said, "Nothing happened. I just couldn't." Mary was happy about it, and so was he. I got a lot of mail from that show. The temptations in life are something a lot of people understand, and they let me know it.

I also got a lot of mail on the episode where we adopted a Vietnamese boy. That was a beautiful thing with Joyce and me, to play parents in that sort of a situation. A lot of people also wrote in about the episode where I was moonlighting. Murray wanted to buy his wife a new car. He was gone so much, she thought he was having an affair with somebody. She finally confronted him, and he said, "No, no, honey." The punch line is that even with a second job, he can't afford to get her a new car. "You know that 1967 Chevy you always wanted? Well, that's what you're going to get." Of course it was 1970-something! That got a big laugh. People could relate to this stuff. It was so real, and so humble. Murray was an average Joe, and the audience seemed to enjoy whenever he got the spotlight. I think they felt like they were getting a little spotlight too.

I got such a kick out of the writing on that show. The episode called "Not a Christmas Show" was one of my all-time favorites. All of the characters got snowed in at work, and the Happy Homemaker (played by Betty White) was preparing to do her Christmas program. None of us could go home, so she said, "Everybody come down to my set, and we'll have a Christmas party!" (Can't you just hear her voice when you read that line? It's amazing how strong of a voice she has!) The problem was that everybody in the newsroom was angry at everybody else. The characters were so upset with each other that we didn't want to look at each other, didn't want to talk to each other, didn't want to see each other.

But we all went and sat around the table, and Betty said, "The first thing we have to do is put on our hats." So we each put on a terrible hat, and the audience just roared. We were just sitting there, still so angry at one another, but wearing these ridiculous-looking hats on our heads. I swear, it took everything I had not to burst into laughter right along with the audience. It was hard to keep it in!

"And now we're going to sing!" she said, and we all protested, "No!

We're not going to sing." But finally Georgie started in that lispy voice of hers, "On the first day of Christmas . . ." and slowly we all joined in and started singing. Eventually the mood changed and we all stopped being so angry. That episode was an insightful look at friendship, and the strains we all go through, and the ridiculousness of life and work and how it all mixes together. John Chulay directed that one. He was our first assistant director, and—in another instance of small-world Hollywood—he was also first assistant director on *Kelly's Heroes*. He was from Yugoslavia and joined us on that shoot because he could speak the language and knew his way around the culture. What a great guy, and what a great episode to get to direct!

As the show grew and grew, we had all kinds of talent come through. Walter Cronkite came on the show one time. We were doing a television news show. We talked about him all the time. He was the pinnacle of a newsman. And when he walked through those doors, the audience went crazy. They stood up and cheered. They cheered for so long, we had to stop the cameras and start again.

There were so many talented actors who worked on that show. You might not remember this, but a little girl by the name of Helen Hunt played my daughter. Once she grew up, my "daughter" got more nominations for Emmys, Oscars, and SAG Awards than I could even dream of! She's an amazing actress.

Johnny Carson did an episode too. Mary's character was known for having her parties fail. She never knew how to give a party. So she came to the office this one day and said, "You'll never guess what happened. Johnny Carson's in town and he said he would come to my house for the party tonight!" We were all so excited, we got there early and were waiting and waiting for him, and then all of a sudden the lights blew out. There was a power failure. You hear a knock at the door and someone comes in: "Hello, Mary? Mary? This is Johnny." (Chances are you can hear his voice in your head, too, can't you?) He came in and we played the whole scene in darkness. Talk about the genius of the writing on that show! That one was Jim Brooks's doing. Jim Brooks, who would go on to co-create *Taxi* and become an Oscar-winning film writer/director with *Terms of Endearment* and *Broadcast News*. When I tell you we were working with the best of the best on that show, I mean it. It was really something special!

Johnny came in for one afternoon, shot his part, and that was it. He was fabulous to work with. He was friendly and nice to everyone. I met him at a party at Chasen's restaurant one time, and he seemed like a very affable guy. And boy oh boy, when he got in front of an audience? Magic. Just humble, brilliant, magic.

The First Lady, Mrs. Ford, came on the show once. Gloria Steinem used to come by just to watch us and see what we were doing. I tell you, it was heady stuff!

And then there was the episode titled "Chuckles Bites the Dust." *TV Guide* once called it the funniest half hour in the history of comedy. David Lloyd wrote that episode. David Lloyd, who would go on to *The Bob Newhart Show, Taxi, Cheers, Frasier,* and *Wings*!

Jay Sandrich, who was our primary director, didn't want to direct it. He said, "Death isn't funny." So they got this talented actress on board instead, Joan Darling. She directed it—and got nominated for an Emmy for it.

Mary was absolutely brilliant in that groundbreaking episode. She is a fabulous actress. She can do anything. The plot was all about Chuckles the Clown, who we'd talked about quite often on the show. He was sort of a mythical character you heard about but didn't really see. The story went that he was walking in the parade that morning, and he was dressed like Peter Peanut, and the elephant that was walking behind him got hungry and tried to "shell" him. And he *died*!

Lou comes in and says, "Isn't that terrible?"

Sure, it was terrible. But the circumstances were so outrageous, some of us just couldn't stop laughing.

I said to him, "Yeah. It could have been a disaster. You know how hard it is to stop after just one peanut!"

Wow! That was the first major laugh of that episode. It brought the house down. It was the only other time I remember when we had to stop the cameras. The audience wouldn't stop laughing! Murray rarely got guffaws, but some of his wit was really something, and that was easily the biggest laugh I got on the whole series.

If you've never had the privilege of watching *The Mary Tyler Moore Show*, that is certainly one episode not to be missed. It turned comedy on its head and was simultaneously so moving and real. What a treat to be a part of something so special.

The producers of that show were smart too. They brought in new writers every year to join the regular crew, to bring fresh ideas to the table. What a gift! Especially considering that those core writers we had were some of the most incredible minds in the business. Besides Jim and Allan, there was Ed Weinberger, who would go on to co-create *The Cosby Show*. Dave Davis would co-create *Taxi* with Jim, and *The Bob Newhart Show* with Lorenzo Music. David was also the guy who created the little "meowing" kitten that came on at the end of the show under the MTM logo—a funny play on the MGM lion; and he's been in a relationship with Julie Kavner (the voice of Marge Simpson) since sometime in the mid-1970s, when they met on the set of *Rhoda*! Don't you love all the history, and the way these people meet and develop careers and relationships?

Stan Daniels, another one of our brilliant writers, passed away in 2007. He had parents in vaudeville and wrote for *The Dean Martin Show* before coming to *MTM*. Stan was really important to me, personally, and I said so when I spoke at his funeral.

Because my father had died when I was a kid, it had always been important to me to get a compliment or a pat on the back from an older man. And whenever I had a good show on *The Mary Tyler Moore Show*, Stan would come over at the end and say, "You did good, kid." It brings a tear to my eye just thinking about it. That meant so much to me.

He was one of the most creative men I ever knew. And I don't know if he ever knew that what he was doing was so important to me, but he made me feel like a mensch. This guy was brilliant too. He wrote musicals; he wrote everything. He was a tennis player, strong as can be. To warm up the audience before our Friday night tapings, he would go out and perform "Old Man River" as an old Jewish guy with a thick accent. He rolled and spat those *R*'s out, and half-spoke/half-sang each line, "He just keep rrrolling, just keep rrrrolling along."

The *audience* would be rolling!

I performed a little bit of that in his style for him at his funeral. Patti and I made a donation in his name to the Actors Home out there too. There are certain people you can still see in your mind's eye, as if they're still alive. Stan was always kind. Always nice. And I'll never forget what he did for me.

During those seven years, people got married, people got divorced, people had children, and people died. All of that happened in that *MTM* family, and by family, I mean much more than just the actors you saw. Our *MTM* family was the writers; it was the prop men; it was the costumers. It was a huge group. It's so much more than what you see on TV. And we all shared in the show's success, whether we won awards as individuals or not.

Funny enough, in all those years I played Murray Slaughter, with all of the Emmys that show picked up, I never got one myself. I was never even nominated. When every other actor on your show gets a nomination (or two or three) and many of them actually *win* one of those golden-winged statues (or two or three) and you don't? I tell you, it builds you as a human being.

Whether a person wins only has so much to do with a person's talent. I've come to realize this through the years. Certain parts are written in certain ways that attract attention and votes. Murray wasn't written that way. He wasn't flashy. He was low-key. But I was sad about not being nominated, for sure. Who wouldn't be? Especially after that final season, when I knew I wouldn't have another chance. I couldn't imagine I'd ever get to act on another show that was so well written, let alone so culturally important. Not getting nominated didn't crush me, but it was a letdown.

Remember what I said about our writers taking cues from our real lives? Well, in the last season, they wrote an episode for Murray, addressing the fact that he never won an award. The fictional TV news awards on our show were called the Teddies. Ironically, in the fictional storyline Murray had at least been *nominated*. Who would believe that he wouldn't even get nominated? But he never got the chance to go up on that stage and accept one of those awards. So on this episode, Lou heard a rumor and said, "I shouldn't tell you this, Murray, but I heard you won!"

"I *won*?"

Murray could hardly believe it: he won for Best Writer! So they all went to the awards show, and the announcer said, "And now for the Best Writer . . ." As Murray started walking up to the stage, they called another writer's name. Lou had heard wrong. Murray was heartbroken.

There was a party at Mary's house afterward, and Mary tried to cheer Murray up. She said, "Well, tell us what your speech was going to be." And my character said, "You know, this means so much to me, but I could never do it without my coworkers. Mary is the best, and Lou, and Ted . . ." It was a heart-wrenching moment, because it was the truth! If I ever got the chance to give an Emmy acceptance speech, it would have gone just like that. I was so thankful to each of those actors, and to those producers, and to those writers, and to our whole *MTM* family for giving me the opportunity to play that lovable brown-bagger, Murray.

After all, the real reward for playing that part was a gift like no other: I had a *name* now. Regional theaters all over the country wanted well-known TV stars to come anchor their plays and musicals. Now I could help draw big audiences. Can you begin to imagine how excited I was when those calls started to come in? Being on the *MTM Show* meant that during every vacation, during every hiatus, I would get to go on the road and do live theater—the thing I loved most in the world.

And the real blessing was, more often than not, I'd get to do it with Patti.

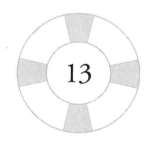

LEARNING TO QUIT

M Y LIFE WAS ON THE UPSWING ALL THROUGH the mid- to late 1970s, and I'm pretty sure I know one of the reasons for it: I stopped drinking.

I've already mentioned the night I nearly drove off a cliff as I wallowed in self-pity in that inebriated state in my car on Mulholland Drive. I've mentioned how I stayed up all night drinking with Carroll O'Connor on *Kelly's Heroes*. I talked a little bit about how I could get ugly, and get in fights with my wife when I drank.

It's not that I drank a lot, as I've said. I would have a little taste and I'd be out. I never had a capacity for a lot. And hard liquor? It only touched my lips when I was doing *Operation Petticoat*, when Arthur O'Connell invited me to the place he was living in down in Key West. A couple of us went down there, and he said, "You've gotta drink some Ballantine's Scotch!"

"Oh, who wants to drink that kind of stuff?" I said.

"You gotta try some," he insisted. "You're not a man 'til you try some!"

So I tried it and said, "Ick, this is like medicine!" But before you know it, we were there for a long time and I said, "Maybe I'll have another one." Even then I remember thinking, *I don't like this stuff. Why am I drinking it?*

I didn't drink a lot—until I got on *McHale's Navy* and was so unhappy. But after I was off that show, once my career was going a little better for me, I didn't drink quite as often. But I still drank, and sometimes I drank too much.

Just before we got married, Patti and I went to Reno, Nevada, to see our friend Kaye Ballard—the brilliantly talented actress, comedienne, and singer. I had done a run of *Gypsy* with Kaye earlier, in 1973 in San Diego, in a burlesque theater with Linda Kaye Henning. It was a terrific show, everybody will tell you. But that's another story.

Kaye was playing this gig in Reno with the Lennon Sisters, and she invited Patti and me to come see her. We met her afterward and had a good time, and I got to drinking some kind of alcohol. I don't even remember what it was, but whatever it was, it went down easy. I lost track. I kept slurping them down until I was sloppy drunk. I remember thinking how much fun we all were having! Until afterward, on the way back to the hotel, when Patti said to me, "I want to tell you something. I don't like you when you're like this. My first husband was an alcoholic, and I'm not going to marry another one."

Boy, did that hit hard.

An alcoholic. Was that what I was? I never wanted to be an alcoholic. I vowed that I wouldn't be like my father. Whether or not I *was* an alcoholic, I certainly didn't want to be *perceived* as an alcoholic, by anyone, and especially by the woman I loved. *What am I doing?* I thought. *Am I turning into my father? Am I following in the gutter-bound footsteps of his father?*

I woke up the next morning and said to Patti, "I've got something to tell you. I really love you, and I'm never going to drink again."

That was 1974, and I haven't had a drink since. Not one. I've never wanted it, never even craved it.

Where did I get that sort of willpower? I think it had been there all along. I remembered that my grandfather did the same thing, so I knew I could do it too. Or maybe I just wasn't a lush. Maybe I didn't *need* alcohol like a lot of people do. I was just careless with it, and my carelessness was costing me.

Or maybe, just maybe, it was God's help once again.

My grandfather, Jimmy Shea, the Irish master carpenter with the bald head, my mother's father, had made that deal with God. When his son, Johnny, came home safe from the war, he never drank again. That story sure resonated with me that weekend.

"I wasted forty-eight years of my life," my grandfather had once told me. Here I was, already forty-two years old. I had let the bottle interfere with my first marriage already. I knew I didn't want to waste any more of my life, so I resolved, "If my grandfather could do it, I can do it." He was my blood. He's part of me. And it was astounding to me to think about how much he changed once he stopped drinking. He was a scary, mean guy before that. Without the alcohol, he became funny. He became charming. He became loving. That real man was there all along, only the alcohol was hiding it! (What was it hiding in me?) My grandfather was alive, and when I took Patti back east to see him for the first time, he said, "Did you bring your daughter to see me?" That Irish charm was there all the way 'til the end.

I knew when I made that promise to Patti, it was a promise I could keep. *If Grandpa could do it, I can do it.* And I did it.

Not drinking in a town full of drinkers, I did run into some resentment from some of my friends. I would go to parties and they would get high on booze, and one in particular—a big-name actor—came over to me once. I was just standing with Patti and he said, "You think you're smart, don't you? You're not drinking and you're looking down on us." I thought, *Why are you so unhappy?* I couldn't understand how my decision not to drink was somehow hurtful to *him*!

I did the same thing with cigarettes. I haven't talked about the fact that I smoked because back then we didn't think it was a big deal.

Everybody smoked in those days! I tried maybe one cigarette in high school and then really started smoking in college. I remember once I saw a cigarette butt on the street and I picked it up and smoked it. That's how bad the cravings got. After a while I was smoking two packs a day.

When I first met Patti, she said, "Smoking is not good for you." (Patti is responsible for cleaning up a lot of stuff in my life!) After I first started on *The Mary Tyler Moore Show*, I went to a doctor and he said, "I watch the show you're on all the time. You're in bad shape."

I said, "I am?"

He said, "Yes, you are. I've run some tests, and you've gotta stop smoking. Do you want to see your grandkids?"

"Of course I want to see my grandkids!"

"You'll never see 'em if you don't stop smoking."

I was shocked. But I decided to listen to that doctor, and to Patti. I went home that day and said, "Kids. Look at these." I held up my pack of cigarettes and declared, "I'm never going to smoke again." I put down the box, and I never smoked again. I joined the nonsmokers' side of the big worktable at the *MTM Show* and never felt better about a decision.

If I can do it, anybody can do it. Willpower is strong! I believe that. You just have to have faith in yourself—and God—and make sure you know where your priorities stand.

Years later I was forced to give up coffee for my health, and I did it the same way: cold turkey. When you have to make a decision in life, and the answer is just as clear-cut, black-and-white as a decision that could cost you your health or your love or your life, why would anyone hesitate to make the right decision?

After quitting drinking, quitting smoking, even the painful "quitting" of my first marriage—after all of that, I was finally ready to start taking steps in the right direction with my life.

It felt good. *I* felt good, for a while at least.

They were only the first steps, though. I had no idea how much farther I still had to walk.

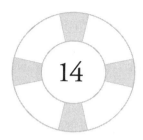

14

THE FAME GAME

LL THE ACTORS ON *THE MARY TYLER MOORE*
Show had millions upon millions of adoring fans throughout
the 1970s. It's not like TV today, where just a fraction of a percentage point of Americans watches any given episode at any given time.
In those days, you had millions upon millions of viewers, all watching at
the *same* time. There were no DVRs. Heck, the *VCR* wasn't even around
yet! There was no competition from the Internet or anywhere else. So
you watched your shows when they were on, and then the next day
everyone talked about them.

I gotta tell you, being in America's living rooms week after week was
a gift from God to me! People felt they knew me. *Really* knew me.

Murray represented all the brown-baggers—not just in newsrooms,
but in all sorts of professions. He was the kind of guy who never got a
raise and had to get an extra job to buy something for his kids, or to
buy something nice for his wife. In some ways, that made him one of
the most approachable, relatable characters on TV. Being that relatable

brings a very different kind of fame than people like Steve McQueen experienced.

Speaking of whom, the last time I saw Steve McQueen in person I was on my way to work at *The Mary Tyler Moore Show*, and I was getting well known. A car pulled up alongside me on Vincente Boulevard. It was Steve and his bride, Ali MacGraw, who now lives in Santa Fe. She did *Love Story* with Ryan O'Neal; she's wonderful. He waved and smiled, and gave me a thumbs-up. He was clearly aware of what I was up to and all the fame that was coming my way.

Then he got cancer. He went to Mexico and all over trying to find a cure. I remember he filmed this Swedish play. He had a beard on, and he was big, and you would never know it was Steve McQueen. I didn't see it at that time, because I just couldn't. It was too heartbreaking for me. But years later I watched it. Even in that state he had that vulnerability—that power in the close-up of the camera lens.

Thinking back to the Steve McQueen I knew, the thing I really remember is that he never knew his mother. His aunt had raised him. He had heard that his mother was in California, so he came out here to find her, and she died the day before he got here. So he had a chip on his shoulder. The story goes that he was in a Boys Town over in Chatsworth. And I tell you, whatever he learned in the Actors Studio about "making moments" as an actor, he used—and he made them on film. In film you can take all the time you want in the world, which you can't do in theater. He used that to his advantage. But the vulnerability he had, you're born with that. And that's really something.

The thing that really struck me, though, was this: fame couldn't keep him from cancer. Fame couldn't keep him from heartache. Fame couldn't keep him alive. Thinking about the meteoric rise of Steve McQueen, and the sadness of the end of his life, made me wonder. To be close to a guy like that, even briefly, put a lot of things into perspective for me.

Fame, for me, in the way I achieved it with the down-to-earth character of Murray, didn't put me up on some kind of a pedestal. People would approach me in a friendly way, as if they knew me. They were happy to see me. Not giddy, not screaming like people did for some big-screen idol, but just happy. I've always enjoyed meeting people, and I'm always gracious signing autographs or taking pictures. Why wouldn't I be? This is the best job in the world! Being on TV allowed me to be on the stage, whenever I wanted. What a gift!

As our salaries went up on *The Mary Tyler Moore Show*, and went up significantly in the series that followed that show, my fame also allowed me to buy some nice things. I fell in love with real estate and architecture, and I would move Patti and the kids into a series of ever-bigger, ever-nicer houses as the years went by. (Rootie and our kids were content to stay put in the house in Granada Hills, where Rootie still lives to this day.) I picked up a fabulous apartment in New York City, just east of Central Park and across the street from the Metropolitan Museum of Art. We moved into the Pacific Palisades at one point, on the western-most edge of the United States, on the brink of the Pacific Ocean. And Patti and I bought a house in Palm Springs, where we could get away from the hustle and bustle (and traffic) of Los Angeles.

But the best house that TV-fame money would buy wasn't for me. It was for my mom: I was able to buy her a nice condo back in Pleasantville. It was right down the street from the Catholic church, within walking distance of everywhere she needed to be. Years later, when she was forced to give up her driver's license, that turned into a bigger blessing than either of us ever could have imagined.

I counted my blessings all the time as my fame grew. I counted those blessings because I also knew that fame could bring plenty of curses.

My friend Ted Knight wound up experiencing the curse side of things because of the very same show we were on together. Ted was brilliant in the role of Ted Baxter. Audiences loved him. But I'm glad I saw him prior to that in his dramatic work, because he would never get to do that sort of work again after *The Mary Tyler Moore Show*. That really bothered him. He would say, "The character's name is Ted, my name's Ted, and when I walk into places everyone says 'Ted' and starts laughing." It was over for him after that. He was never accepted again as a serious actor. And I've gotta say, when I saw him play Hornbeck in *Inherit the Wind*, he was better than Tony Randall, and even Gene Kelly, who played the role in the movie version. I didn't know Ted back when I saw him in that, so I'm impartial when I say this: he brought so much to that role, he even took on the *look* of Hornbeck. He was just so powerful. And then I saw him play the DA in the play *Compulsion*. He was great in that too. He did a movie about the Lincoln-Douglass debates. So many incredible dramatic roles!

Ted was heartbroken over being typecast, and his experience proved to me that your success can also be your downfall. It can keep you from doing other work that you love. In that regard, I was very glad I played Murray. He was so relatable, so approachable, so friendly, and so real, I had a feeling it wouldn't harm my career going forward one bit.

Boy, would that be an understatement!

Jessica Tandy once said that as an actor, you often get paid the most for the roles that require the least amount of work. That was certainly true of Murray. This was nothing like playing Leach, or Big Chicken, or any of those tough character roles I had once played. In a lot of ways, Murray was a lot like me. I knew this guy. He was an underdog. He worked hard. He cared deeply about his family and friends. He wanted to do the right thing. So I just sort of played myself a lot of the time, and as a result, theaters all over the country were thrilled to have a "big television actor" grace their stage. They had no idea that I probably would have done those plays for free, just to get the chance to take lead roles in some of those fabulous musicals. I was living the dream. And Patti was right there at my side.

Patti and I created our first nightclub act during my *MTM* days. We put together a whole song-and-dance show, and we took it to a beautiful theater in Texas. My fame allowed me to not only do what I love but do it with my wife. I was blessed.

Fame also got me noticed by some people who really meant a lot to me.

When Bing Crosby was in the hospital, not long before he died, Mary Tyler Moore went to pay him a visit. She came back and told me that Bing wanted her to tell me something: he was "proud of me." More than a decade had gone by since I'd had my little moment with Bing on the set of *High Time*. I had no thought in my brain that a guy like that would even remember who I was. But he did. And he was *proud of me.* What a fantastic feeling that was.

Yet, in some ways, all the fame and attention I was getting scared me a bit. I was acutely aware that fame wouldn't protect me from illness, or from loss, or from any of the heartache that I didn't want to feel in life.

I often think of the losses that Mary Tyler Moore has endured. This fabulous actress and wonderful human being lost her sister right after the *MTM Show* ended. Two years after that, she lost her son in a horrible accident. She lost her brother in the 1990s too.

During the 1970s, I didn't know how I would handle that sort of loss in my life. I was terrified. Where would I turn if something terrible happened? I didn't even have the church anymore. As a Catholic, once you get a divorce, you're excommunicated. You're out! So throughout my rise to fame, I stumbled, spiritually speaking.

Patti was exploring New Age religion when I met her, and we got into that whole thing as the 1970s progressed. It was great, on the surface at least, the whole idea that everything revolved around the self. *You* have the power to be healthy. *You* have the power to be fulfilled. *You* have the power to bring happiness into your life. It was all about *you*! And there was no such thing as sin. Boy, if that isn't appealing to an actor who loves the spotlight, tell me what is?

The thing I was coming to realize is that fame doesn't give a person fulfillment. Fame doesn't protect a person from heartache. At its best, it opens some doors. It allows you to touch an audience. But making the most of that opportunity isn't easy, and I sometimes wondered if I should be doing more with this gift that I had been given.

Increasingly I was seeing and interacting with people who had all the money in the world. I was starting to feel as if *I* had all the money in the world. Yet it started to set in that money didn't matter. Money wasn't an answer. Fame wasn't an answer. There were days when I would know in my heart that I should feel as though I were on top of the world, but I *didn't* feel that way. I felt a certain emptiness. A "hole." A longing for something more, just as I had felt during my drinking years, in the years when my first marriage was struggling. It didn't have anything to do with Patti. I loved her, she loved me, and the two of us were fabulous together. We had so much fun everywhere we went. We were always laughing, and that is certainly one of the most important ingredients in a successful marriage.

It was just a feeling that something was missing.

Fame and money were not providing the answers I was looking for. I didn't really know I was looking for answers, to tell you the truth. I didn't know I *needed* answers. Come to think of it, I didn't even know what the *questions* were!

In the coming years I would experience fame unlike anything I ever imagined. Yet the more I "had it all," the closer I would come to losing everything.

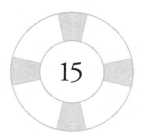

CLIMB ABOARD

THE MARY TYLER MOORE SHOW CAME TO A CLOSE,
and our final episode was a classic. The collaborative spirit we
all had behind the scenes played out in pure physical comedy, as our whole group gathered in the newsroom, arms around one
another, holding so tightly that we didn't want to let go. Under new
management, all of our characters (except for Ted) had been fired from
the six o'clock news! And when the tears started to flow and some of us
needed a tissue, rather than let go of one another, we all shuffled across
the floor in one mass toward the tissue box on Mary's desk.

Boy oh boy, that moment when Mary was the last to leave, and she
looked back into the empty newsroom for a moment before turning out
the lights—*wow*. The end of an era for American television.

Not to mention the end of an era for me. I was out of a job!

Valerie had *Rhoda*. Ed was going directly into the one-hour drama
Lou Grant. Ted was joining a new show called *Too Close for Comfort*.
No one had any doubt that Mary would go on to anchor another hit

show after all those Emmy wins. Everyone seemed destined to go on to big things!

Me? I was happy to take a break and to head to Palm Springs with my wife. Patti and I were spending more and more time in that beautiful desert oasis, and we were thinking of putting another nightclub act together. I wasn't really interested in doing TV anymore. The stage was where I found my joy, and the opportunities just kept rolling in. I had my choice of choices! It was fabulous.

So we had our final *MTM* party, and at the end of the night, as I was packing a few final things from my dressing room into the trunk of my car in the parking lot, Mary's manager walked up to me. "I'm so sad for you, Gavin. What are you going to do next?" I was shocked. I said, "Arthur, are you kidding? I feel like a bird that's been let out of a cage. I'm going to land someplace and be very happy." I meant it too. That whole notion of doors closing and opening had really sunk in by the time 1977 came around. I had a good feeling I would have plenty of opportunities going forward—and I was right.

Within days of our final *MTM* taping, my agent started calling me, trying to talk me back into television. He was getting offers, he said, and he convinced me to take a look. *If the right thing comes along*, I thought, *who knows?*

The first pilot to come my way was a cowboy show starring Jeff Bridges. I took a look at the script, and wouldn't you know it? The character they wanted me to play was just like Murray Slaughter, only in a cowboy suit! It's amazing how people can't think outside the box. I read it and immediately said, "That's not right for me." The last thing I wanted to do was to be typecast.

The very next offer I got, my agent called and said, "Aaron Spelling wants you to do this pilot called *The Love Boat*." This was just a couple of weeks after *The Mary Tyler Moore Show* finished shooting. "He wants you to play the captain of this cruise ship."

I said, "Wasn't that done before?" My agent wasn't sure. I looked into it and in fact there had been two separate pilots for *The Love Boat*, both of which aired as TV movies, and both of which featured different captains. *If the show hasn't taken off after two pilots already, what hope does it have of getting on the air?* I knew Aaron Spelling was a big deal. He was well on his way to becoming the king of television in those days. Nonetheless, I had doubts. I hadn't seen those previous pilots, so I asked my agent for a straight-up answer.

"Did you read the script?" I asked.

"Yes," he said.

"Well, what did you think of it?"

"I think it sucks." God's honest truth! Those were his exact words.

The fact that Aaron Spelling was interested in me was an enormous compliment, though, so I asked to read the script myself. I had him send it over, and I read it—and I started weeping at one of the stories.

There were three distinct stories in the pilot episode, but the one that got me was kind of like *Love, American Style* set on the water. The story went like this: an old Jewish man (who would be played by the great Phil Silvers when we shot it) was at the end of his life, and he had lost all of his friends. There was no more space in the cemetery. They're piling 'em up! So he planned to go on the ship, die, and be thrown overboard. In the meantime, there was an older lady who showed up on the cruise by herself. (Audra Lindley, the actress who played Feldman's wife on *Three's Company*, would play the part.) These two met onboard, they talked, they danced—and they fell in love. These two old people. It was beautiful. It just touched my heart. And then she went to meet him toward the end of the cruise, and he was gone. He had passed away.

It made me cry.

There were two other stories in the pilot, one a sophisticated comedy, one a broad comedy. And I remember thinking, *If there are three stories like this in every episode, and one of them is a poignant one like this, I'm in!*

I read that script down in Palm Springs. I gave it to Patti to read too. I trust her judgment like no one else's. "If they cast it right, and put it on the right time—there isn't anything on television like this," she told me, "and I think it can really make it."

So I made an appointment to go see Aaron Spelling at his estate.

In the meantime, my agent called with another show for me to consider over at NBC. I wound up going to NBC first, to see Aaron Ruben, who produced *The Andy Griffith Show*. Turns out he wanted me to be the lead in his show too—a show about three guys who haven't made it in life, who sit around making cryptic comments. They were unhappy guys. It was a good script, but like so many things I've read through the years, I just didn't think it was for me.

So I went to Aaron Spelling's house. I had never met him in person before, but I respected him so much. There he was, this little guy from Texas who used to get beat up, and now he was a huge success, becoming Mr. ABC. He was friendly as could be. The kind of guy who would never forget where he came from, no matter how much success he had.

I asked him whether *The Love Boat* would have those three storylines in every episode—two humorous, one serious—and he said yes.

In my mind, I knew I wanted it right then.

Aaron was very aware that I loved the theater, and he knew I didn't want to give it up. He had also seen me do guest appearances on game shows like *Hollywood Squares*. I got a kick out of all that stuff, and I was honored to even be asked to be a part of those fun television moments. "I know you like diversification," Aaron said. "I can work around you. I can make your part small one week so you can do what you want to do. I can make your part bigger one week. You can go do a game show, or theater, or other things. We can work around you. We'll have a lot of guest stars. But we want *you* to play the Captain."

I was thrilled. I was jumping up and down inside. *Me? The Captain? The guy at the top?* It seemed almost too good to be true! But I played it cool. I said, "I told my agent I wouldn't say yes while I was here, and I've got another script by Aaron Ruben to read. So can I have a little time?"

Aaron said okay.

I went back to my agent, and I read Ruben's script, and it had all these lines making fun of Jimmy Carter, who was president at the time, and it just wasn't funny to me. It was too negative. I told my agent I didn't want to do it. "They're guys who don't have a desire to make it. Why are they even alive?" I said. I wasn't interested in doing something negative. *Why would anybody be interested in watching something so negative?* I turned it down, and that show never aired on TV.

So we called Aaron Spelling back, and we put together a deal to shoot the pilot for this show called *The Love Boat.*

In the meantime, Gower Champion called—the famous musical theater director who did *Hello Dolly* and so many big musicals on Broadway. He and Blake Edwards went to high school together. They had a part open in a production of *Annie Get Your Gun* that they were getting ready to do in San Francisco, and they wanted me to come in and audition for the second lead male role!

Have I mentioned before how everything seems to happen all at once in life?

The Love Boat was moving fast. Both Aaron and the network (ABC) were already happy with three of the cast members they had used in the second pilot: two young guys I had never met before, Fred Grandy in the role of the ship's purser, "Gopher" Smith, and Ted Lange in the role of bartender Isaac Washington; and Bernie Koppel in the role of "Doc," the ship's doctor, Adam Bricker. I knew Bernie! I'd known him for a million years. He was one of those Hollywood actors who was all over the place, like me, so we'd cross paths everywhere. He had even done an episode of *Mary Tyler Moore.* Bernie is one of the funniest actors ever, and he's an excellent dialectician. He can do any dialect in the book! If you saw him in *Get Smart,* that alone would tell you what he's capable of. I was excited to work with him, and excited to meet the new guys too.

There was just one problem: they couldn't find the right girl to play the cruise director, Julie McCoy. That part just didn't click in either of the first two pilots, and both Aaron and the network wanted someone special. They wanted a "today" girl—a girl who looked like the living embodiment of a vibrant young woman in 1977. It's funny, you would think that all sorts of vibrant young women who were hanging around Hollywood in 1977 would embody the look and style of 1977, wouldn't you? But the show had something very specific they were after. They auditioned eleven girls opposite me, and that was after weeding through hundreds of potential actresses, and even flying some in from New York! They just couldn't find her.

Two weeks before cameras were set to roll, we did our first reading—without a Julie. Someone on staff filled in and read her part as we sat around a table. Ted and Fred were both fabulous guys, and it was clear from the moment we started that Bernie and I clicked. We'd be the "old guys" in the cast, without question. We were in our forties! That's over the hill, man! But who on earth was going to play the role of Julie?

It really came down to the wire. In fact, I wouldn't meet our Julie McCoy until the first day of shooting. We shot the first scenes for our pilot aboard the *Queen Mary*, that massive, beautiful old ship docked down in Long Beach. The interiors and even the pools were built on the Twentieth Century Fox lot and were exact replicas of the interiors and pools on two real-life Princess cruise ships. Cruising wasn't a popular industry in those days. Princess only had two ships, total. Having never been on a cruise myself, I instantly became intrigued by the whole idea. The only thing we cheated a bit on our sets was the size of the rooms: the cabins on real ships aren't as big as the ones on our show. We needed room to fit people and cameras and lights, and for the actors to move around. Once the show became a hit, we'd get letters from people who took cruises, complaining that their rooms were small! They accused us of false advertising.

Anyway, the first time I laid eyes on Lauren Tewes—whom we all called Cindy (she was born Cynthia Lauren Tewes, and only used Lauren professionally)—I understood exactly what Aaron and the network had been looking so long and hard to find. She was perfect for the role of Julie! And you know who finally found her? Candy Spelling, Aaron's wife. She had a flash of genius one day when they were talking about how tough it had been to cast Julie. She remembered a girl who had played a one-day role on Aaron's other megahit, *Charlie's Angels*. She thought this girl, whoever she was, would be perfect. So Aaron listened to his wife. They looked her up, tracked her down, and just like that this young actress with just a handful of one-off credits to her name got a call to come in for a starring role on this pilot.

With Cindy on board as Julie McCoy, we got to work. I put on that captain's uniform for the very first time and stepped into the role of Captain Merrill Stubing. The captain had originally been conceived as a stern, authoritative boss—but I saw him as something different. I saw him as a leader: the kind of guy who cares deeply about his crew, and his passengers, and who takes *responsibility* for his crew and his passengers in a loving way. So in that sense, Merrill Stubing would become more of a father figure in my hands. I thought that was important. To me, *that* seemed like the type of guy people would like to watch week after week on TV.

The cast got along well on that shoot. Bernie and I had a million laughs. We shot that pilot over the course of about a week, we all said good-bye and good luck, and then we went off to wait. Lots of pilots are shot every year. Very few get made into TV shows. That's just a fact. So I didn't get wound up or worried about it. I just did my job, hoped for the best, and moved on.

I auditioned for Gower Champion, and he cast me in *Annie Get Your Gun*, starring Debbie Reynolds as Annie Oakley—Debbie Reynolds, whom I had fallen in love with in college when I first saw her in the movie *Singin' in the Rain*. I could not believe I had this opportunity! Over the course of the coming weeks, this musical started really turning into something big. We were set to open in San Francisco with a twenty-eight-piece orchestra. It was a dream come true for me! I'd never worked on a musical of that size and scope before. This was Broadway quality, and Broadway big. Finally I had achieved the melding of my musical interests and acting interests, going all the way back to those childhood days when my uncle Al brought me to the theater in Manhattan. The costumes, the makeup, the orchestra, the lights—and I was in the center! I couldn't believe it was happening to me. I was so excited, I almost forgot about *The Love Boat*.

Six days before our big opening in San Francisco, I came home from rehearsal and Patti met me at the door, excited. "Aaron wants you to call," she said. "They sold *The Love Boat*!"

I panicked. I didn't think it would sell so quickly. I said, "Patti, if I have to pick, I'm gonna stay with *Annie Get Your Gun*. I've been waiting a lifetime to do a musical like this."

She understood completely. If it had come down to a choice, I would have turned down *The Love Boat*. That's how much I love the stage.

I called Aaron and he was so excited: "Gavin! I can't believe it! They saw it today and they pushed the buttons on the computers for the Captain. The buttons went through the roof!" He was talking about a test screening they had done of the pilot episode to gauge audience reaction. They pull a random selection of the viewing public into a room with ratings buttons on their seats, and the audience members push buttons to express how they're feeling as they watch a show, in real time. TV was getting more and more sophisticated. And apparently, the moment I appeared on screen in that captain's uniform, the audience went nuts—in a good way. "They couldn't believe it was *you*! They loved it. You're gonna be on the air! We're gonna start shooting!" Aaron said. He was like a kid, he was so enthusiastic. I love that kind of enthusiasm in a person!

Plus, I'm an actor. Getting high marks from an audience was as flattering as could be. I was thrilled. When he finally let me get a word in, though, I said nervously, "Aaron, I'm gonna open up in San Francisco in a few days in *Annie Get Your Gun*." I was scared to death. I wasn't sure what he would say.

"Well," he said, without skipping a beat, "I told you I'd work around you, so I'm gonna work around you."

Simple as that. Aaron Spelling, this powerful mogul of a man, would let me do the musical at the same time we were shooting the show. So we made the deal. *The Mary Tyler Moore Show* went off the air in the spring of 1977, and *The Love Boat* came on the air that same fall. As far as viewers were concerned, it was almost like Murray Slaughter got a promotion. A promotion to the number one position on a show: the Captain. *Murray struck gold!*

Murray was the underdog, the guy who works hard but never catches a big break—and now here I was, Gavin MacLeod, suiting up and getting to be the boss. They were two completely different shows, on two different networks, but there was something about that underdog, everyday guy making good that resonated with audiences. And to think that two previous pilots of *The Love Boat*, starring two different and capable actors in the role of the Captain, had failed! It makes you wonder sometimes: *Why me?*

Looking back on it, the only explanation I have for how any of this amazing voyage of my life has unfolded is that it was all part of God's plan. He had bigger things in store for me. Bigger things than I possibly could have imagined. I mean, honestly, can you imagine anything bigger than landing the top role on a primetime television series that would become a huge hit? I certainly couldn't have imagined anything bigger than that in 1977. It would take decades for me to understand the true path I was on.

The whole thing was also rather ironic, given the fact that I never picked up so much as an Emmy nomination during my seven-year run on *MTM*. I started *The Love Boat*—and wound up having the longest-running show of any of the *MTM* cast members. Who'd have thought?

And I still got to pursue my first passion—live theater!

Let me explain to you just how accommodating Aaron Spelling was with me. Every day I would shoot *The Love Boat*. About four fifteen in the afternoon, one of his drivers would pick me up and take me to LAX, where I'd fly to San Francisco and go right to the theater. I'd have something to eat. Do the show. Fly home late at night.

Patti liked to say, "There's a man that gets into my bed at one thirty in the morning and leaves at six. I hope to *God* it's my husband."

I'd do that schedule during the week, and then on the weekends I would stay up in San Francisco and do the musical full-time. We would close up there after five or six weeks and then open in downtown LA So I was still doing both things, but at least I didn't have to fly. At that particular time, *Annie Get Your Gun* made more money at the Dorothy Chandler Theater than any other musical before. Aaron worked around my schedule, exactly as he said he would.

Good things happen to people who keep their word. Aaron Spelling could've said, "Look kid, come on. You're gonna be seen by the world here. What are you doing, a little *facacta* musical?" But he didn't say that. He worked around it.

He used to be an actor, so he knew.

He also knew how to make a hit—despite what the critics thought. The critics *hated* us! I'm sure most viewers have forgotten, but reviewers referred to *The Love Boat* as "mindless television." They predicted it would sink like the *Titanic*!

In fact, at one of our presentations before the show launched, a critic asked me directly, "Why would you want to do *this* show?"

"Because I liked it," I said. "I think I'm an ordinary person, and I think I would like to see a show like this, with big stars on the water, and life changes, and happy endings every week. What do you want for an hour of television?"

Sometimes the critics don't know what they're talking about. Plain and simple. Their tastes are often very different from those of the general public. That "mindless television" show not only became a hit, lighting up living rooms all over America every Saturday night for the next nine years, but it caught on in countries all over the world. It had something special that reached across borders and appealed to many cultures.

Oh, and one more thing: it gave birth to an entire industry. Cruising would become a new vacation option for millions of Americans. People everywhere started calling up their travel agents and saying they wanted to take a vacation on *The Love Boat*!

The original cast of
The Mary Tyler Moore Show

New girls on
The Mary Tyler Moore Show

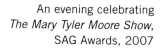

The one and only
Mary Richards,
sleeping on the job

An evening celebrating
The Mary Tyler Moore Show,
SAG Awards, 2007

Ted and Murray—
dig those crazy
'70s shirts!

Murray at his typewriter

Final bow of last season, 1977—real tears flowed

Love is wonderful
the second time
around—with
Shirley and Pat
Boone as matron
of honor and best
man, June 1985

With my daughter
Julie at her wedding

Nothing makes me cry more than
being the father of the bride!

With my daughter Meghan at her wedding

With my stepdaughter,
Stephanie, at her wedding

First *Love Boat* publicity photo, taken in 1977 at ABC

Andy Warhol, special guest— what a thrill to work with this artistic genius!

Patti and the Captain on board *The Love Boat* in Australia

Pinching myself! Ethel Merman, Ann Miller, and Carol Channing—does it get any better?

Uncle Miltie and the two captains— me and Alan "Gilligan's Island" Hale Jr.

Helen Hayes, first lady of the American theater

Raymond Burr, one of my favorite actors

Kyoto, Japan—that's me in the authentic kimono

After cruising a few years on *The Love Boat*, Jill Whelan joined the crew. She was adorable and talented.

Ted, Fred, and me at the Forbidden City, on location in China

Cruise to Alaska with stepdaughter Stephanie Steel guesting with Mark Harmon

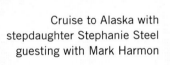

Accepting the People's Choice Award in 1978— "The people loved us!"

Sharing a TV Land Award with my
favorite TV doctor, Bernie Kopell

"The *Love Boat* Follies"—
a dream come true

Patti and me
waving bon voyage

I guest-starred with
Linda Evans on
The Bob Hope Show.
Bob was right:
"We're pretty good
bookends."

Mike and the "Moon River" great, Andy Williams

Mike and me singing "She's Too Fat For Me"

Patti—she's not too fat for me!

At a party in Bel Air with Betty White, George Burns, and David Wayne

This role I was playing would turn into something much more than just a role. Over time, I would become part of the cruising industry—an industry I still remain a part of all these many years later. I mean, come on! Who would've thought?

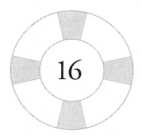

16

SHIPMATES

YOU KNOW WHO WAS MAKING THE MOST MONEY on all of Aaron Spelling's various productions back in those days? John Forsythe—and yours truly. Can you believe it? Me! This bald-headed kid from Pleasantville, New York, who mowed lawns for one dollar apiece, became one of the highest-paid actors around.

My salary wasn't anywhere near what TV actors get paid today, believe me. Not even close. But Aaron paid me good money to play the Captain. His thing was that he would give you the money up front—and not a percentage on the back end. Not the residuals. You hear about the cast of *Friends* and some of these other shows in the decades that followed making more money *after* their shows went off the air and went into syndication than they did when they were actually doing the work. That definitely wasn't the case with any of us. We only got residuals for the first six showings, and the amount of that residual payment would decrease each time the show aired. So I realized pretty early that

I'd have to be careful to put my pennies away for the future. Who knew when all of this fabulousness in my life might come to a halt?

The thing is, the money almost didn't matter. I know that sounds ridiculous, especially coming from someone who grew up poor, but it's true. I was still getting to do live theater during our breaks and vacations, and I was getting more invites for bigger shows at bigger regional theaters all over the country. Plus, I was filled up and "paid" many lifetimes over simply by the experience of being on that show—by getting to act (and interact) with all of those fabulous stars of the stage and screen who came on each week as our guest stars.

How many men can tell you for certain that Joan Collins is a good kisser? I can! She came on the show and played this Elizabeth Taylor–type of character who wanted to make the Captain her tenth husband. It was fun to work opposite that fabulous lady.

I got to work with some of the hottest stars of the day, too, including Barbie Benton, who was dating Hugh Hefner at the time, and Farrah Fawcett, whose poster was pinned up in every teenage boy's room in America. Boy, was *that* fabulous! We did a whole crossover episode with *Charlie's Angels* in our second year, which was a pretty cutting-edge thing to do at that time (and certainly savvy marketing on the part of Aaron Spelling, as a creator behind both of those shows).

But for me, the biggest thrill I got was when we brought on some of the older talent. The show was such a gift to so many actors who had "passed their prime." It was a godsend to old Hollywood. The only show that's ever come close to us in featuring so many guest-starring roles for actors was *Murder, She Wrote*. But we had three story arcs per episode, and love stories, and opportunities for so many actors from the stage and screen to come aboard each week, there was truly nothing like it. I was so proud to be there, to glimpse that history, and to see these men and women, whom I'd admired from afar, up close and in action.

Given my love of musical theater, you can probably imagine the joy I derived from an episode we did called "The Love Boat Follies." I got to do a musical number on my show with Ethel Merman, Carol Channing,

Ann Miller, Della Reese, Van Johnson, and Cab Calloway! All legends, and many of whom have passed on now. Oh, the memories. I wore this sparkly silver jumpsuit in the big number at the end. Behind the scenes I remember Ethel and Carol argued over who'd get picked up first by the limo each morning—divas to the end.

I tell you something that bothers me, though: Carol Channing has never been honored at the Kennedy Center Honors. They've honored Chita Rivera and all of these other actresses for their legendary stage roles. Why not Carol? Think about *Hello Dolly*. She must've done that show more than anybody else in the world. To think I got to work with that fantastic talent. I saw her do *Hello Dolly* in her prime when I was younger, and now here I was working with her!

I felt the same enthusiasm for Ethel Merman. Sure, I got to meet her and go to her engagement party way back when I was on *McHale's Navy*. But this was different. She was here now, on *my* show, and we were performing a musical number together. I was pinching myself the whole time. I should also mention that Ernie Borgnine did a *Love Boat* episode at one point too. To think I had played a "glorified extra" aboard his PT boat, and now I was welcoming him aboard my cruise ship as the Captain! It was great to see him. We had a few laughs reminiscing about the old days, that's for sure. We had both come a long way.

I think my pure joy during the making of that "Follies" episode was balanced by the views of the critics when it aired: the reviewers hated it! The guy at the *Los Angeles Times* wrote, "When Gavin MacLeod finished his number, they should have torpedoed the ship." Ha! I laughed my tail off at that comment. Fred Grandy got so mad, I can't repeat what he said. But I was beyond worrying about the critics anymore. We had the love of the audience. That's all that mattered. That dichotomy would be the story of *The Love Boat* from day one: the critics hated us; the people loved us. But it's the people who kept us on the air.

The parade of talent seemed endless. One morning I arrived on the set to find some of the biggest legends from the theater world, the very people I wanted to be like when I grew up, all sitting together at the

Captain's Table—including Helen Hayes, the First Lady of the American Theater, and Maurice Evans. I could hardly talk! Yet *they* were the ones saying, "We're a little nervous for this first scene." *They're just like the rest of us!* I thought.

I never stopped being in awe. Ever.

Milton Berle, Uncle Miltie himself, came on when he was getting older. He was still full of such wit, yet his memory wasn't quite what it used to be. He was one of only two actors who came on who had to use cue cards (the old-fashioned kind that a guy would hold up with his hands, next to the camera). The other was Phil Silvers, whom they hired back a few years after that pilot episode he did so he could play the Captain's father—mainly because he was bald, like me!

When Helen Hayes did her episode, we threw her a big party, on February 22, 1980, which also happened to be my sixth wedding anniversary with Patti. Oh my word, Patti was so vivacious. We both wore tuxedos to that party! There were all kinds of photographers and our picture wound up in the papers. We were in the papers a lot in those days. Ron Galella, the famous paparazzo, and lots of other paparazzi followed me around quite a bit, snapping pictures of me out on the town, or attending events in New York and LA. I was on a big TV show now, and the papers all wanted to know more about me. I think they were all hoping there would be some kind of a scandal to write about. Especially since I played such a nice guy on TV. They would sell a lot of papers if the "nice guy" Gavin MacLeod turned out to be not so nice, wouldn't they? I did my best to ignore that part of the business, and to concentrate on the parts that I love.

My jaw dropped to the floor week after week seeing what kind of guests would come on this show. Lillian Gish came on one time. *Lillian Gish!* The First Lady of American Cinema! This gorgeous creature with the fabulous eyes who lit up the screen when screens were first being lit up. An actress who had worked with D. W. Griffith, way back at the dawn of the film industry. I remember we were rehearsing a scene and she said, "Cinematographer? I can't see his eyes. If I can't see his eyes, I'm not going to do this scene. You have to see his eyes." She made our cine-matographer relight me so she could see my eyes! I was simply in awe.

In 1984 they flew Luise Rainer all the way in from France to do an episode. She was the first actress to win back-to-back Oscars, for *The Great Ziegfeld* and *The Good Earth*. She was ninety years old by then, and *The Love Boat* gave her a chance to play dual roles, one an elegant woman, one a maid. She was *fabulous*. All of that talent, sitting quietly, unused, untapped, was suddenly uncorked and allowed to breathe on the decks of the *Pacific Princess*. What a gift.

They brought on Joan Fontaine, who had starred opposite Laurence Olivier in *Rebecca* and wowed everyone in *Jane Eyre*; and not long after that they flew her older sister in, the grande dame herself, Olivia de Havilland, from *Gone with the Wind* and *Robin Hood*. These two sisters and megastars of the silver screen had stopped speaking to each other. Yet they both wound up acting on our show in their later years. My grandmother had taken me to the movies just to see Olivia de Havilland in *To Each His Own* in 1946—and here I was, holding her in my arms.

I thought, *If my grandmother could see me now.*

Lew Ayres and Janet Gaynor came on for one episode. She won the first Oscar in the history of Oscars, and this was the third time I got to work with Lew. The first was on *The Big Valley*, playing the heavies, and then he came to play my father on *MTM*. Janet Gaynor's husband had produced the last play that I did on Broadway, way back in 1962—the one that closed so quickly it left me desperate and worried enough to sign on for the "glorified extra" role on *McHale's Navy*. Such a small world. They were both such talented actors, and I'm humbled to think that her role on *The Love Boat* would mark the very last role of Janet's life. She died in 1984.

I swear I could live off the richness of that history alone.

I mean, Douglas Fairbanks Jr. and Ginger Rogers were on our show. What a treat! I was talking to Ginger Rogers—which was ground-shaking for me to begin with—just before the shoot and she said, "Who's going to play my boyfriend on this?" I said, "Didn't you hear?

It's Douglas Fairbanks Jr." She said, "My God, I haven't seen him since we were engaged." Turns out they had broken up long ago, and they were reunited for the very first time on our show.

Raymond Burr came on—what a thrill *that* was for me. I had done small roles on *Perry Mason* and *Ironside*. *And now he's coming on my show?* I was enamored of his talent. He had such a great presence. (Did you know he raised orchids as a hobby? Interesting side note for such a big guy.) He brought his friend on the boat as well. He was an older guy. It was nice that we had an atmosphere on that set in which people could bring their significant others along and no one would mind—and no one would talk about it, since it obviously would have caused some controversy back in the day. (Burr's homosexuality wouldn't be revealed until sometime after his death in 1993.)

Susan Strasberg came on the show too. She was a delight to work with. You think of *The Diary of Anne Frank*, all this beautiful work she did, and the friendship she shared with Marilyn Monroe, and then all those years later she killed herself. Why? Someone of such talent. I can never understand why.

So many of the great actors who came on our show have passed on. I don't want to dwell on it. It's too sad to even think about. Especially since I had such laughs on that show each and every week.

I got to work with the hilarious Phyllis Diller one time. She played an inspector or something and she started coming after the Captain. There was one scene where she climbed up on the desk trying to get me! We had so much fun on that shoot. And Rue McClanahan was one of my favorite comedic actresses. I just loved her. She came on cruises with us and would pick up all sorts of young sailors everywhere she went. Her *Golden Girls* character (a few years later) would turn out to be a lot like she was in real life! I remember when I first came to California, one of my costars in *A Hatful of Rain*, John Patrick Hayes, knocked on my door and said, "Look what I got!" He had picked up an Oscar nomination for Best Short Subject—but what he really wanted to show off was his girlfriend. It was Rue! What a hot ticket she was.

The older ladies loved to come on our show, in part, because we had a phenomenal makeup guy, Larry Darr, "The Cowboy," a real artist who would do everything in his power to make them look good. He used something called "facelift tape" to give them a little lift when necessary. He just loved working with older women, especially the grande dames of stage and screen, and there wasn't a one of them who didn't look great on our show.

I was able to bring my friends onto the show at times too. Ted Knight came on a couple of episodes, one in Japan, and once when I had broken my leg. I had fallen in Australia while we were shooting, and he and I played captains together. We both got to wear a uniform! That was fun. We laughed and laughed, like we always did. He also took a cruise with us up to Alaska one time, where our characters competed against each other in a dogsledding competition. (Only the dogsledding was filmed on the back lot at Warner Brothers Studio!)

Valerie Harper came on and joined us on a cruise to Egypt, of all places. It was so great to spend time with her again, and on a journey like that. One of the big perks of getting to do this show was taking real-life cruises. We would shoot most things at the studio, and we would take seven-day cruises to Mexico on one of the two Princess ships to get exterior shots, usually returning to some port at the end of the day. Then, every once in a while, especially as the show grew in popularity, we would take off on a trip somewhere in Europe. As the Captain, they'd always put me up in the biggest, most beautiful cabin on the boat. When Valerie came on that trip to Egypt, she brought her husband, Tony, along, and I offered my cabin to them. "Take it! I'm just one guy. You'll enjoy it. It's the chance of a lifetime!" I said. But Valerie wouldn't hear of it. She insisted that I keep that big room.

"You earned this," she said to me.

I have to tell you, that was an incredibly sweet thing for her to say. I'll never forget it. She has always been someone special to me.

Of course, the best friend of all that I got to bring aboard so many of those cruises, and to bring to the set for a whole series of roles on the show, was Patti. The first time she landed a role was a surprise. The two of us were invited to Cindy's (Julie McCoy's) first wedding, in 1977, and Aaron Spelling happened to be sitting in the pew right in front of us. Out of the blue he turned around and said, "Patti, I've got a great role for you on next week's show!"

I had never asked about having Patti on the show. As much as I loved working with her, and was actively working with her onstage every chance I got—we had a whole second nightclub act that we put together during my *Love Boat* years—it just didn't seem kosher to ask your boss to give a role to your wife, you know what I mean? But that's just the kind of guy Aaron was. Patti would come on and play six different roles on different episodes of *The Love Boat* over the years. She would even take a cue from my old days and wear different wigs at times, so no one would recognize her. It was fantastic, and we would cherish those moments together, working and laughing and setting sail to foreign lands.

I went to Japan, where I performed Kabuki in full makeup and robes for one segment of the show. I saw the Great Wall of China. (Fred said it was a "nice" wall.) I traveled through Greece (where young Prince Albert II of Monaco developed a crush on Jill Whelan, our little Vicki, and followed her all over). I went to Russia. And I'll never forget that trip with Valerie, in Egypt, where I saw the pyramids, and the Sphinx, and the Kissing Camel . . .

"What's the 'Kissing Camel,'" you ask? Let's hope you never have to find out in person. One day in Egypt, we had wrapped up the shoot, and my producer Doug Cramer came running over to me: "Gavin, we've got this camel here. They call him the Kissing Camel. I want you to take off your hat and let him kiss your bald head!"

I said, "Oh, Doug, are you *crazy*?!"

"It will make *Time* magazine!" he insisted.

Alexis Smith was on that episode. That husky-voiced actress who'd had so much acclaim for her roles opposite Cary Grant and Paul Newman and so many others in the 1940s and 1950s did a few episodes of *The Love Boat* over the years. I turned to Alexis and said, "Isn't this awful, what we do?"

She just laughed, knowingly. Anyone who's been on top has had to do some embarrassing things for the sake of publicity. It's just a part of the business.

Anyway, I relented, and the camel came over. I took off my hat, the camel puckered its lips, and its handler pulled it closer and closer. Those beasts—they regurgitate their food, and their breath is just awful—but I swear that camel's handler had worse breath than the camel! Finally, it planted a big, sloppy, beastly kiss on my bald head. They took the photo, and wouldn't you know it? It really did make *Time* magazine. There it was, for the world to see. So I guess it was worth the embarrassment. And the stench.

Getting to see all of that history all over the world was amazing. And getting to *make* history on our show was amazing too.

We had Sir John Mills and his daughters, Juliet Mills and Hayley Mills, all on one episode at the same time. We were the first show to have all three members of that acting family working together, ever. Juliet Mills and I played opposite each other, and we revised our "relationship" on a show called *Hotel* later too. But I'll never forget when I welcomed John onto the ship. His hand was wringing wet. We stopped shooting and he said to me, in that charming British accent of his, "It's rather like going back to school, isn't it, old boy?" *Even a famous actor like that can still get nervous coming onto a new show,* I thought. *How about that?*

In 1984, we had Vanessa Williams on our show—*after* her Miss America crown had been stripped. Someone had unearthed some controversial photos of her in rather un-ladylike poses and sold them to *Penthouse* magazine, so to have that former Miss America on a show as wholesome and family friendly as *The Love Boat*, playing herself, in a segment titled "Hit or Miss America," was very controversial.

In a way, every show we did was historic. Think about this: we had the Temptations, Hulk Hogan, and Andy Warhol all on the same episode. Can you even *imagine* that? All on the same hour of television?

When would that ever happen today? All of those fantastic talents from completely different worlds, colliding on one ship. I can't imagine any show that could bring such diverse personalities together, let alone have a broad-enough fan base to want to *watch* all of them together in one show!

Andy Warhol and I wound up posing for the cover of *L.A. Weekly* magazine. He was dressed all in black (of course), and I stood in my Captain whites. I liked him a lot. He wrote about me, too, in his book called *Andy Warhol's Party Book*. He and I spent an entire lunch hour taking pictures together. I had first met him a few days earlier at my producer Doug Cramer's house. Doug threw a big party to welcome him to town. Andy was a very shy guy. He had four or five people who traveled with him to protect him and all that kind of stuff, and he wore that strange hairpiece. But he was very sweet and dear to me. It was quite an honor to spend a lunch hour with Andy Warhol. He didn't talk that much, though. I probably said more to the photographer, Jim McHugh, who was doing the shoot!

It's almost surreal to think about how popular *The Love Boat* became, and how my role of the Captain became sort of iconic in that era. I was just an actor, playing my part, learning my lines, trying to make Captain Stubing as honorable and likable a guy as I could. Yet here I was being photographed with Andy Warhol, an icon of that era if there ever was one; and sharing the TV screen with The Temptations, that iconic group, and Hulk Hogan, the most iconic professional wrestler of all time—the guy who set the bar for everyone else!

It's hard to see it for all it is when you're in the middle of it. I felt the same way about *The Mary Tyler Moore Show*. I was acting, learning my lines, prepping for stage work during our breaks. It was the critics and audiences who had the luxury of indulging in the cultural meaning of the work more than any of us actors—until it was all over and we could look back on it, I suppose. Even so, I never let go of the awe and wonder: the fact that little old me got to stand in the presence of so much greatness.

MY CREW

EVERYBODY LOVED THE CAPTAIN. PART OF IT, I think, was that no one could believe that this tanned Captain in dark glasses could possibly be the same guy who played Murray. I think that's why the transition worked. Everybody knew Murray. And when we put in the extra effort to make Merrill Stubing a likable guy on every level, that really went far in embedding this Captain in the consciousness of the audience.

I talked to our producer, Gordon Farr, about the Captain's sternness in the early scripts, and he's the one who first said, "We want to soften him up and make him more like you." I said, "Okay, let me start working on that." And I did.

I love playing the stern guy, the heavy, the deeply flawed character. That stuff is great to play as an actor, much more rewarding than playing a nice guy. But playing Captain Stubing as a man who was caring, who helped people with their problems, was better for the show.

He was the antithesis of Murray in some ways. Murray had a

typewriter. This guy had a whole ship and thousands of people under him. He had to have authority, and in that regard, I don't think it was my acting so much as my uniform that made an impact. I've found that uniforms say a lot. If you put a guy in a uniform, people will listen to him more than if he's in street clothes, or even his sailor whites. Even though I was only acting, I emanated a sense of authority whenever I put on that uniform. The uniform itself was what did it. It's a symbol of authority. And the writers made sure the Captain lived up to that authority.

When you think of a captain's responsibility in real life, it's not just for himself; it truly is for every single person on that ship. You may not have noticed this when you watched the show, but the Captain never drank. Not a drop. We tried to make that point, subtly. It was mentioned once on an earlier episode, when Ray Miland, a young Mark Harmon, Lorne Greene, Eleanor Parker, Charlene Tilton, Donny Most, and some other wonderful actors—including our daughter Stephanie—were on the show. We hit some terrible waves on that cruise up to Alaska. It was frightening. We did our best to keep it from the press because we didn't want people to think cruising was dangerous. But it wasn't until a later show, when Raymond Burr came on and played a heavy drinker, that the Captain got a chance to pull his character aside and reveal his full history: Captain Stubing had been an alcoholic when he was younger, and he spoke about how you can ruin every moment in your life, and not even remember them. It was certainly a truth that resonated with me, as an actor and a human being.

Putting lessons into a TV show isn't easy without sounding corny, but *The Love Boat* made it work. In fact, we got letters from viewers who decided to quit drinking after that episode: "If the Captain can do it, so can I!" Talk about humbling.

Patti and I were walking to church one Sunday in New York City, and this lady stopped me and said, "Aren't you the Captain?" I said, "Yes." She said, "I want you to tell those writers something." I thought, *Uh-oh. Here we go.*

To my delight, she said, "I looooove their messages—because they cover them with cotton candy." I thought that was so interesting for a fan to say, because that's a difficult thing for writers to do. That lady was right. Mary Tyler Moore used to say, "You don't have to get hit over the head with a turkey bladder to make the laugh. The laugh is there!" *The Love Boat's* approach to some very serious messages was handled in the same subtle way. Granted, some shows were better than others, but we had a great team.

Captain Stubing was a single guy, of course. He couldn't be a "player," the way Bernie was with his character, Doc. It wouldn't be becoming of a Captain to be sleeping around with lots of different women. But the writers didn't want him to seem loveless, either, so for one storyline they did a flashback. It showed Merrill in his younger days, having an affair with a beautiful girl. It was a warm scene in front of a fireplace, and very lovey-dovey. And he said to this girl, "Will you marry me?" She looked at him and replied, "On one condition. It's either me or the sea."

He couldn't do it. The Captain couldn't quit his job. His first love was the sea. His first love was being the Captain. That's why he was still a bachelor.

I asked a real ship's captain from England whether that storyline rang true. "Would this really happen?" I asked.

He said, "Gavin, I don't want to tell you this, but it happened to *me*. I had to make a choice. It doesn't mean that I haven't stopped thinking about her. But somehow, the sea was in my blood."

The depth of the Captain's character, and the truth that served as the foundation of that character, resonated far and wide.

During the show's second season, Aaron called me into his office. "Gavin, we have an idea about something, and I want to know what you think about it. What do you think about us bringing on a young girl as your daughter, to help us get the younger audience?"

I was confused. The Captain didn't have a wife. I said, "Aaron, where is she going to come from?"

"She's going to come from that affair you had with that beautiful girl who made you choose between her and the sea. This could be your daughter from her."

It was brilliant.

I said, "If you think it will help the show, I'll do it." So they wrote an episode with a little girl who came aboard the ship. She had her aunt with her, and the aunt looked familiar to the Captain, but he couldn't quite place her. She even went so far as to say, "Look at you; you both have the same blue eyes!" Then there's a scene where he talked to the aunt, and the aunt didn't reveal very much, but it was enough to raise some questions in his mind. When they docked, the little girl went missing. The Captain went looking for her and wound up at the house where the little girl and her mother used to live, before her mother passed away. He recognized the house. He'd been there before. He found the girl. She was sitting with her mother's diary. She'd read it. That's when the little girl said, "Tell me the truth. You're my father, aren't you?"

The Captain looked at her, knowing the answer would be life-changing. He thought back to the scene in front of the fireplace with his former lover, and he put it all together in his mind. He said, "I am."

Those were some beautiful scenes. Very emotionally moving. A father and a daughter, discovering each other for the first time. The two of them decide they want to be together, so she joins him on the ship to live with her daddy as he sails the high seas. What a life for a little girl! Can you imagine? A lot of kids all over America suddenly wished the Captain were their dad!

Jill Whelan was cast in that role, and she was a natural-born actress. It marked the beginning of her career. In another small-world moment, she and her mother, Carol, had actually seen me in *Annie Get Your Gun* in San Francisco just as *The Love Boat* first set sail! Boy, time flies. Little Jill has her own kids now, sings at a club in New York, and has a successful radio show in Los Angeles. She was married to a very handsome guy she met in an elevator (which sounds like something right out of a script on our show), but she divorced him. She eventually remarried—on a Princess ship!—and her new husband is just great.

Want to know a really interesting fact? Every regular character on *The Love Boat*, including little Jill, my daughter, has been divorced at least once in real life. All of 'em. I'm surprised some tabloid journalist hasn't jumped on that fact and dubbed it "The Love Boat Curse" or something! But you know what? It wasn't a curse. Not at all. We're all happier now. We've all found new love and moved on to great things in our lives, even if we went through some major ups and downs before we got there.

Jill was the youngest of us regulars. I was the oldest. Bernie's a little younger than me, and the older guys, the writers, the producers—so many of them are gone now. Aaron's no longer with us. I remember how sad I was when I heard that he had throat cancer. One can only guess it had something to do with his smoking a pipe all those years. I can't believe I smoked cigarettes for as long as I did. I might not be here if I kept smoking. (Praise be to God for Patti's influence!)

It's strange to think that so many of those people are gone.

I was so blessed to spend all of those years with that brilliant cast. We really became an extended family to one another: I was like the father; Bernie was the uncle; and Fred, Ted, Cindy, and Jill were the younger generation.

Like any extended family, you all grow apart a little bit after the kids leave the nest. But we've all stayed in touch through the years, and it's always such a joy to see one another when we get the chance. I'm so proud of all of them!

Fred Grandy was brilliant. He had an Ivy League education and had learned some hard lessons from the school of life. His mother and father died in a crash and he was raised by his older brother. Through all of that, he emerged as this bright, go-getter of a guy. He was a speechwriter in Washington and wrote some off-Broadway plays, and *then* he came out to Los Angeles with his wife, had two little kids, and got this big hit TV show where his character, Gopher, would get tons of laughs. A year or so before our show ended, Fred was determined to do something bigger than acting. "I have to do something with my life that's important.

I want to help people from where I came from," he told me. He wound up running for the House of Representatives from his home state of Iowa. I was proud to campaign for him up there. In fact, I gave him his first check! I went home and told Patti after he first brought up the idea, and we gave him a check to get started. He said, "I'm taking this to Washington with me. This makes me a viable candidate!" He was so excited.

He called me after the election and told me he won by a small percent. I was thrilled for him. Plus, I had never been close to a congressman. I remember he told me, "Now you know somebody in a medium-high place."

The next time he ran for office, I heard he won by more than a 60 percent margin, and he served four consecutive terms. By the time we got together for a *Love Boat* reunion on *The Oprah Winfrey Show* in 1997, he had become the president and CEO of Goodwill Industries. He has a radio program out of Washington, DC, too, and I have a feeling he'll always serve as a bright voice in the conservative landscape. What a fascinating guy.

Ted Lange was very, very, very popular on our show, playing that lovable bartender Isaac. Ted was such a wonderful actor and seemed to absorb everything when he came on that show. He and Fred used to call Bernie and me the "old farts," but they both liked hearing our stories of life in Hollywood and all the great actors and directors we had worked with through the years. I enjoyed hearing their stories too. Ted made his Broadway debut in the breakthrough musical *Hair*, in 1968. He had attended the Royal Academy of Dramatic Art in London. He had quite a pedigree!

The role of Isaac was so distinct, Ted easily could have been typecast for the rest of his life, just the way Ted Knight almost was with Ted Baxter. But he wasn't. He fought hard to keep his serious side going after *The Love Boat* ended, and he has since become a prolific writer and director.

You know who always had faith in him? His mother. Right after we started the series, this woman came backstage to see me in *Annie Get Your Gun* up in San Francisco, and she introduced herself: "Gavin? I'm Ted's mother."

"Oh!" I said. "You must be so proud of him, getting a job like *this*."

And she said, "I've always been proud of him."

That was so cool. I'll never forget how nice it was for me to go back and tell him how proud his mother was. I'm sure he already knew, but it's always nice to hear that someone's proud of you, isn't it?

He directed a whole bunch of *Love Boat* episodes in our later years, plus episodes of *The Fall Guy*, and later *Moesha* and *Dharma & Greg*. He was busy directing multiple episodes of two big shows in 2012–2013, *The First Family* and *Mr. Box Office*. He also directed a stunning *Othello* for the big screen back in 1989 and puts on new, original plays all the time. I saw an original of his called *George Washington's Boy* back in 2000, and it was brilliant. It was about the relationship George Washington had with one of his slaves and raised the question of whether our first president was actually the father of this young man.

Ted's first wife was a dancer. They married in 1978, and he has two grown boys now, and he's married to a lovely woman named Mary. I'm so proud of him too!

I never got as close to Cindy Tewes as I would have liked during our years together on that show. She has faced some terrible ups and downs in her lifetime. We talked about her background when we first got to know each other. She had gone to Catholic school, but she got involved in all kinds of rebellious stuff during high school. I could hardly believe the stories she told me. I felt like such an innocent by comparison!

She met a guy on a commercial shoot that first year, and Aaron Spelling paid for her whole wedding at the Hotel Bel Air. (As I mentioned, it was at that wedding when Aaron first asked Patti to come play a role on the show.)

The wedding was gorgeous. *She* was gorgeous! But there were problems already starting behind closed doors, stuff that nobody knew about. She got involved with substance abuse—something she would later admit, which I admired her for doing. She and her first husband divorced after only three or four years. She met an Italian drummer, Paolo, a great guy, on one of our cruises, and the two of them would eventually marry.

She left the show in 1984, and there were two different actresses who would try to fill her shoes. Neither of them caught on with the audience like she did. Cindy *was* Julie. She *was* that "today" girl. And it was so sad to see her spiral down. The tabloids were relentless. They followed her all over the place and made her life far worse than it had to be.

Eventually, she escaped from Los Angeles and the whole Hollywood scene. She divorced the drummer and found true love with a man whom Patti and I would get to know when we all reconnected nearly two decades later.

I'll talk more about Cindy a little later on, because the two of us would grow much closer in the end. It's funny how people can come into your life, and then leave, and then come back. We were in each other's lives for a reason, I think—but that reason wouldn't become clear until each of us had gone through some major life changes.

And that leaves Bernie—my fellow "old fart." Bernie's only a year younger than me, but playing that role of Doc made him into a sex symbol. Can you believe it? It was the first time in his life he got all kinds of attention from the ladies! Boy, did we laugh about that. You just never know in life. One minute you're a character actor wanted more for your savvy use of dialects than you are for your looks, and the next you're a stud in the eyes of millions of women all over the world! Women sure do love a man in a uniform. It's true.

Bernie was married to Yolanda, a beautiful girl, when we started, and they stayed married all the way through the end of the series. Then they divorced. I couldn't understand it. I always thought they were great together.

Anyway, he went down to Florida, did a play at Burt Reynolds's theater, and met this talented woman from upstate New York who was the producer/stage manager. They fell in love. He told me all about her.

Next time I saw him, I finally met this fabulous woman named Catrina, and I couldn't have been more pleased. He was happier than ever. And before you knew it, they were having a baby! They had a second boy after that too. Can I remind you again that Bernie's only a year younger than I am? I can't even imagine having little kids at that age. It floored me! It floored *him* too.

He told me a funny story once. After their first boy was born, Bernie was headed out of his local CVS drugstore with a box of diapers, and the woman checking him out recognized him and said, "Oh, Mr. Koppel, I'm so sorry."

"Sorry for what?" he said.

"The diapers."

"They're not for me!" he said. "They're for my baby boy!"

The fact that he's surrounded by the love of his children and enjoying a happy marriage makes me happy. He and I had more scenes together on that show than either of us had with anyone else. That's a lot of time you spend with someone over the course of nine years, and I couldn't have spent it with a better guy.

The fact is, during those years, I spent far more time with my *Love Boat* family than I did with my real one. I guess that's inevitable. It's the nature of being the top guy at work, whether you're the Captain of *The Love Boat* or a top manager at some corporation. I would leave my house when it was dark, and come home long after it was dark again. Twelve-hour, even fourteen-hour days were the norm. Most hourlong dramas take ten days to shoot a single episode. That's the schedule Ed was doing over at *Lou Grant*, for instance. Not us, though. We were doing an hourlong show every *seven* days! With forty-eight extras! We went into what they call "golden hours" on Saturday many times in order to get the show finished. Imagine only having seven days for a big show like that—with all those extras, the boarding scenes, the big scenes in the carousel lounge. It was a massive undertaking, week after week. An hour of TV is like half a film each week.

Luckily, we had good background players. We had great stand-ins too. They're the folks who fill in for us actors while the crew sets up the lights and gets the shots arranged, so we can run lines and do other things and no one is wasting time just standing around. I had the same guy for years, Lee, a Jewish man who used to work in vaudeville. (I envied him for that!) He gave me a beautiful Jewish Bible with jewels on it as a gift one time, which I cherished. He was very efficient on the set, and he worked so hard. He would watch me, this professional stand-in, and learn my mannerisms and my stance, so everything would be perfect when I came out there to do my part.

All of those guys and gals were part of my *Love Boat* family. This show, just like the *MTM Show*, was life-altering for everyone involved. We worked together for nine straight years. That's a long time! Two years longer than *MTM* lasted. So once again, there would be romances, heartbreaks, marriages, divorces, even deaths. The show marked each of us in different ways.

No matter where we went for the rest of our lives, we would always be a part of that big, crazy *Love Boat* family. In so many ways, this was the big one. For all of us. And we'd all have to learn what to do with that massive gift of a hit that Aaron Spelling gave to each and every one of us.

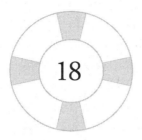

SEEING STARS

W ITH *THE LOVE BOAT* LAUNCH A BONA FIDE
success, and the Captain's smile seared into the American
mind-set, the doors of opportunity swung open for me
like never before. When you're popular, suddenly everyone wants to be
your friend—and everyone wants to have you at their party. In my case,
because I was well known for my work in live theater, I wound up field-
ing invites to perform on all kinds of shows, to make guest appearances
all over, and to lend my talents to some of the charitable efforts that
some really big stars and politicians were involved in. I was so excited
to meet so many of these amazing people, I said yes to just about everything! Wouldn't you?

Of course one of the biggest stars *and* politicians all rolled into
one was Ronald Reagan, and my encounters with Reagan began all the
way back in 1960. I remember I got a call. Universal was producing *GE
Theater* at the time, and Reagan—who was the president of the Screen
Actors Guild during that period—was also the show's producer. It turns

out they wanted me to do this show as the heavy, opposite the gorgeous Peggy Lee. I jumped at the chance!

I was nervous to meet Ronald Reagan, though. The president of SAG holds a lot of sway in Hollywood. I wanted him to like me. I wasn't sure what to say to him. Well, wouldn't you know it, on the first rehearsal day Reagan said to me, "You want to have lunch?" He brought me down to the Universal Commissary and I never knew I had so many friends! Here I was, sitting with this great actor and the president of SAG, and *everybody* kept coming over wanting to say hi because they wanted to meet him.

He was taller than I had imagined, and I have to say, he and Robert Redford were the best raconteurs I had ever run into. He made me feel so good and wonderful and important—on that very first day of rehearsals. Can you imagine? We talked about *everything*. He told me he loved radio, and he loved announcing sports. He *loved* sports. He used to be a lifeguard! I asked about his mom and dad, and he told me that his mom had died of Alzheimer's. I had never heard of that before. He was telling me all of this very personal stuff.

Anyway, we did the show, and it was a big hit. And then Peggy Lee invited me back to her place at the end of the shoot. I didn't go! My goodness, it was nice to be asked. But I was married with a new baby on the way. What kind of a guy did she think I was?

Flash forward some seventeen years or so, and I'm the Captain of *The Love Boat*. I'm out one evening eating chili at Chasen's, one of our favorite restaurants, and Maude Chasen asked me to host an awards show. I had never emceed before. But the producers of the event were glad to run into me, and sure that I was capable of pulling it off. The big honoree that night was going to be Nancy Kissinger, and her award was going to be presented by none other than Nancy Reagan.

As luck and fate would have it, the organizers sat me at the Reagans' table for the dinner. Patti got all dolled up, and a jeweler let her borrow a magnificent set of diamonds just for the evening. We got there early and we sat there waiting, all excited to think we were about to sit next to the former governor of California and his wife. I forget the exact date of this event, but there was already buzz that he was going to run for president of the United States. You can imagine how excited we were to see them both and get to sit with them. We were nervous! Yet as soon as Ronald Reagan arrived, he turned all of that nervousness we had right on its head. He charmed the spit out of both of us: "Well," he said, "I've always wanted to dine at the Captain's Table, and tonight's the night!"

I could hardly believe it: he was still that same raconteur, *and* he remembered who I was! *Wow!* "It was so great to act with you in that show all those many, many years ago," I said, and we reminisced a bit about the days of live dramatic television. Nancy and I were seated next to each other, and we talked about our kids all night. A few years later I traveled all over the country as a representative of her "Hugs Not Drugs" program. I was so proud to do that work, because I knew how much she believed in it, and I knew how much she loved kids.

On that night, I opened up the festivities with a song and then I introduced Mrs. Reagan. I said, "I'm going to introduce this fabulous person, who I was a big fan of when she was acting at MGM. But she doesn't do that anymore." I said a few other nice things, talking about her bio and what kind of a person she was, and then I added something that wasn't in the script. I said, "She's a lady who many of us hope will be this country's next First Lady . . . Nancy Reagan."

The applause was immeasurable.

At the end of the night, two guys came over to me: "Mrs. Reagan wants to see you."

"Did I do something?"

"No, no," they said, "but she won't leave until you come over to see her."

I walked over to Nancy Reagan, and she put her arms around my neck and said, "You made me feel so wonderful when you said 'First Lady.' I'll never forget that."

I'm not sure if anyone had said those words to her in public before. It didn't even occur to me when those words left my lips, but I think it was a first! I was humbled and so glad that she didn't mind. "That's what we believe," I said. "We believe in your husband, and we believe in you. You're a team."

The next time I saw them, he was president.

It was Christmastime at the White House, the big event where they have a tree for each state and they put on a show. *Today Show* weatherman Willard Scott emceed the event, and I sang something with Jill Whelan, the little girl who played my daughter Vicki on the show. Afterward we were in the Red Room. (You understand how surreal and spectacular this is, right? To be standing in the Red Room. At the White House. As a guest?) And all of a sudden the Bushes, the vice president and his wife, came down. "We just wanted to say hello," they said. They were fans of the show! "The president will be down soon and he wants you to be first in the line," they told us.

How does this happen? It just blows my mind.

So Patti and I got in place at the head of the line, and before we knew it, President and Mrs. Reagan walked in and came right over to us with a big, "Hello! It's so nice to see you again." We were being kind of stiff and formal, as I thought you were expected to be at this sort of event with the president, but Nancy said, "Give me a hug!" And we hugged. We got a picture together, and they signed it for us later on. By this time I was right in the thick of making appearances for the "Hugs Not Drugs" program, and I told Nancy I was out there doing whatever I could for her. She said, "I know!"

The First Lady of the United States of America not only knew who I was, and remembered who I was, but she was aware of the work I was out there doing on her behalf. It's difficult to explain what that feels like, because I still can't fully comprehend it myself.

We stayed for a long time, mixing and mingling with people that night, until a guy came over and said, "You're wanted downstairs."

"What did I do now?" I said.

Patti and I went downstairs and it turned out that the head chef wanted to see me. He was Swedish and had worked on cruise ships, so he thought it would be fun to meet the Captain. He gave us cookies to take home from the White House. And they were delicious.

I saw the president another time after that, too, during his second term. It was just as special, and I was in just as much awe. Years later I would see President George H. W. Bush down in Fort Lauderdale. They were taking a cruise, and they had security all over the place, and they wanted to meet me on the bridge. Mrs. Bush came in first: "They said you were here, and I didn't believe it!" She gave me a big hug.

This was just after he lost his bid for reelection. I said, "Mr. President." And he said, "They didn't want me. That's the way it is." He gave me a presidential tie clasp, which I later gave to my grandson.

Mrs. Bush suffered a fall on that cruise. I remember that. It made headlines. Thankfully she was fine. I would see them again when I was doing a play at the Ogunquit Playhouse up in Maine, not far from the home they have in Kennebunkport, and they came to see me yet again in a production of *Gigi* down in Houston. They visited and took pictures at intermission—as if *I* was the famous one! It's just astounding to me that this role of the Captain would garner the interest of presidents and First Ladies.

Many years later, toward the very end of her life, my mother would suffer from dementia, just as Reagan's mother did, and just as Reagan himself did before Alzheimer's set in. I was invited up to Canada to help raise money to fight the disease, and people from all over Canada came to hear me speak. I used President Reagan's farewell speech as part of my message. I've mentioned before that I tend to cry at the drop of a hat. Well, I sure cried at that podium. I thought of him. I thought of my mother. I remember looking out at that audience full of people who had been touched by this terrible affliction, and I said, "We're all in this together."

I ran into Michael Reagan later on, and I told him I had used his father's speech for that purpose. He responded by telling me a story I will never forget. He always used to hug his father whenever he would see him, he said. The last time he saw him, his father was lying down on a sofa, with a pillow, and Michael told me, "I could see that Dad didn't know who I was, and I just said, 'Good-bye. Thanks for being a great man and a great dad.'" I'm paraphrasing here, of course. It was so beautiful the way he told it. I don't tell the story nearly as well, I'm sure, and I hope he'll forgive me for not having his eloquence. But it touched me very deeply, so I want to share it. "I went out the front door," he continued, "really feeling lousy, thinking I'll never see my dad again, and all of a sudden the front door opens—and it was my father. He was standing there looking at me, with his arms open for a hug. He didn't know who I was, but he knew I was the guy who hugged him. That was my last moment with my father."

What a story. It just showed the love of a son and a father, which—well . . . by now, you know what that means to me.

Ronald Reagan was so good for this country, and so good for this world. He made us a strong power again, and that's what we have to be. America can't be second or third. What's happening to us these days?

I was a Democrat until he ran for president, and then I became a Republican. I'm an Independent now, and I won't get into my political beliefs any more than that in these pages—mainly because I'm sure you don't want to hear it. I just think it's interesting the ways in which each of us can change our perspective through the years. I've certainly changed mine, in part because I was blessed to spend time with these incredibly influential and wonderful human beings.

At the other end of my legendary celebrity experience spectrum, let me set it up in the form of a famous film title: *Guess Who's Coming to Dinner?*

Our friend Kaye Ballard, whom I've mentioned already—the fabulous actress, singer, and comedienne I had the great privilege of working onstage with in *Gypsy* in 1973, and with whom Patti and I are still dear, dear friends to this very day—called us up one day out of the blue. This was 1980, or maybe early 1981. Patti and I lived in a beautiful house on

Burlingame in Brentwood at that time, and Kaye had become a very good friend since we had purchased a second home in Palm Springs. She lived close by.

Anyway, Kaye said, "Gavin, I just ran into a friend, and I wonder if you might have her over for dinner."

It was an odd way to phrase a request. I said, "Um, Kaye—who is it?"

She said, "Bette Davis."

I said, "*The* Bette Davis?"

"Yes, *the* Bette Davis. She's an old friend of mine."

"And you want her to come to our house for *dinner*?"

"Yeah. I mentioned it to her and she went crazy," Kaye said. "She said, 'I can meet the Captain? When are we going to go?'"

The thought that Bette Davis knew the Captain really knocked me over. Kaye said, "I ran into her at a function and said, 'How're you doing, Bette?' and she said, 'Oh, I'm very lonely. Nobody ever asks me out to dinner anymore.' So I thought it would be nice for you and Patti to have her over. Patti could make her eggplant parmigiana!"

Patti makes an amazing eggplant parmigiana. Dom DeLuise once said it was the best he'd ever had in his life. And Patti's not even Italian! (Yes, we had Dom DeLuise over for dinner, too, one time. I'm dropping names like hot potatoes now!)

I said, "Well, I can't believe this. Sure. I'll ask Patti."

The only other thing Kaye said was, "Be sure to have some Chivas Regal Scotch for her."

I said, "We can do that. All we have to do is feed her?"

"Oh yeah," Kaye said, "she just wants to meet you, and she's so wonderful, and she's so lonely."

I couldn't believe it. *Bette Davis!* Patti of course said yes.

We set it up for a Sunday. Kaye was going to bring a friend named Jerry Lang, a big-deal photographer from New York City, and one of his friends. And we invited Stephanie, Patti's daughter (who I very much considered my daughter at this point too). And that was it. We wanted to keep it small. Simple.

The night before, we could hardly sleep! *Bette Davis is coming to our house for dinner!*

Sunday arrived. We got all set up. We didn't even go to church. That house had never been so clean. We brought in a special kind of caviar from the store where we shopped. We had special crackers to put the caviar on. We had Chivas Regal all over the place, and wine. Patti prepped all the food so all she'd have to do was heat it up a little bit. We got dressed to the nines. Finally the doorbell rang, and who was standing there but Bette Davis. *The* Bette Davis!

She was tiny! She came right over and gave me a big hug. I was struck that this giant of the screen was just about Patti's height. "I'm so happy to meet you," she said. "I love your work."

I almost choked.

"Well, I love your work too!" I said.

I had heard that she once worked as an usher at the Cape Playhouse on Cape Cod, and so I mentioned that. She said, "Yes! I started out there before I started acting." I told her I was on the board of directors there now. It's one of our country's great regional theaters, a place I had performed and a place I longed to return to again and again.

Kaye came in with Jerry and his friend, and we all went into the living room. There was one big sofa under the window, and two love seats, and tables, and Patti started putting out the hors d'oeuvres. I asked Miss Davis if she wanted a little Chivas Regal, and she said, "Thank you, yes."

She started drinking a little bit. Stephanie came in, and they were all sitting on that sofa while Bette sat over in a chair, all by herself. We had a little French poodle named Rose that kept jumping up, but the thing I remember most is that Bette Davis just kept eating. She was dipping into this caviar as if she hadn't eaten for days!

We started talking about the business, and Jerry said, "I'll never forget when you were doing *Two's Company*," which was a revue she did in New York. He said, "I went to see you after a matinee one day, to ask you for an autograph, but you weren't there."

Bette got very serious for some reason. "I never left the theater after the matinee."

Jerry said, "Well, okay, but on this day you weren't there."

She reiterated, very sternly, "I never left the theater after the matinee!"

Jerry seemed confused. "Okay, but Miss Davis, I went there, and you—"

Bette leaped to her feet. "Did you hear me? I never left the theater after the matinee!" She was belligerent!

Jerry let it go, but I whispered to Patti, "I think you'd better get the food ready."

I fixed her another drink and asked if she'd like to see the house. "I'd loooove to!" she said, very dramatically.

Our house was filled with antiques and vintage pieces. A friend had redecorated the entire place after we bought it. I had enough money to do that sort of thing for the first time in my life, so I indulged a bit. One of the pieces we had was an old, handmade sled from Paris, Maine. Bette saw it and said, "Well, look at that."

I told her where it came from and said, "Don't you have a home near there?"

She responded, "I own Cape Elizabeth."

"You own Cape Elizabeth?"

"I *own* Cape Elizabeth!" she said.

I don't think it's true that she actually owned an entire coastline in the state of Maine. But I didn't argue, and I couldn't understand why she was getting so angry. She said she wanted another drink, and this time she went and poured one for herself.

We walked around some more, and eventually walked into the bedroom, where she said, "Oh! I love those lamps!"

They were inexpensive lamps with a patchwork design. Patti and I were planning to throw them out and build something into the wall on either side of the bed instead. I said, "You really like them?"

"I *love* them!" she said.

I told her we were going to get rid of them and asked if she wanted them. She said, "Yes! You know where I live, up on Harper Avenue?" I said, "Yeah, I've heard about where you live."

"I think the food's almost ready," she said, and she headed toward the kitchen. It was all so strange!

After dinner we all retired to this rustic room we had with a fireplace, with blue-and-white walls—it was very Cape Cod–ish. Everybody sat near the fire, but Bette Davis sat way, way across the room on a little bench by the door, all by herself. Then she looked at Patti and said, "Why do you have the fireplace on?"

Patti said, "Well, I thought I'd give you a little taste of New England."

Bette looked her in the eye, and in the snarkiest voice said, "Well, you haven't."

Kaye started laughing. She's the type of person who laughs whenever somebody's in trouble. I couldn't take it anymore. I walked out of the room.

The phone rang. It was my director, Allen Baron. He said, "I've got your new script. You want me to bring it over?"

I said, "Allen, you'll never guess who's here. Bette Davis!"

"You're kidding."

"No! Bette Davis is here for dinner, and she's a major pain in the tush!"

Allen rushed right over just to see her. When he walked in, Bette was suddenly all friendly again. "Oh! You're the director!" She turned on the charm for *the director*!

Poor Patti was a basket case. She tried to do everything she could, and Bette Davis was just miserable. She got more and more miserable as the evening went on, and then she left. She just left! Patti was crushed.

The whole thing turned into a case of, "Guess who came to dinner . . . and you wish she hadn't!"

Kaye called us later on that night just laughing and laughing. She thought it was hilarious! Patti sure didn't. I was flabbergasted by the whole thing.

Then it got worse.

Sheila MacRae, the actress and former wife of actor Gordon MacRae, was a good friend of ours, and she called us two or three weeks later. She said, "What's going on here? You had a party with Bette Davis at your house and you didn't invite me?"

Patti said, "Well, it was just with Kaye and the kids. It was small."

Sheila said, "I know. I just read about it in the paper!"

Turns out, somebody did an interview with Bette Davis, and in that interview she said, "The new Hollywood is not like the old Hollywood. Gavin MacLeod, the Captain of *The Love Boat*, invited me to dinner and it was a *disaster*. They don't know how to entertain anymore."

She ripped us!

I couldn't believe it. I called Kaye and said, "Kaye, remember you told me nobody invites her to dinner anymore? I think I know why now." Who would want to be around that kind of a personality, no matter how big of a star she is?

Oh well. We got a good story and a good laugh out of it. Patti eventually laughed too. It was just so ridiculous. I mean, come on: How many people ever have Bette Davis over to their house for dinner? We tried to make her happy, but nothing made her happy. I thought the Chivas Regal would make her happy, but it only made her angry. Maybe if Jerry didn't say what he said about the matinee she would have been fine. Sometimes you have no idea what sets people off. But I was floored.

By the way, we never sent her those bedroom lamps.

You never know what you're going to get with certain celebrities. There are a lot of nice people in the world—actors and actresses who stay grounded and keep smiles on their faces and never forget where they came from. Then there are others.

I flew up to do the *Donny & Marie* show in Orem, Utah, one time, and I just love Donny and Marie Osmond. I love their whole family! They came on *The Love Boat*. Marie and I have made other appearances with each other through the years. I went to her wedding when she first got married, and went to Las Vegas to see them when they opened their show just recently. They're fabulous, loving people. I'm not sure how many people remember, but they had the hottest show on television in their day. I wish everyone could be more like they are with all of that fame.

I tried never to be demanding or belligerent, no matter how well-known I got. Grateful is my middle name. I was grateful to have the job. Any job. My managers or agents would do what they did, of course. They demanded a certain salary and everything like that. But for me? If somebody wanted me to come and do the stuff that I love doing, what more is there?

Right after *The Love Boat* caught on, I got to cohost with Mike Douglas for a week. For a whole *week* he had me on his show! In fact, it was showing off my singing and dancing skills on *The Mike Douglas Show* that helped me land that emcee gig for the Reagans.

His talk show was the greatest. He had so many guests from so many walks of life on that show. Old legends, new artists, cutting-edge comedians, sports figures, you name it! The greatest times were when he had 'em all on together—kind of like what we did on *The Love Boat*—and I was fortunate to be there for one of those perfect, unimaginable occasions. I got to sing with Ella Fitzgerald. I couldn't believe it! It was Mike Douglas, Tommy Lasorda (from the Los Angeles Dodgers), Ella Fitzgerald, and yours truly, all singing "You Gotta Have Heart" from the musical *Damn Yankees*. We each took a verse, and then we harmonized all together. It was magic, man! Another time I was on the show, and Ray Charles was a guest. He said to me, "Maaaaaaan, I watch you every Saturday night." I didn't know blind people say, "I watch you." But that's what he said.

Being the Captain opened so many doors for me. The reach I had, the notoriety I had, the ability to interact with so many legends of stage and screen. If I recounted every story, I'd fill this whole book!

But let me share just one more from those early *Love Boat* years— a meeting I had with one of the greatest singers who ever lived: Frank Sinatra.

We were doing *The Love Boat*, and Patti had just gone away to do summer stock in Pennsylvania. I got to the set, and there was Frank Sinatra Jr. He was doing a guest role on our show. "Frank! Welcome. Nice to see you!"

We spoke for a few minutes, and I just couldn't resist. I said, "Can I tell you, I love your father, man. He's been such a major part of our lives."

He said, "You really like him?"

"Yeah!" I said.

"You want to come see him? He's recording tonight."

He told me that Billy May was going to be conducting the orchestra, and they were working on this new album called *Trilogy*. "Wow, what an honor, Frank." Since Patti was gone, I said, "Can I bring my secretary?"

He said sure, so I invited my longtime secretary, Judy Van Herpen— who was a big fan. She was thrilled!

After work, before we headed to the studio, I called Patti. "How was your trip?"

She said, "Oh it was all right . . ."

"Well, you'll never guess where I'm going. I'm going to see Frank Sinatra record a new album!"

She squealed. "I can't believe you! I only left a few hours ago and you're going to see Frank Sinatra?"

I told her that Frank Jr. set it up. She was jealous. Who wouldn't be?

We got there, and we walked in past that big, big orchestra and into the recording booth where we were out of the way in the back. And in came Frank Sinatra. I can hardly explain what it felt like just to sit there and watch him and his producer, Sonny Burke, talk. It was so exciting! He said, "We'll start with 'Surrey with the Fringe on Top.'"

And then we watched him record that famous song. To see him in person, up close like that—it was breathtaking. Every phrase he sang just rang out. Every note was powerful, or subtle, or just what it needed to be. I've done my share of singing onstage, but I could never *dream* of having the gift that he has.

When the song was over, he walked back into the recording booth to listen to the playback with the producer. He said, "I don't like it. Let's come back tomorrow and do something else." To any one of us, it was the most beautiful recording we'd ever heard. But to him? It wasn't quite right. He wasn't satisfied. He was a perfectionist.

That's when Frank Jr. went over to his dad and said, "Look who I've got over here."

Frank Sinatra looked over, smiled, and started walking toward me. He said, "It's great to meet you in person." Then he hit me on the chest with his hand and said, "Kid, you're a hell of an actor."

I didn't know what to say. I said, "Mr. Sinatra, you're a hell of a singer."

I introduced him to my secretary, Judy, and she just about slid down the wall. I don't think I've ever come down from that moment. It was truly one of the great moments of my life, getting to shake that man's hand and then getting a compliment from him.

Some months later, Frank Jr. called and said, "My father's going to be performing at the Universal Amphitheater. Do you want to go? I'll take your daughter for a date." My daughter Stephanie was single at that time. So we went. Sarah Vaughn opened for him that night. I remember her all dressed in chiffon, and it billowed in the wind. Sarah is one of Patti's favorite singers of all time, and it was such a thrill to see her perform in person. Frank Jr. also invited Jonathan Winters and his wife. What a funny guy he was. He started breaking into comedy routines in the audience!

We met Frank again before the show. When the show was over, he always left, right away. That was his routine, his son told us. But before the show, you could see him. So I met him and shook his hand once again, and this time Patti got to meet him too. It was great.

Coincidentally, all these years later, Frank's first wife, Nancy, has become one of my dearest friends, and their daughter, Nancy "These Boots Were Made for Walking" Junior, is my neighbor. She's a friend and confidant. We park our cars right next to each other. I even live on Frank Sinatra Drive. I love them both. That's life! (As Frank used to sing.)

Frank Jr. later told me that his father wasn't just being a nice guy when he gave me that compliment in the studio. Frank was a fan of my work, and he had been a fan long before *The Love Boat* came along. One of Frank's favorite movies of all time was *High Time*, his son told me. "He loved the stuff you did!"

It just goes to show that when you get out there and do what you love, and you do your best, you never know who's watching. All those years I enjoyed listening to Frank Sinatra, I had no idea that he was out there watching my performances up on the big screen.

The Love Boat was now airing in ninety countries around the world each week. And between *Mary Tyler Moore*, which had gone into syndication; *The Love Boat*, which repeated a couple times a week because it was so popular; and the various talk shows, game shows, and TV movies I was doing in between, *Entertainment Today* named me "the most visible star on television." I was being seen on TV no fewer than thirteen hours per week! It was wild.

Maybe it had something to do with being around all of these gigantic stars. Maybe all the fame and notoriety was going to my head, but I felt driven, sort of like I did back in the mid-1960s. I was working all the time. I never stopped. I was getting invited to do so many amazing things, and to meet so many incredible people, each day felt like a new adventure.

Boy oh boy, I tell you, by that early part of the 1980s I felt like I was on top of the world.

And wouldn't you know it? That is precisely when I started to lose my way.

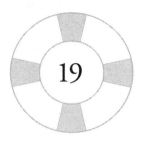

19

MAN OVERBOARD

I NEVER THOUGHT ABOUT ACTUALLY TAKING A VACA-
tion during our vacation breaks on *The Love Boat*. It never even
occurred to me. I think a lot of other actors do that too. After years
of trying, you finally find yourself in a situation where there's ample
opportunity to do the work you love, so you jump at every opportunity
that comes up. In the beginning, I had the added bonus of getting to do
so much of that work with Patti.

We put another nightclub act together, just as we had in the early
1970s, and the excitement of putting that act together as a couple was
great. It's a very creative process to do something like that, working out
the dances, choosing all the songs. To get to work on that kind of a thing
with your wife? I loved every second of it! Doing our act together was
like frosting on the cake of life.

During the months when we were filming, though, I was hardly
ever home. I'd be off doing the series all day, and Patti would wait during those months until we'd do shows together after all of my hectic

shooting was over. That worked well for a good three years. But as we turned the corner into 1981, something started to change.

We started the year off just fine. We had a nice anniversary dinner at Chasen's, that famous celebrity restaurant in LA. We could hardly believe we were celebrating seven years together! Time was flying, and we were enjoying the fruits of my success. My parents never owned a home when I was growing up, and here I was with the opportunity to own multiple homes, and to keep trading up and up. I think I may have overcompensated!

We moved into a sprawling condo overlooking the Pacific, at Ocean Towers in Santa Monica. Patti took on the bulk of the work in setting up each of our new homes, since I was so busy at work. And it started to feel like we were apart a lot. So much so that when we were together, it started to feel like it was all business: talking about what goes where, which plan had to be finished, what was happening next week, which friends we were having dinner with. Patti didn't see me all day, so when I got home I felt like she was bombarding me with all kinds of questions and all kinds of orders. They weren't "orders," of course. She was just trying to keep track of the details and keep our household going. I know now that those questions were just her way of trying to connect with me. I didn't appreciate that fact when I was in the middle of it.

The sad, horrible truth of it was maybe I didn't appreciate *her*.

In my first marriage, when I was drinking, I would sometimes get in moods that I would describe as "nasty." I was unhappy. I didn't *want* to act that way, but I did. With Patti, it was different. She would get on me once in a while. I was working, working, working. I was more interested in my work than working on our marriage at that point, but it wasn't a fighting situation. We didn't hate each other. It was more a matter of priorities. I think because of the New Age thinking I had embraced, I kept putting all of my focus on myself—as if *I* were "number one." When you embrace that sort of thing fully, sometimes all you think about is *you*.

Once again I felt a longing for something more in my life, just as I had back in the late 1960s. I felt that tug, that pull, the feeling that something was missing—and I started to pin it all on my wife. I felt like Patti was nagging me, and because of that, I felt like I didn't want to be around her very much. I want to be clear: as I look back on it, I don't think that she *was* nagging me. It was this feeling that something was *missing* that was nagging at me. Patti was trying to love me. She was trying to connect with me. The only one to blame, truly, was me—because "me" was all I cared about.

The chain of events that unfolded as we headed into the summer of 1981 is very difficult for me to look back on. I'm ashamed of my own behavior.

Patti and I were planning to go on the road together in a summer-stock production of *The Music Man*, on the famed Kenley circuit in Ohio—where a cavalcade of great actors did summer stock over the years. Wouldn't you know it? That spring, I broke my leg during a *Love Boat* cruise down in Australia. That changed everything. I would likely be out of my cast by the time the show started, but there was no way I could dance those parts and do all the movement that con-man Harold Hill has to do in *The Music Man*. The risk of reinjury was too high. So we backed out. I got offered another play, a murder mystery down in Florida where I wouldn't have to sing or dance; I could just walk. And Patti picked up an offer of her own: to star opposite Ken Berry in a summer-stock production of *George M* for the same Kenley circuit.

It was the first summer since we married that we didn't spend together.

I wonder sometimes if we had done *The Music Man* together if things would have turned out differently. I wonder how life might have played out if I hadn't broken my leg. I don't know about those things in life. All I know is that once I got down to Florida, my whole perspective on our marriage shifted, and shifted quickly.

I rented a place on the beach. I took long walks with no one to rush back to. I could do whatever I wanted to do. I found I enjoyed operating on my own schedule. I enjoyed simply being alone in my own space. For the first time since I first got married at the age of twenty-four, I spent a few weeks not answering to anyone else—and it felt like heaven.

That's the selfish space I was in when I decided I wanted a divorce from Patti.

I thought of that episode of *The Love Boat*, the flashback scene when the young Captain chose a life on the sea over the love of his life. It's sort of what I was feeling in that moment, only instead of dedicating my life to the sea, I was dedicating myself to showbiz. I was giving myself to it. I didn't want to share it anymore. I wanted it to just be mine. I thought it was time that I answered to no one.

It's easy to forget in life that we're always answering to someone, isn't it? How foolish we can be at times.

Patti was shattered. She couldn't believe it. It all happened so fast. She was blindsided. I still can't believe I did that to her, out of my own selfishness.

Of course, the tabloids had a field day. *The National Enquirer* had already been focused on the cast of *The Love Boat* in 1981, spreading false stories about arguments on the set, saying each of us actors was vying for bigger and better storylines. None of it was true. We got along well—and as the Captain, I set the tone. I took cues from Mary Tyler Moore about how a leader should act, and I always came to the set with a smile. I always arrived early. I made sure everyone was taken care of. I acted like the Captain of my show, and I swear to you, it was 99 percent smooth sailing on that set. But the *Enquirer* was relentless. They were determined to dig up dirt behind the scenes on this happy-go-lucky show.

Well, guess what? They finally got what they wanted: a negative story about the Captain of *The Love Boat*. Stories pop up about you wherever you go in times like those. I would innocently walk through a lobby some-where or go to some restaurant, and the next day my whereabouts were reported in the gossip columns. It was nuts. It's easy to understand why some stars become paranoid. I never knew who was gonna dime me out!

So Patti and I divorced. It was over. As far as I was concerned, there was no turning back. I barely even talked to her about it. We just split. It was all my decision.

As the months went by, I dated some other women. No one serious. No one I thought about settling down with, that's for sure. I wasn't interested in settling. I wasn't interested in sharing my life. I was interested in calling my shots, all on my own.

The press told a different story.

My friend Diane Ladd came on *The Love Boat* during that time period. (If you remember, we were in *A Hatful of Rain* together back in the late 1950s.) Diane had broken up with her husband, Bruce Dern, at that point, and her publicist put something in the papers claiming she and I were an item. "Reunited after all these years!" it said. It showed up in the *Hollywood Reporter.* Everybody believed it—even my mother. My mother was the type of person who says, "If it's in the paper, it must be true." I tell you, if it's about Hollywood and it's in the papers, you should take it with a grain of salt!

Diane and I didn't date. We were good friends. On the episode, I played the Captain's brother, wearing a hairpiece and fake moustache, which was so much fun to play. It was just like the old days. That *brother* romanced Diane on the ship. It was acting. Nothing more.

Back when we were in *A Hatful of Rain* in Boston, after the show I used to walk her across Boston Common at night so she could get to the nunnery where she was staying. That's how it was in those days! We were in our twenties when we worked together. We started our careers together. There was no romance, but boy oh boy, it was nice to see her.

During that same time period, Ruth Warwick came on the show. I don't know how many people make the connection between the Ruth Warwick who was in *Citizen Kane*, considered by many critics to be the best film of all time, and the Ruth Warwick who was on the soap opera *Days of Our Lives* for many years. They were one in the same! She was fabulous no matter what she did. I was honored to work with her. But her publicist took one of our on-set pictures together and put it in *The Examiner.* The headline read, "Hot romance!"

Ruth Warwick was old enough to be my *mother*!

Years later she came to see me in a play in Cape Cod, and I asked her, "How did that thing get in the paper about you and I having an affair?!" She said, "Dahling, it was so wonderful!" She was one of those actresses who survived all that time by keeping her name alive. That was just the old Hollywood way of doing things, I suppose.

Jessica Walter came on the show too. What a wonderful actress. I was a big fan of hers. She took over for country singer Tammy Wynette, who left before the shoot was finished. They got Jessica to come in and sing and everything else on short notice. I actually *did* take Jessica out a few times. In fact, we were photographed by Ron Galella, the celebrity paparazzo. He snapped me out and about with a couple of other women during that time too—women who weren't actually "dates," but just companions who joined me so I wouldn't show up to red carpet events all alone. Agents and managers and publicists set up those sort of "dates" all the time. It's good for the actors on both sides of the equation. Once you're a celebrity, your whole life becomes part of the act!

I found out pretty quickly that I wasn't too keen on participating in the "act" for the sake of celebrity. It felt like lying. But more than that, it felt destructive to the parts of me that mattered most. Especially when the *Enquirer* kept calling Patti, and calling Rootie, and calling my kids. My daughter Meg, my youngest, would call me on the phone crying, "Daddy, they're on the phone again. Why won't they leave us alone?"

Once it started, it seemed there was nothing I could do to stop it.

I ignored as much of the tabloid press as I could, and I asked everyone I knew to ignore it too. I wouldn't read the tabloids myself, but then someone would always talk about them whether you read them or not. It was a real nightmare, to tell you the truth. Remember, I was never in this to get famous. I just wanted to act. I was perfectly happy being out of print and on the stage.

Perhaps that negative stuff that was happening all around me was a sign that something in my life needed to change. We bring misery upon ourselves when all that we're focused on is ourselves. That seems obvious to me now, but I couldn't see it then. I had spent half of my life married, always having someone else there. I just wanted to be "me." I didn't want to have to put someone else first, except for my children. I did want to spend more time with my kids, and for some reason I felt that not being married freed me up to do that like never before. I went on some really great camping trips with my son David, traveled to see my daughters, and hung out with Keith. It was wonderful to bond with them as they blossomed into adulthood.

I was still just as busy with work, and busy living my life with gratitude whether it was on the stage, on the set, or out on the high seas on *The Love Boat*. I was just "happier" doing it on my own.

After the split, I didn't talk to Patti. At all. I never called her. Not even once. I didn't *want* to call her.

She stayed in our place in Santa Monica, in that high-rise overlooking the ocean. I went out and bought myself a huge house in Beverly Hills, thinking bigger is always better. I had the place beautifully decorated. I turned it into a real showplace—a home befitting the Captain on one of television's biggest shows.

And every night, I would go home to that big house. Alone.

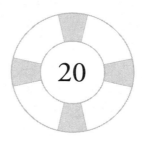

THE LIFE BOAT

N THE SPRING OF 1982, I TRAVELED TO NEW YORK
City to perform in the *Night of 100 Stars*, a big celebration of the
one hundredth year of the Actors Fund. The whole show was
happening on my old stomping grounds at Radio City Music Hall. It
was great to get back there!

Our daughter Stephanie was living in New York at the time, and I
contacted her to let her know I'd be in town. She came over and visited
with me for a while, and she told me something I didn't quite understand.
"Mom has really changed a lot," she said. "She's left the New Age teaching
and become a Christian." She said her mom was like a different person
now. She thought I should give her a call.

I listened, and I told her I'd think about it, but I knew I wasn't gonna
call Patti. I had already gone out on some dates with other women. I was
so involved in my work. I was enjoying my time alone—and frankly, I
just wasn't interested.

For the next two and a half years, I would go on living that same selfish life, putting on a smile, living out my dreams onstage, seemingly enjoying every minute of it. *All I want to do is act!* I kept telling myself. But that emptiness I felt, that hole in my life, that longing for something more—it never, ever went away.

In September 1984, I learned that my mother had a cyst in her brain. It was the size of a baseball, they told me. If the doctors didn't get it out, they were afraid they were going to lose her. As a result, they planned to operate right away. Yet the surgery itself was extremely risky, they said, and there was a chance—a very real chance—that she wouldn't make it through surgery at all.

My mother went into surgery on the morning of September 14 at a hospital in Palm Springs. She was staying with my brother at the time, and my brother and his wife had been taking care of her. I couldn't get to the hospital. There wasn't enough time to get there and back. I had to work. I had no option. For all the accommodations Aaron Spelling had made for my schedule on *The Love Boat*, all the juggling I had been able to pull off for the sake of my work in the theater, and on game shows, and talk shows and more—this surgery came up so suddenly that it was impossible for the producers to rearrange my schedule. Too many other people's schedules were tied directly to my presence. I *had* to show up on that set, no matter what. I had no choice.

I went to bed the night of September 13 feeling completely lost and empty inside. After all that my life in showbiz had allowed me to do for my mother—sending money back home, buying her a nice condo—it was my life in showbiz that now kept me from being at her side in her time of need. I couldn't be with her because of my job—the job that had been my sole focus for the past three years to the exclusion of just about everything and everyone else in my life.

I woke up that morning praying to Jesus, which is something I hadn't done in a very long time. With all the New Age stuff I had been practicing since the mid-1970s, I thought I was in charge of everything! Suddenly, I wasn't. I was helpless. Completely helpless. I was alone in my bed, in that gigantic house in Beverly Hills. More alone than I had ever been in my life.

That is the moment when everything changed—at 7:15 a.m. on September 14, 1984. I said, "Jesus, if you give my mother more time, I'll turn my life over to you. I don't care if I act anymore. Just give my mother more time."

Thoughts were coming out of my mouth that I had never even considered before. Acting, the thing I thought I cared about most in the world, meant nothing to me in that moment. It was inconsequential. I was willing to trade it away without any hesitation. I was willing to do anything to save my mother—and the one thing I wanted to do, the one thing I felt I *needed* to do, from the bottom of my heart, was to give my life to Jesus. I didn't even know what it *meant* to give my life to Jesus. I just somehow knew it was the one thing I wanted—and needed—to do.

I was ready. I was willing. For the sake of my loving mother, who had already led such an impossibly tough life. My mother, Margaret Theresa Shea See.

I prayed to Jesus. I offered my life to him. And the moment I laid my head back on the pillow, I sensed a voice saying, *Call Patti*. I had no idea where that came from, but suddenly it was the only thing that mattered.

Enough time had gone by that I didn't have Patti's number.

I called my secretary, Judy. "Judy, are you awake?"

"Yeah, boss."

"Do you have Patti's phone number? I've gotta call her."

Judy had been there through it all. She knew I hadn't spoken to Patti since we split up. She was baffled by the request. "Why do you have to call her?" she asked.

"I don't know! But I have to."

In the past, whenever I called Patti from work or from the road, she always hit me with a lot of questions. When we were married, I used to feel as though I had to prepare myself before I called. To get ready. She'd want to know how things were going, what was going on, where I'd been, what I'd done, how I was feeling. I know in retrospect she just wanted to feel connected to me—at a time when I wasn't allowing myself to fully connect with her. I know that now. I didn't know it then. But on this morning? I didn't even think about it. I wasn't nervous. I wasn't worried. I just knew I had to do it, because that voice said, *Call Patti.*

I prayed to Jesus at 7:15. It was barely 7:20 when Judy gave me the number. And I dialed.

"Hello?"

"Patti, this is Gavin."

"I was just thinking about you!" she said.

It was breathtaking. I still tear up at the memory.

I said, "Can I see you?"

I didn't understand why I was saying this, or where it was coming from. But I continued. I said, "Can we be friends?"

"That's all I ever wanted," Patti said.

My eyes filled with tears. I could hardly speak. "Can I see you?" I repeated.

"I would love to," she said. "But I belong to a support group called LADIES—it stands for 'Life After Divorce Is Eventually Sane'—and this support group, we travel all over, and I'm just getting ready to leave. I have to be gone for a week."

I was flummoxed. She didn't say no!

So I said, "Okay, well, how about next Monday?"

"I'll be home," she said.

"Should I come down?"

"Sure," she said. "I'll have dinner for you."

That is how it all began. Again.

Later that day, I got the call: my mother's surgery went well. In fact, it went perfectly, the doctors said. She was doing fine. She was going to be okay. My mother was already in her late seventies. To survive a surgery like that was a big deal. Recovery would not be easy. But to know that she was alive, to know that she was still with us, meant one thing and one thing only to me: *Jesus had answered my prayer.*

That Monday of the following week, I drove straight to Santa Monica after work. Our Ocean Towers apartment was on the third floor, and you had to walk past all the people downstairs and the desk staff in order to get to the elevators. With all of the stories about me in the *Enquirer*, I was worried about who might see me, and who might say something, and all that.

There was no way around it. They all saw me, they all knew me, and they were all very friendly. I just hoped no one would dime me out to the tabloids. *Not today. Not now.*

I went up and knocked on Patti's door. No answer.

Second knock. No answer.

My heart sank. I thought, *She's standing me up. I don't blame her.*

I knocked a third time, and the door opened—and there she was, standing there in an apron—my beautiful Patti. Without a moment's hesitation, we hugged each other. We held that hug for what seemed like an eternity. I didn't want to let go.

Finally, Patti spoke to me. "I'm sorry your dinner's cold," she said. "It's been waiting for three years."

Patti invited me in, and we never ate that dinner. We sat down and just started talking. She seemed so centered. So happy. So together. Here I was feeling like a complete mess of a human being, and Patti was just glowing.

"What's happened to you? You have it all together!" I said.

"I've been born again," she answered.

"What does that mean?" I asked her.

And she explained it to me.

She shared passages from the Bible, and specifically spoke about a man named Nicodemus, a Jewish leader who went to see Jesus in the dark of night—afraid to be seen in Jesus' presence in broad daylight, fearing someone might report him. (Suddenly this felt familiar to me.)

Nicodemus asked, much like I was asking, "How can you be 'born again'? What does that mean? You can't go back into your mother's womb!" And she explained that Jesus said, "No. You recognize me as the Son of God. I eradicate all your sins." She explained to me that sins are "mistakes." I'd rather call them "mistakes" than "sins," because that's more understandable, especially to those of us who were raised in a way that made us fear God, and fear punishment.

I'm clearly paraphrasing everything here, because I want it to make sense the way Patti made it make sense to me. But you can pick up any Bible and look this up for yourself in John 3. Patti basically explained that being "born again" is to recognize Jesus as your Lord and Savior. "You recognize me," Jesus said, "acknowledge me as the Son of God, and then eternity is yours." After you die, Jesus said, "You'll see my Father. There is only one way to the Father, and that's through me, and he sent me here to teach you that."

Patti went on. To be born again is to start over, she said—to begin life anew. Your past mistakes are forgiven, and you begin with a clean slate. With Jesus as your Lord and Savior, the life you once led is put behind you, and you begin a new life in his name.

"I want that," I said. "That's what I want, Patti!"

She turned on the TV and we watched televangelist Kenneth Copeland for a little while, and the Trinity Broadcasting Network, and all of these sorts of programs that she had been watching for the past two years. I had never seen this sort of kindness in the name of God. It was very different from anything I had ever known from the church.

Patti had become very good friends with Shirley Boone, Pat Boone's wife, and she talked about how Pat and Shirley had helped her. They introduced her to a ministry called Born Again Marriages, which was made up of people who stood up for their marriages. People who had been dumped, walked out on, left behind. People, I'm ashamed to say, like Patti.

She told me she had been praying for me to return. Outside of Born Again Marriages, there was a whole different group of supportive women who prayed with her, and who prayed that I would come back to her. In fact, this group—led by Bonnie Green, the wife of the talented musician and composer Johnny Green, and a wonderful woman named Louise French—had prayed for me on the night of September 13. Up until that time, so many people, including Patti's therapists on both coasts (we still had an apartment in New York at that time), had told her to "let go." To "forget about Gavin" and "move on." But she wouldn't hear of it. She knew that our love was real and that for some reason I had gotten lost.

The story gets even more interesting, because on the night of September 13, I went to the theater with Bernie Koppel and his wife, and when we left that theater—that very night—I thought, *I wonder how Patti is doing?* It was the first time I had thought about her in a very long time. I think the power of their prayers was already at work!

As I sat in that apartment, Patti handed me a Bible with my name printed on it. She had kept it there, waiting for me. She told me that each time she came home to our apartment, for all that time, she would walk in and say, "Honey, I'm home!" as if I were still there.

She wanted me to meet all of these people who had helped her, and I agreed. I was so moved by the whole experience. I was so moved that Patti would not only open that door for me but let me walk through it.

To think that she had been praying for my return, after what I had done to her.

To think that we had both given our lives to Jesus, at different times, and for different reasons, and that Jesus had now brought us together again.

We talked for hours. We fell asleep. We woke up and talked and talked again. We fell asleep again. We woke up the next morning, and kept right on talking. There was nothing physical at this point—this was a very different kind of reunion. It was just us and our words—and the Word of God.

Patti and I were together frequently from that day forward. Jesus and I were together too. Even though I had already given my life to Jesus that morning when I prayed in my bed for my mother, I wanted to make sure it was legit. I wanted it to be "official." Patti laughed at me for that, but she also thought it was absolutely fantastic. So we made an appointment for me to go see Pat and Shirley.

Pat Boone was the number one entertainer in the world at one point. He had his own TV show while he was still a student at Columbia University, and he still managed to graduate at the top of his class while juggling that career. *Who does that?* I would come to learn that Pat is one of the greatest, smartest guys I've ever met in my life. He has a heart for the Lord and a heart for people unlike any I've ever seen.

The following Sunday they took me to a place called Church on the Way, on Sherman Way in the San Fernando Valley. It was so unlike any church I had ever entered. So big. So full of love. I felt as if the entire congregation embraced me the moment I walked in! And that morning, I made it official. I publicly acknowledged my commitment to Christ.

It was a wonderful, uplifting day. In fact, everything Patti and I did from that moment on was wonderful and uplifting.

A short while later, I decided I wanted to be baptized. Patti had already been baptized, but she offered to come along with me—so we could both be baptized together. Oh, what a moment that was. I couldn't stop crying! The whole thing was just so moving. I realized that I had been living my life the wrong way, living selfishly, for almost as long as I'd been alive, and I was so glad for that to be over. I was so elated to be starting again. Patti was happy, too, but she wasn't crying in that moment. She was laughing! She wore these loose, flowy pantaloons into the water, and they kept floating way up to the surface. They were billowing all around her! She just laughed and laughed, while I cried and cried.

Right before that moment when the minister dipped us into the water, he said, "Nothing before this moment has ever happened." So you are washed clean. Washed *clean*. I know not everyone who reads this book will fully understand what that means, but I hope you'll think about it for a minute: Everything you've done wrong in your life is forgiven. You're given a fresh start. For me, it meant my drinking. My first divorce. My second divorce. My selfish ways. All of it. Wiped clean.

I didn't stop crying for three days. To think that such a thing was possible, that I could be given a whole new beginning. I wasn't a bad person. I think I lived my life pretty positively most of the time. I never purposefully hurt anybody in my life. But it was that selfish nature inside me that put me before anyone else, especially God. Until that moment when I gave my life to Jesus, I didn't realize just how much guilt I had been carrying around inside of me. How much sadness. How much disappointment in myself. All of the mistakes I made—and you can call them "sins" if you want to—but all of those mistakes, *all* of them were forgiven.

At the age of fifty-two, I was starting over—with Patti at my side—determined to make the most of every bit of this gift I had been given.

MOVING ON

THE YEAR 1984 WAS ALL ABOUT CONNECTIONS: new connections and reconnections.

When I returned to the set of *The Love Boat* after being born again, people noticed a change in me. I had always been positive. I had always been the Captain of our show, but I was truly becoming a new person. Just like that. I didn't want to hear people's off-color jokes anymore. I was hearing with new ears. I also smiled a deeper smile, and people noticed.

Two of our new producers, Michael Warren and Bill Bickley, came up to me. They had heard what happened, and they told me they were born again too! It was wonderful to connect to two members of my *Love Boat* family in a whole new way. Some of the cast and crew were curious about what had happened to me, and some were even a bit uncomfortable with it. It was understandable. I might have felt a little funny being around someone who was "born again," too, before I understood what it meant, what it felt like, what it did for my own life. I suppose some of them worried I would judge them, or try to sway them to my faith. That simply wasn't the case. I would never force my beliefs on anyone, and I didn't even talk about it all that much those early days. It would take time for me to fully understand what Paul said in the Bible: that when you're born again, you become an "ambassador for Christ." For me, that role would evolve and grow stronger with each passing day, as I lived my life to the fullest and gave thanks to Jesus for this new life I had. But it would take some time before I stood comfortably in those shoes.

Instead, I just kept living. I woke up every day not only grateful for what I had, but grateful to Jesus for blessing me with all I had. There's a big difference in that!

One of the great blessings that came into my life during that time was the woman who would eventually become my manager, Susan Munao. We met at Church on the Way, and she was a sister in Christ from the start. She managed Donna Summer, Nell Carter, Tony Orlando, and The 5th Dimension, and was such a force of nature! For someone to become involved in your work life after being introduced through your spiritual life is a wonderful gift. She's been with me for almost thirty years now. In fact, her sister, Anne Marie Merz, eventually became my secretary. She runs my office and takes care of all my fan mail, and she loves Jesus too! I love them both dearly.

It's a funny thing: as we entered that second-to-last season of *The Love Boat*, the writers decided it was time to give Captain Stubing a serious love interest on the show. Here I was on a show about love, having come from the *MTM Show* with the theme song "Love Is All Around," and now I had found Jesus who was all about love! I was surrounded with nothing but love, love, love!

The producers came to me with some ideas for casting this love interest, and they had some pretty popular actresses who were ready and willing to do it. But I had the perfect actress in mind, and they were so thrilled when I mentioned her name: my old friend Marion Ross. "Mrs. Cunningham? From *Happy Days*? That's fantastic!" they said.

Marion signed on, and she and I played opposite each other for the next two seasons, working together week after week and culminating in the final show, where Captain Stubing and the love of his life get married on the deck of the *Pacific Princess.*

Oh, and guess who I convinced my producers to cast in the part of the minister who married the two of us? Jan Peters! One of my dearest, lifelong friends (who, I'm sad to report, passed away while I was writing this book). He was my pal in college, and in New York, way back in the beginning, who helped me pick out the name "Gavin MacLeod." I loved having the sway to be able to pull favors like that and to get to hang out with old pals again as we got a chance to act together. What a dream this whole experience had been!

Yet I wasn't sad when the show was over. When *The Love Boat* shot its final episode in the early part of 1986, I felt very much as I did at the end of *The Mary Tyler Moore Show*: like a bird set free from a cage. Only this time, I knew for certain I would be happy wherever I landed, because now I had Jesus in my life.

No matter where life took me from that day forward, I would never walk alone.

Patti and I remarried on June 30, 1985. I wanted to get married in Pastor Jack Hayford's office, with just us and the kids. Small. Simple. But a lady we met at Born Again Marriages, a wonderful older woman named Beulah Ward, whom we met through her daughter, Vida, kept talking to us about it. She would always say, "When are you two young'uns going to get married again?"

She was fantastic. We didn't have anything in common, artistic-wise or anything else, but we had the Lord in common. That was enough.

I had told her a few times that we weren't sure when it would happen, or where. We were waiting for the Lord to tell us. Then one day, Beulah Ward said, "Well, *I'm* telling you: you should get married at the

Born Again Marriage conference in Omaha, in front of all those people. Give them hope."

It was a beautiful idea—to use our remarriage to give hope to others. So we did. Pat and Shirley Boone served as our best man and matron of honor at a ceremony in front of a thousand people at the Red Lion Inn in Omaha, Nebraska. We got married in front of people who had gathered in prayer for the sake of their own marriages. We served as an inspiration to all of those people. It was incredibly moving.

The conference was led by a married couple who hosted a program on TBN called *Marriage on the Rock*. They themselves had been inspiring people to believe in love, and to believe in their marriage—even when their partners had lost their way. All was possible through Jesus, including the fixing of broken marriages. It was wonderful to be a part of that inspiration.

This marriage was different for Patti and me, because it wasn't just about us. There were three of us in the marriage now: Jesus, Patti, and me. That first pillar of strength is so powerful. We were all in this together. None of us would leave. None of us would walk away. I wouldn't walk away from the marriage because I wouldn't walk away from Jesus. Patti wouldn't walk away from the marriage, because she wouldn't walk away from Jesus. Neither of us would walk away from each other, because we had this bond with Jesus. And Jesus, well, he would never walk away from either of us. It was a marriage of safety, security, and love far greater than either of us had ever known.

In the spring of 1986, after we had completed shooting *The Love Boat* but before the final episode aired, my boss, producer Doug Cramer, had this idea to use a Princess ship for a fund-raising gala. Doug was heavily involved with the new Museum of Contemporary Art in Los Angeles, and our show was so hot, the idea of throwing a gala on a Princess ship in San Pedro Harbor drew lots of press and attention from all over. The plan was for all of these beautiful, wealthy people to pile into limousines, motor down to the harbor, and have a magical evening on the ship—and I, as the Captain, would be there to greet them as they came aboard. Some of Aaron Spelling's other big stars served as greeters too, including Linda Evans, Joan Collins, and John Forsythe.

The night was incredible. Diahann Carroll was singing in one room while Bobby Short was singing in another—there was fabulousness everywhere you turned. Once I finished with all of my duties, I finally had a chance to join my wife and daughter at a big, round table in the dining room. Right after I sat down, the door opened and who should walk in but Cary Grant and his young wife. He was eighty-one, maybe eight-two years old at the time, and he had that white hair and those horn-rimmed glasses—the picture of old Hollywood elegance. Everybody stopped and looked. He had so much grace and power and presence, and he held so much respect and reverence from all of us, it was astonishing to witness. Even among all of those stars, he shone bright enough to stop you in your tracks. You didn't hear a glass tinkling in the room until he finally sat down at his table.

That's when Patti leaned over to me and whispered, "That's Cary Grant!"

I said, "No, really?"

She said, "I want you to introduce me to him."

"What?" I said. "Patti. He doesn't know *me*."

"Well, you worked with him," she said.

"That was twenty-five years ago. He doesn't even know I'm *alive!*"

Patti really poured it on: "I'll never ask you for another thing," she said. Then my daughter started in: "Please, Pop, please!"

If any husband believes that his wife will never ask him for another thing, I've got a bridge to sell you. But Patti was so charming, I wanted to please her. I stood up and my heart was pounding out of my chest like a cartoon character. I was so nervous to approach him. I walked over to Mr. Grant's table, and I took a deep breath and thought, *God, give me the right thing to say.*

"Excuse me, Mr. Grant?"

He looked up at me, and much to my delight, he recognized me right away. He smiled and turned, and grasped my forearm. "Gavin, Gavin, Gavin!" he said. "I'm so proud of you."

I tell you, I almost lost it. Cary Grant knew who I was. I still thought of myself as that young actor who played that role with him in *Operation Petticoat*. I had forgotten, *He's a human being! He watches television too!*

I introduced him to Patti, who was shaking all over, and my daughter, who was blushing. It was a wonderful moment for all of us. (My wife has since asked me for other things, by the way. Don't be fooled, fellas.)

The reason I tell this story is because it's an example of a moment when I took a risk. Cary Grant was at that time maybe one of the biggest living movie stars on the planet. For me to bother him at dinner like that, he could have put me down. He could have said, "Please don't interrupt me." But he didn't. He said something amazing. I took that risk of embarrassment for the sake of my wife and my daughter, and I've carried this lesson ever since: if you take a risk for somebody else, take a chance; don't be afraid. It can give you a moment that can last for the rest of your life.

That brief encounter with Cary Grant has helped me for the rest of my life too—when I'm down sometimes, when I'm doubting myself, I think of what that giant of a man told me. And I smile.

Just a few months later, Cary Grant was out on the road showing his films and giving talks about them—connecting with his audience, live and in person, which was something he loved to do. And on one of those nights, in Davenport, Iowa, he had a stroke and died.

Just like that, the great Cary Grant was gone.

If I didn't take that risk, if I didn't reach out that night when we saw him, if I didn't say hello, and *then* he had died? I would have felt guilty about it for the rest of my life.

Sometimes you don't get a second chance. You need to take a chance when you have the opportunity. Always.

With *The Love Boat* over, Marion and Patti and I decided to join forces in a play. We would spend the summer performing *Never Too Late*, first in Denver and then all the way out on Cape Cod. My friend Jan Peters would join us on the road, too, and I could hardly imagine a better group with whom to spend my summer.

I was worried about another friend of mine, though: Ted Knight.

Ted had cancer. He had been fighting it off and on for years. He had an operation for it but never let anyone know back when we were on *The Mary Tyler Moore Show*. Patti and I were the only ones who knew outside of his immediate family.

That's how close we were. We laughed and cried, and we just had a complete relationship, Ted and I. He really was like an older brother who gave me advice about everything. He was just wonderful.

In the early part of 1986, his cancer came back in a more aggressive form. I said, "Patti, I think we should go see Ted before we go away." We hadn't seen him for a couple of months. He had been in treatment, but he was home now.

So I called him. I said, "Listen, how you doin'?"

"Well," he said, "I'm still here!"

"Patti and I are going on the road," I told him. "Can I come over and see you before we leave?"

"Yeah! Of course. I want to see you."

I offered to come over that Sunday and he said, "Sure."

Ted didn't have Jesus in his life. He didn't adhere to any faith whatsoever.

We went to church that day before we went to see him. I knew I wanted to talk to him about his choices, and about eternity. I saw Dean Jones at church with his wife, Lory. Dean's a great actor, known for his Disney roles in *The Love Bug* and for so much more, but he became a born-again Christian in the early 1970s and had a powerful influence in the church. He's quite a guy. I asked them both, "If you would just say a prayer for Patti and me, because we're going to go over and see Ted, and I know he's not doing well." Dean prayed for us—and I know he also prayed for Ted.

Ted was living in Pacific Palisades, in the house he always dreamed of. We pulled up and Dottie—his wife, who was one of the first people to tell me to stop drinking, way back when—came out to greet us. I loved her for that, and so much more.

I asked her, "How is he?"

"He's not doing well," she said. We talked for a couple of minutes, and then I heard Ted shouting, "Well, are you going to come in this house, or aren't you?"

We went upstairs and he was in bed, surrounded by bookcases full of books—and he was so thin. He reminded me of my father, when my father was home before he went to the hospital for the very last time.

It was so good to see him, and he was so happy to see Patti and me. I told him that we were going out on the road and would be gone for four or five months. He was thrilled that the two of us were back together, and for some reason, on that day, he asked us how it happened. "You both seem so happy," he said. "How did you do it?"

That question opened the door.

I told him, "The reason we're back together is that God did it. We have a relationship like we never had before—because it's not just Patti and me. It's threefold. Jesus is here too. It's the three of us. Nobody's going to leave. He's not going to leave us, and we're not going to leave each other. There's a secure feeling now.

"But more importantly, Ted, have you thought about eternity? The afterlife?"

He said, "Well, look at all these books. I've been reading all these books."

That's when I told him, "You want to know why Patti and I have this peace? It's because we know where we're going when this is all over."

"You mean heaven?" he said.

"Yes, heaven. That's eternity, Ted. That is forever. Our lives here are like nothing, like two seconds. Heaven is forever. And if you accept Jesus into your life like we did, eternity in heaven is a promise," I said. "Would you think about that?"

He looked at me and said, "You know, I've been reading all these books . . ."

He paused. He clearly hadn't found the answer he was looking for in any of those thousands of pages.

"What do I have to do?" he asked.

"You just have to repeat a prayer after me," I said.

He teared up. He said, "I think I've waited long enough."

I tear up now just thinking about it.

He bowed his head. Patti and I were on one side of the bed, and Dottie was on the other, and we all held hands and I read from what they call a tract, a little prayer card. I didn't want to make a mistake! This was too important. I read it, he repeated it, and he started weeping. And of course I started weeping too.

It was quite a moment.

"Well," I told him, "now you can, as they say, 'rest in peace.' Because the rest is going to be a blessing for you."

Dottie left the room, and Ted said, "Gavin, there's one thing. I believe what I just did. But Dottie doesn't believe there's a God."

"Well, Ted," I told him, "maybe she does now."

The tears started up again.

"This is the most wonderful day," he said. "I feel peace already."

"I'm telling you, Ted, this was the most wonderful day for me too!" I cried. And we hugged. I could feel the weight lifted off of his shoulders. He had accepted Jesus into his life, and the change in him was instant.

Man, I could have packed it up right then and been happy. To think that you could be used that way by the Lord, for one of your very best friends. Every time I start to think about it I start weeping—out of joy!

Patti went downstairs with Dottie, and Ted asked me to help him get to the bathroom. This incredibly strong, strapping Polish guy was on a cane now. So I helped him get out of bed, just like I used to with my father when I was a kid.

When he came out, he said, "I want to show you something downstairs."

"Can you make it?" I asked.

"Yeah, yeah!" he said. We went down through the kitchen and out to the backyard. He said, "Look. I finally have my dream: my own black-bottom pool!" He had talked about wanting his own pool for as long as I'd known him. It really was a dream come true. And it was beautiful. It was different from a lot of ordinary pools, and he pointed out why. "They wanted to put stairs here, but I made it smooth so I could go in in my wheelchair."

It broke my heart. Can you imagine a strong guy like Ted saying those words? He finally had his dream come true, and he couldn't walk on his own to get into that water. I was happy for him, of course. He had made his dream come true. But the irony of it stung.

We visited a little while longer, and then we left. Ted stood in the hallway and waved good-bye as we were leaving. He had a smile on his face. A peaceful smile.

Once we were in the car, I said, "Patti, I don't think we're gonna see him again."

Patti was quiet for a moment. She took my hand.

"We'll see him again," she said. "In heaven."

A few days later, we hit the road. We went to Denver to rehearse and then put up the play for the first time at this wonderful theater. When that run was over, we flew to Cape Cod, where we had a whole week off before we opened. It was the first vacation Patti and I had taken in what felt like forever. It may well have been the first vacation that didn't involve at least *some* aspect of my work in our entire relationship! And as we tooled around the beautiful eastern peninsula of Massachusetts, we fell in love with the whole area. We just flipped for it. All that history, all that beauty, surrounded by the ocean—Cape Cod is one of the most beautiful parts of the whole country, as far as I'm concerned. It captivates you. Just think of the history alone. Route 6A, the King's Highway there, was named after the king of England. The first church in the entire United States is *right over there!*

Within days Patti and I decided that we wanted a house on Cape Cod.

I happened to meet a real-estate agent at our opening-night party, and I told her we were on the hunt. We thought we wanted to live right there close to the theater in Dennis, so we could walk to our shows, just to make it easy. But thanks to that agent, our house hunt would take us a little farther than we expected.

A few days into our run of *Never Too Late*, during a point in the play where I went backstage to change my jacket, I noticed there were some notes on my desk in the dressing room. One of them read, "Associated Press wants to talk to you after the show." I had no idea what the AP might be calling about—until our producer, Charlie Forsythe, came running in. He was weeping.

"Gavin," he said. "Ted died."

"What?"

"Ted died."

That's how I found out that my best friend, Ted Knight, was gone.

Ted had played the Cape Playhouse years earlier in a show called *Generations*, which I would perform myself eventually at a theater in Traverse City. So Charlie knew Ted. They all knew Ted. They all loved him.

In between scenes, word got around to every member of that cast. We were all a mess—but we had to finish the show. *The show must go on!*

When the curtains closed, we finally let it all set in—and the tears flowed like crazy. No one could believe this vibrant man had been taken from us.

Losing a friend in show business brings an added layer of difficulty, in that the press often wants to talk to you. Reporters want the story, they want the scoop, and they want it right away—before you've had any time to grieve, or even to let the news sink in.

"I don't want to talk to the press right now," I said. But someone convinced me to speak with just one reporter from New York City.

The guy got on the phone and said, "Tell me, um, Ted Baxter did a show about conquistador boots?" I said, "Yeah, it was one of the funniest shows. He bought some boots that were called 'conquistador boots,' and they made him taller, and it was a very, very funny episode."

"Well, what's so funny about that?" the guy said.

I just couldn't. My dear friend, this incredible man I had known and loved since 1957, was gone, and this reporter was just—I'll reserve my words here about how crass and clueless certain members of the press can be.

"I'll tell you something, mister," I said, "I don't want to talk to you right now." And I hung up the phone. I didn't want to talk to any of 'em. My heart was broken. I needed to grieve in private.

Dottie called with a message. She said, "I'd like you to do the eulogy."

Unfortunately, I told her, I wouldn't be able to fly to California for the funeral. Patti and I were committed to this play. There were too many people who would be let down if I didn't show up. Summer stock is a tricky business, and to miss even a night or two could be devastating to one of these theaters. Dottie understood. Ted would have done the same thing if our roles were reversed. But she wanted me to write the eulogy regardless, and to send it to her. She said she could have someone else read it.

I prayed to God for the right things to say, because I knew there would be plenty of nonbelievers at Ted's funeral. I would have to word this carefully. I decided the best way to do it was to pen the eulogy in the form of a letter directly to Ted.

My daughter Stephanie went to the funeral. Mary Tyler Moore attended, as did a whole bunch of others from our *MTM* family. And our great writer David Lloyd read the words I wrote:

Dear Ted,

... Patti and I cried rivers of tears when we heard the news, but forget our mourning. I want to celebrate your life. I want to thank you for having shared your entire being, not only with me but with the world. If laughter is healing, think how many millions you helped heal. That alone is tribute enough for any ordinary mortal, but you were far from ordinary, Ted....

You were blessed with success in all areas of your life. But your two Emmys, all your accolades and awards, pale in comparison with the award you received the last time we were together, just a few weeks ago, when you asked Jesus to come into your life. Because of this, we know where you are at this very moment. You are in our Father's arms and if I know you, Ted, the angels are smiling their biggest smiles ever. You have finally done it all....

Dottie sold the big house with the dream pool and moved into a smaller place. She had a nice garden. We had dinner with her every now and then. Then, about three years later, she died too. I spoke at her funeral. They buried her right next to Ted, in a plot overlooking the whole San Fernando Valley. It was strange to stand there looking down at Ted's stone, knowing his body lay under the ground beneath my feet. The stone was marked with his birth name, Theodore G. Konopka, and right underneath it, in quotation marks, "Ted Knight."

I guess you never really get used to people dying. You cry for yourself sometimes, because of your loss. But Ted was a bright, creative friend in my life, and I cherish every memory I have of him. In my heart, I know he's not dead. He's in heaven, where I hope to be going someday. That's what I believe. But I still miss him.

So much in my life was changing all at once in 1986.

After Patti and I got married in front of all of those believers the summer before, Pat and Shirley Boone invited us to share our story in front of a number of different church groups. And we did. It was wonderful. Audiences of hundreds and hundreds of people responded in an emotional way to our story of reconnecting through Jesus. It was just so powerful. I wondered if the Lord wanted me to quit show business altogether and start a ministry!

That thought crossed my mind again after Ted died, yet I kept thinking back to an encounter I had in April of that same year. I guest-hosted *The 700 Club*, and I met a man named Dr. Ed Cole, the founder of a movement called Maximized Manhood. His book of the same title encouraged men to find strength through the Lord. It had sold over a million copies. He said to me, "I believe God has called you to the entertainment world, Gavin. Just be the best actor you can be for Jesus."

I'll admit that I didn't really know what he meant. *How can a person be an "actor for Jesus"?* Show business seemed so very different from the business of my faith.

I would certainly find out in time.

As it turns out, 1986 wasn't nearly finished with me yet. And neither was my Lord and Savior.

BACK IN PORT

AGAINST WHAT WE THOUGHT WERE OUR WISHES— our expressed desire to stay close to the Cape Playhouse—the real-estate agent brought us miles away, to a whole other town, to show us a big piece of property set back all by itself. As we drove up we saw an old saltbox-style home standing there, next to a big barn with a carport, and a main floor I could turn into an artist's studio (I was getting back into painting at that time), and a top deck with a full apartment where our guests could stay, all overlooking a beautiful marsh . . . and we fell in love. Patti and I bought that property and turned it into our primary residence. We would keep a place to go back to in California, and our real-estate adventures wouldn't really slow down until thirty years later, when we downsized to the place we now call home in Rancho Mirage. But in 1986, that home in Cape Cod, far from Hollywood, far from our old life, was the place where we would start our post–*Love Boat* life together. A life focused on theater. A life focused on each other. A life focused on family. A life focused on doing the work that God wanted us to do.

We were just barely settling into that new life on the Cape when a guy by the name of Max Hall called me up. He was VP of public relations for Princess Cruises. "Gavin," he said, "we'd like you to be our spokesperson. What do you think about it?"

Princess Cruises had seen such a bump in business because of *The Love Boat*, they wanted to do all they could to keep it going. What better way, they thought, than to hire the Captain to do commercials and make appearances for them! I thought it was the greatest thing ever. I said, "I don't even have to talk to Patti, Max. This is such a great fit." Captain Stubing was truly the role of a lifetime. Now here I was, accepting an opportunity to extend that role into real life—to keep on sharing the Captain's smile with the world.

Princess Cruises only had two ships at the time, but they were getting ready to expand. Massively. So we made our deal in that busy, busy year for me, and we shot our first television commercial.

"Princess . . . it's more than a cruise. It's *The Love Boat*," I proclaimed, as I walked the deck in black tie while beautiful music played and they showed romantic couples in scenes from around the world and out on the water. That commercial won awards for best cruise commercial, and best international travel commercial—and Princess's business soared.

Before I knew it, Princess Cruises bought Sitmar, the massive Italian cruise line. They acquired new boats, and kitchens full of Italian cooks, and a new set of captains from Italy who operated in a laid-back, friendly fashion—similar to the way I had approached the character of Captain Stubing.

Suddenly, my life became a lot more than just acting. I was a spokesperson for this incredibly vibrant, growing company. I was traveling the world, speaking to audiences on the ships, greeting cruisegoers at autograph sessions, attending sales conferences and shindigs for travel agents all over the place. And to think it all grew out of my role on a TV show. How does this happen?

It's funny, but a lot of shows on television now give you nightmares. *The Love Boat* did just the opposite. In fact, a young girl in New York once told me what the show meant to her, and it sums it up pretty good. She said of *The Love Boat*, "It gives me something to dream about."

That dream translated right over to the cruise industry in real life. And the effect of that has continued to this day. People dream about going on cruises. They save up their pennies. They wait to go on a cruise with someone special, or they go on a cruise to *find* that someone special. People use cruises to mark special occasions, from weddings to golden anniversaries. How many lives have been changed on cruises?

I personally have had this experience, and I can only imagine how many others have too. How many times are you assigned to sit at a table with somebody you think you don't want to sit next to, and by the time the cruise is over, you're best friends? Most cruises have open seating now, but it still happens. Cruising breaks down all kinds of barriers. Thanks to the crews alone, you can experience the whole world on a single cruise. I used to do a lot of the training films for the stewards and everyone else who join the ships from just about every country. Even in the dining room, you never know where your waiter will be from: perhaps Russia, India, Bosnia, the Philippines, anywhere!

Princess Cruises had already been a part of my life for the nine years I was on *The Love Boat*. I had already been on some amazing cruises. But I'll never forget, just after Patti and I were reunited, in 1984, we were onboard the second-ever sailing of the brand-new *Royal Princess*. Princess Diana had "named" that ship—which is how Princess referred to the glorious ceremony on the day of a ship's launching, instead of the more old-fashioned and religious-sounding "christening" of a ship. Patti and I stayed in the same suite on that ship that Princess Diana had stayed in. I said to Patti, "Do you realize something? We're the first ones to sleep in the bed that Princess Diana slept in! Can you believe these opportunities they're giving us?"

In all seriousness, I think the reason God gave me that job is I'm a people person. I not only enjoy people saying hello to me or wanting an autograph, but I love it! Everybody needs love, and I love 'em up! I give people hugs. I find out about their families. I love talking to people and interacting with people, especially onboard those magnificent ships. It's just the way I am. That part of the job is not a "job" for me—it's an experience!

Of course the rest of my "job" with Princess Cruises is pretty sweet too.

Right after they purchased Sitmar, Princess flew Max Hall and me and some other executives, including his new associate, Julie Benson, over to Paris for meet-and-greets with the press. (Funny how a character named Julie was the Captain's right-hand girl on my show, and now a real-life Julie was about to play a big role in my real life.)

I had been to Paris once before, for an episode of *The Love Boat*, but I didn't get to see very much of it because I was working. This time? I was working, *and* I got to see the city. I could hardly believe my life.

When we first arrived, Max's bag was missing. It went to the wrong airport. He had to buy a scarf, and he put it on his credit card, and when he got home he got the bill for it: it was $385! He called me up, so frustrated. He used to wear a little bush jacket and scarf. I used to wear them too. We were fashionable men in those days.

Because he was tied up trying to deal with his missing suitcase, Julie and I decided to leave the hotel without him and take a little walk around Paris. We tried to get into the Louvre, and we couldn't get in, so we started walking the back streets of that beautiful city—until we came across a little place that sold hot dogs. Of all things! Julie and I had a hot dog in Paris, the first time I ever met her. Today, she's the VP of public relations for the whole company. We had only known each other a few hours then, and I've known her all this time. She's like one of my daughters now. Patti and I went to her wedding—she married a fellow Princess Cruises executive, the handsome Bruce Krumrine. We also went to her father's funeral. It's a very familial relationship, and it all started over hot dogs in Paris.

Again, a hot dog serves as a nice memory for me.

We went from Paris down to the lower part of Italy, where they were starting to build our new ships at the Fincantieri shipyard. Witnessing the formation of one of those giant floating palaces from the inside out is quite an experience. They took me into the hull as hundreds of men buzzed about, working day and night. There were seemingly millions of wires hanging down from the steel bones of the ship, yet the guide could say, "This is where the elephant bar will be," and so forth. Six months later they'd take me back, and it was all done. It was magnificent.

Max was a great guy. He wasn't much of a world traveler, but he loved to go on cruises. He had met Cary Grant, too, because Cary Grant used to take Princess Cruises long before *The Love Boat* came along. He used to mingle with the guests, and was nice to everyone, Max said. I wasn't surprised.

Max and I would travel all over the world for Princess Cruises in the coming years. We would even travel together when I shot an episode of *Lifestyles of the Rich and Famous* in Puerto Rico—timing my speech on the beach just right so one of our Princess Cruises would come into frame and pass behind me as I spoke.

One of the best parts of the gig was that Princess hired me to serve as emcee and host for a whole series of ship-naming ceremonies. Just like on *The Love Boat*, I found myself welcoming a cavalcade of well-known movie stars and personalities onto these brand-new, real-life "love boats."

The star who came aboard to name the first ship I was involved with was Audrey Hepburn. In 1989, Patti and I spent seven days with that beautiful actress on the *Star Princess*, and she was absolutely delightful. Her boyfriend, actor Robert Wolders, was with her, as was one of her sons. It was the first time I heard someone actually name a ship. I wish I had a recording of it, in that fabulous voice of hers: "May God bless this ship and all who sail upon her," right before smashing that bottle of champagne.

Patti and I had dinner with Audrey and Robert, and she was just everything you could ever want Audrey Hepburn to be. (Had I known then that she had had an affair with my old pal and castmate Ben Gazzara, I might have asked her about it!) In fact, when the cruise ended and we were getting ready to disembark in Fort Lauderdale, I saw Robert and said, "Where is Audrey?"

"Oh, she's upstairs packing for us," he said.

Audrey Hepburn, as famous as she was, packed her own suitcases—and packed *his* suitcases too. I don't know why that struck me, but it did. *She has a servant's heart*, I thought.

Funny thing is, I had an "almost" acting experience with Audrey in my career, thanks to Blake Edwards once again. He almost used me a couple of times. He *almost* gave me the part of the Asian guy in *Breakfast at Tiffany's*, but it went to Mickey Rooney instead. And if Peter Falk didn't do *The Great Race*, I was next in line for that leading role. But everything worked out just the way it was supposed to. Meeting Audrey Hepburn aboard a beautiful, brand-new Princess cruise ship was exactly where I was supposed to be.

The actress who named our next ship in 1990 was just as well known: Sophia Loren! The night before the ceremony, there was a big function on the ship, which was launching from Brooklyn. She was supposed to appear, but she wouldn't come out of her room. She was staying at the Waldorf Astoria, and Max had to trek over there to get her. She just wouldn't come out. According to him, she said, "I'm afraid to meet all those people." He said, "You have to!" They had spent all sorts of money, and bought jewelry for her and everything. Aaron Spelling's designer Nolan Miller, from *Dynasty*, even designed an outfit for her, just for the occasion.

Max finally talked her into coming, and she wore that custom dress and a golden cape—and when she walked down the main staircase on the ship the paparazzi went crazy. She was radiant. She looked like a goddess!

Patti and I met her and her husband, Carlo Ponti, at the bottom of those stairs, and they were kind enough to take a picture with us. We didn't get to spend a lot of time with her, and while I could see she was shy, I could also tell she was a smart lady.

The next morning, on naming day in Brooklyn Harbor, they positioned me on a platform so the press could shoot their cameras past me, over my shoulder. There were dozens of chefs lined up with their tall hats, and a gigantic crowd, and all the staff of the gigantic new *Crown Princess* standing at attention, and Lord Sterling, CEO of Princess Cruises, came riding in with Sophia Loren in a horse-drawn carriage. Everyone began yelling, "Sophia! Sophia!" It was like a Fellini movie! I tell you, art imitates life and life imitates art sometimes. It was magnificent.

The godmother of Princess Cruises' next ship was an entirely different sort of celebrity. A political powerhouse of her day: Margaret Thatcher.

It was August 8, 1991, and because Ms. Thatcher had a cavalcade of bodyguards and handlers with her, they put her up in the suite of the *Regal Princess*, where Patti and I normally would have spent the night. Princess apologetically put us up in the Waldorf Astoria Hotel instead. Boy oh boy, we were really slumming it that night. (Ha! That hotel is glorious! Are you kidding me? What a treat!)

That first night they held a dinner in her honor, and President Reagan shared a taped message on a big screen, because he and Margaret Thatcher were very close.

Max told me, "We're going to get a great shot of you and Margaret Thatcher, so come with me."

This wasn't an actress. I had a feeling she might not know who I was and might refuse to take the publicity shot he was imagining. I said, "You're kidding." But Max pulled me into a big room and said, "I want you to get up on the stage. When she comes in, I'll introduce you, and we'll take a picture—and it will make *Time* magazine!"

I said, "Okay." At least it wasn't a kissing camel!

Margaret Thatcher came in with a whole group of people, and I saw them whisper something to her, and she looked right at me, sizing me up, and then shook her head no. I felt like I was a nobody. She didn't want to come over. She didn't know who I was.

Max was a persuasive guy, so he convinced her people and they brought her over to me and introduced her. They helped her climb onto the stage and I said, "This is a great honor."

We posed for a picture, and I swear she is the only person in my life I've taken a picture with whom I didn't touch. I wasn't going to touch the prime minister!

When the flashbulbs stopped, she said—in her distinct British accent—"I understand your television show is very popular."

I said, "Yes, we're on in ninety countries. We've been on many years now and we're all over the world. But in all my years, to be able to meet someone like you, this is a thrill for me. It's a great honor that you would take the time to take a picture with me."

She said, "Well, they tell me this picture will be in *Time* magazine!"

Ha! They sold her on the idea of posing with *me* the same way they sold *me* on the idea of posing with the Kissing Camel back in Egypt! (I certainly hope my breath was better.)

Well, guess what? It worked. *Time* ran the picture of the two of us. There I was, smiling with Margaret Thatcher, and it looked like we were buddy-buddy—but I wasn't even touching her. Oh, it makes me laugh. After our photo session, she said, "It's so nice to see you." She was so polite. Then somebody brought Patti over to meet her, and Margaret Thatcher said to Patti, "Do you know that your husband's show is on in ninety countries?"

Patti said, "Yes, ma'am. I know that."

Perhaps politics isn't all that different from showbiz: we'll do anything for a little good publicity.

In 1997, for the naming of the *Dawn Princess*, we pulled together a reunion of the entire cast of *The Love Boat*. Eleven years had flown by since that show went off the air, and though we all kept in touch, and a few of us had seen one another here and there, it was the first time the whole cast had reunited in all that time. Jill Whelan was all grown up! The Captain's little Vicki wasn't so little anymore. It was wonderful to reconnect with her, and to hear about everything that had happened in her life. Of course Bernie and I connected like old pals from the moment we saw each other, and Ted and Fred got along like Frick and Frack, man. It was just like old times. When you think about it, we were on that show more than twice the number of years that people go to high school or college together. You might not see those people every day anymore, but when you reunite, there's a magic and a spark unlike any other—because you all shared that experience together. That's just how it felt on that day in Fort Lauderdale.

I'm saving Cindy (Lauren Tewes) for last as I speak about this, because Cindy and I reconnected in a very different way at this reunion. I mentioned the troubles she had been through. It's hard to imagine what it's like to go through everything she did as a young actress in Hollywood. By this time she had been through two divorces. But in 1996, she met and fell in love with a wonderful actor by the name of Robert Nadir. She was happier than I had ever seen her. Patti and I connected with the two of them, and it felt great to launch this wonderful new friendship.

Robert had been suffering some health issues in the past year. He was fatigued. He started tripping over his words, to the point where people accused him of being drunk. He wasn't.

In 1998, Robert was diagnosed with ALS, more commonly known as Lou Gehrig's disease. Later that year, we all got together again to tape a reunion special for *The Love Boat: The Next Wave*, a new series on UPN, starring Robert Urich and Corey Parker. Patti and I came in from Cape Cod, and Cindy and her husband, Robert, came in from Seattle, and we were all in the same hotel.

We had breakfast one morning, and when Cindy left the table to go to the bathroom, I asked Robert how he felt. He told me he felt terrible—not for himself, but for Cindy. He said he didn't want to be one of her tragedies.

It broke my heart.

In the coming months, I wrote to Cindy and called her. I said, "The only thing that's going to pull you through this is faith and belief." I gave her some things to read, and she read them. I'm humbled and so happy to share that Patti and I were able to bring Cindy to the Lord. She found a church up there in Seattle, and started to attend regularly. I communicated with the pastor there, and Patti and I did everything we could to help her through that difficult time from the other side of the country.

Cindy was strong. She gave her husband the most wonderful life she could. And with the Lord by her side, she managed to carry on with her life after Robert passed away in 2002.

She turned her back on acting for a while. She went to culinary school and became an expert on (of all things) cheese! She gained quite a reputation as the "Cheese Lady," and got a lot of press and attention at one point—in a positive way! Lately, she's done some acting again, and from what I can tell, she's at peace. I can't explain why she has been forced to face so many tragedies in her life. But she faced them, and she carries on. And I'm so proud of her for that.

23

THE SEA'S HIGHS

PRINCESS CRUISES KEPT GROWING AND GROWING. In 1998, I traveled to Italy once again, this time to witness the building of the *Grand Princess*, which would be the largest ship afloat in the world when it launched that September. It was named in New York Harbor by the wonderful Olivia de Havilland. I felt so blessed to get to see her yet again! Jesse Norman from the Metropolitan Opera sang. I brought the new *Love Boat* Captain Bob Urich with me so he could get the full experience. Loretta Lynn was there. I took my business manager and his wife, and we all took a little cruise to nowhere—a one-night cruise in which you go out and come back to the same port—on the biggest ship in the world! It was fabulous.

Two years later, on February 16, 2000, Princess Cruises celebrated the launch of the *Ocean Princess* with "*Love Story* meets *The Love Boat*." They reunited Ali MacGraw and Ryan O'Neal from that wonderful film, *Love Story*.

Something surprising happened at dinner that night. I had never met Ryan before, and when I stopped by his table to say hello, he said, "I gotta tell you something, man. When I saw you in the play *A Hatful of Rain*, I was a young man. And you impressed me so much, I decided I wanted to do what you were doing." Ryan O'Neal had seen me in *A Hatful of Rain* at the Players' Ring Theater in 1957! "You made me want to be an actor," he told me. "I saw you and said, 'That's what I want to do.'"

"I can't believe it!" I said.

"It's the truth."

Once again in my life, I learned that valuable lesson: you never know who's watching. You never know who you're going to influence just by doing your work, and giving it your all.

I spent time talking to Ali MacGraw that night too. She was fabulous! Everybody loved her. I said, "Everybody loves you so much, I've got to be careful that you don't take my place here." She had been married to Steve McQueen, of course, and the last time I saw him, she was in the car with him.

We talked a lot about Steve, she and I. We talked about how Steve had given his life to Christ while he searched the world for a cure to his cancer. It felt good to talk about him. It gave me a sense of closure.

I tell you, I never knew what was going to happen on these ship-naming days. For the *Island Princess*, up in Vancouver in 2003, Olympic gold medalist figure skaters David Pelletier and Jamie Salé came aboard. We had dinner together, and I did a photo shoot with this wonderful couple, and I innocently asked them, "When did you get married?"

"Oh, we're not married," they told me.

"Oh!"

Jamie asked for a picture alone with me, to send to her mother (who was a big fan of mine, she said). So I said, "I'll tell you what. I'll do it if you promise me you'll get married."

They laughed and tried to brush it off, but I sent her that picture—and the two of them wrote me back just a few months later: "We did it!" they wrote. "We got married!"

Speaking of marriages, some funny things happen to people on Princess Cruises—and sometimes the truth is stranger than any fiction we could have created on our TV show. I remember I met this old guy on one cruise, a multimillionaire who got married right there on the ship. He and his whole party ate this big dinner in the Italian restaurant onboard, and we got to talking. That night, before he and his new wife headed back to their cabin, he told me, "Boy, am I going to have a time tonight!" I thought, *Are you kidding me? You can hardly walk!*

I didn't see him over the next couple of days, and as we were getting off the ship, I asked someone from the crew how that newly married couple were doing. "Guess what?" they told me. "He had a heart attack on his wedding night. They had to fly him to a hospital in Hawaii!"

I thought, *At least he flew out with a smile on his face.*

Heart attacks are nothing to laugh at, I realize. In fact, I realize it all too well. I've had two of them.

The first came in 1991, while I was riding a bicycle on Cape Cod. It scared me—and scared my whole family too. I felt blessed to be so close to Boston, where some of the best doctors in the world work, and it turned out an angioplasty (where they go up through a vein in your leg and clean out your arteries up to your heart) was all I needed to feel good as new. I felt so good that I got right back onstage and continued to do live theater and TV guest roles and more throughout that entire decade.

I did a production of *Gigi* in that time period with Anne Rogers, Liliane Montevecchi, and a young girl who didn't have any lines named Anne Hathaway—a girl who would grow up to be *that* Anne Hathaway! I made my entrance in a hot-air balloon. Many people said Honoré was the greatest role I ever played, in one of the most beautiful shows they've ever seen. *The New York Post* said, "The best Broadway musical isn't on Broadway. Heck, it's not even in New York. It's at the Paper Mill Playhouse, in New Jersey, and it's called *Gigi*." In 2000 I even went out on the road on a national tour of Barry Manilow's *Copacabana: The Musical*. That heart attack didn't slow me down at all.

Then I got hit by another one in 2004, and that one was a doozy.

I had flown down to Fort Lauderdale for the naming of the *Caribbean Princess*. Jill Whelan was set to be the godmother of that great new ship, and she was getting married on the aft deck that very same day. It was so much fun to see her again, and to be a part of that special moment. Bernie came down just for the wedding too. As I said, that *Love Boat* family really was like a family.

I felt some pressure in my chest while we were there at the wedding. It passed, so I let it go. But I flew back to LA afterward with my friend and manager, the great Lee Mimms, and we were picking up my bags when suddenly I felt like an elephant sat on my chest. I said, "Lee, I can't move." Lee knew immediately what it was; he had suffered a heart attack himself, in the first class section of the lounge at American Airlines. What is it with airports and heart attacks?

I wound up going in for a quintuple bypass on Good Friday.

To tell you the truth, there were moments there when I thought for sure I was a goner. I can't tell you what a comfort it was to know that I had been saved, to know that I had been born again, to know that Jesus would be there to take my hand, and to take me to see our Father in heaven. But God wasn't ready to take me just yet.

Doctors work miracles today. They really do. I was right back at 'em and up on my feet in no time—resuming my schedule with Princess and more.

Martha Stewart named the *Crown Princess* in Brooklyn in 2006. Katharine McPhee was there, fresh from *American Idol*, and she knocked my socks off with her rendition of "Somewhere Over the Rainbow." Micky Arison and his wife also made quite an impression. He's the billionaire CEO and president of the Carnival Corporation, which has owned Princess Cruises and ten other cruise lines since the early 2000s. He also happens to own the Miami Heat NBA team. They were both very nice to me. (And they were dressed to the nines!)

But the naming of the *Emerald Princess* in 2007 turned out to be my favorite moment with Princess Cruises so far. The naming was set for

Mother's Day, in Piraeus, Greece, so Princess (with my help) decided to bring in two of television's most famous moms and daughters: Florence Henderson from *The Brady Bunch*, with her on-screen daughter Cindy, actress Susan Olsen; and my lifelong friend Marion Ross from *Happy Days*, with her on-screen daughter, Joanie, actress Erin Moran.

I hadn't mentioned it before this, but Florence Henderson holds the distinction of having the most guest appearances of any actress on *The Love Boat*. We had a great time working opposite each other through the years, and we crossed paths all over Hollywood during our respective television heydays. So it was great to see her.

Florence had to fly back home after the ceremony, but Marion and her companion, Broadway musical veteran Paul Michael, were able to stay and come along for a wonderful cruise through Europe. It was the first time either of them had ever been to Venice, and I said to them, "You have to see St. Mark's Square." She and Paul and Patti and I arrived at nighttime, when it was all lit up and the bands were playing. We had gelato together at a sidewalk café and laughed ourselves into the evening.

My friendship with Marion through all of these seasons of our lives is such an extraordinary thing. She called me in the middle of writing this book, and she was off in Kansas City doing a show. She said, "Oh, it's great Gavin. It's about Sherlock Holmes at Christmas, and this young actor is wonderful: he gets all the lines—and I get all the money!" Oh, she makes me laugh. She's still working! I'm just crazy about Marion.

After we left Venice, Patti and I, along with Patti's cousin Lenore Marshall (one of many family members we were able to take on cruises with us over the years) stayed in Italy. Princess hired a car to take us up to Lake Como. One of the Princess executives said, "If you're going to be there, call me and I'll show you everything!" So we did.

There we were in our glorious room overlooking the lake, with all the lights reflecting in the water, and Patti looked out the window and said, "You know what I want to do tomorrow? I want to walk around the lake." I said, "Patti, it's gonna take you *two weeks* to walk around that lake. It goes all the way to Switzerland!" But Italy inspires you that way: you just want to tackle the landscape, and then eat everything in sight.

Across the way there was a museum where Napoleon Bonaparte's brother used to live. Everywhere we looked there was history like that, which we love.

George Clooney has a place there, too, and we drove past that. (Royalty of a different kind.)

Our friend who worked for Princess took us everywhere. My work was done, and we weren't in a hurry, so we took a ride and wound up on top of a big hill. We came upon an Italian wedding, and they welcomed us with open arms—and served us food like you wouldn't believe. There must be some Italian blood in me, because I just loved it. We had such a fabulous time in Lake Como. It was one of the most beautiful places I've ever been.

For me, Lake Como and Tahiti are the tops. Of all the cruises, of all the trips, of all the travel I've done in my life, those two places take the prize for most breathtaking.

In Lake Como, Patti and I would sit outside by the lake at night, with the lights strung, and they would make these pizza pies for us, and then we'd go for some gelato. It was just beautiful. And to think: Princess Cruises gave that to us. That's part and parcel of what happens with them.

When I went to Tahiti, my balcony on the ship was as big as my backyard in Rancho Mirage! It covered half the ship in the back. Lee Mimms and I used to have Bible studies every morning. They would bring us breakfast, and then we would sit out there and praise God. Nobody bothered us. It was just beautiful. The ships are huge now! And my stateroom always becomes a refuge. It becomes a place where we go to pray. My own stairway to God. My sanctuary.

There are a lot of people on these megaships, which is one reason some people say they don't think they'd like to go on a cruise. But I tell you, as soon as you close your door, those thousands of people are no longer there. You're in your private room. You can reflect on what you've done for the day. You can read. You can watch television. You can just sit and look at the water. You can sing praises to the Lord. It's all up to you.

The last ship-naming ceremony I participated in was in 2008. We welcomed *The Bachelorette* and her husband, Trista and Ryan Sutter, and they brought their baby with them. They were the nicest people you would ever want to meet. He was a fireman from a small town, in Colorado, I think. I had never seen the show. I'm an actor, from the days of acting. I don't understand this fascination with so-called reality TV. (How can they call it "reality" when all of those shows have writers and there are cameras all over the place?)

Princess has commissioned two more ships since then, neither of which I was able to attend, but I'm already scheduled to help them launch two more ships as I sit here writing this book. The first celebration in October 2013 will mark the American debut of the *Royal Princess*—a ship that was officially named by Kate, the Duchess of Cambridge, with great fanfare and the smashing of a giant bottle of champagne in Southampton on June 13. To think I'll be celebrating a ship named by the daughter-in-law of Princess Diana, all these years later. The second launch will come in 2014, and I tell you, I hope this fun never ends.

I've seen Princess Cruises grow from two small ships in 1986 to the sixteen or seventeen megaships they have now. I've seen it grow from the very first slogan, "It's more than a cruise . . . It's *The Love Boat*," to the newest one, which perfectly captures the essence of cruising in two words: "Escape completely."

I've met so many wonderful people. I've taken my family on cruises, and my friends on cruises. I've done functions up in Santa Clarita where their headquarters are, and had my kids stand up in the audience—where everyone applauded for them.

Julie Benson is still there, as I've mentioned. She's been with the company almost as long as I have. And I get to travel with the nicest people. Karen Candy, who has two little boys and a husband, is like a daughter to me now too. She's the second in command of public relations, and she's juggling a young family. Her little boy says, "Mommy, I wish you didn't have to go," even when she's only gone for two nights! That's tough on a mom's heart. But we all support one another through these things. It really is a family. There are only five people in the Princess public relations office. That's not a lot of people, and they have a lot of work to do. I love them all.

Princess even produced a movie on my life story, which they play onboard, on a TV station that reaches every passenger's room. They called it *The Life and Times of Gavin MacLeod*, and it won a Telly Award in 2009. How many actors get a gift like that? I'm just so grateful. And I know that none of it would have happened if it weren't for Aaron Spelling creating and believing in *The Love Boat* during that golden age of American television—and then believing in me.

In today's world, if you do a series for three years it's considered a hit. Some shows only do nine episodes per season. We did nine *years* of *The Love Boat*, and *twenty-eight* episodes each season. We reached millions upon millions of people because of that. How many actors get to experience such a thing? And then follow it up with a company like Princess?

Every time I go down into a kitchen on a Princess cruise ship, anywhere in the world, one of the chefs will spot me and start singing *The Love Boat* theme song—and it doesn't take long for the rest of that crew to start singing along.

I mean, my goodness, the watch that I wear on my wrist every day was given to me by Princess. It's the best watch I have ever had! Alan Buckelew, the president of Princess Cruises, gave it to me to mark my twentieth year with the company. And Carnival CEO Micky Arison happened to catch my show on one of our ships one day, and he sent me a personal e-mail saying, "I just want you to know how much I appreciate what you've been doing for Princess all these years."

The Princess family has been generous to me in so many ways. They're a caring, personable, wonderful group of people—from the staff in the kitchen, all the way up to the guy at the top. I hope you can understand why my relationship with Princess is among the relationships I hold dearest in my life.

To think, I've spent twenty-seven years so far with Princess Cruises, going all the way back to that first phone call from Max Hall in 1986. What a year that was for me. In fact, I need to step back here because I *still* haven't told you about everything that happened in that incredible year when *The Love Boat* ended. When that one door closed, it wasn't just another door that opened for me—it was a thousand doors!

The opportunities just kept coming.

NEW CALLINGS

THEY SAY GOD WORKS IN MYSTERIOUS WAYS, AND
he certainly started to work through Patti and me in some surprising ways after we rekindled our marriage.

Word of our remarriage spread far and wide in the Christian world.
The fact that we were brought together through Jesus was seen as an
inspiration, and some very powerful people and organizations wanted
us to share our story with the world.

On top of everything else that was happening as *The Love Boat*
ended in 1986, Patti and I were approached about doing a book. We
were excited! We thought the title should be, *I'm Sorry Your Dinner's
Cold. It's Been Waiting for Three Years.* Obviously that's too long for the
title of a book, so we agreed on another title: *Back on Course.*

We worked with a gifted writer, Marie Chapian, who gathered the
story of our lives, and broke the story of our relationship into two parts:
the first from my perspective, the second from Patti's. It told of our
courtship and our breakup, and then at the end, it described how Jesus

brought us together in a marriage that was stronger than either of us had ever imagined.

The book didn't sell nearly as well as we'd hoped. Not enough publicity. It was a tough lesson for the two of us. From here on out, when it came to our faith and our relationship, Patti and I would need to be careful to surround ourselves with people who not only wanted to share our story but would promote us in the best way possible.

Paul Crouch was one of those people. The man who had cofounded the Trinity Broadcasting Network with his wife, Jan, approached us around that very same time and asked if we'd like to host our own TV show. Trinity Broadcasting was a rapidly growing Christian television network that broadcast all over the world. It had, and still has, millions of viewers. In fact, it's known as the "world's largest faith channel."

The idea of hosting a show together, based on our own personal experience and sharing the experience of others who have overcome challenges in their lives and marriages, sounded wonderful. So Patti and I said yes!

We all decided the title of our book would make for a perfect title for our show too: *Back on Course*. And what a course we set: our little show would stay on the air for the next seventeen years.

We were new Christians and didn't know a lot of people in the Christian industry, but the Crouches thought we were the perfect couple to anchor this show. For one, people knew who I was, because to millions of people I was and always would be the Captain. But they also loved our story—that Patti and I had been married, divorced, saved by Jesus, and then married again.

Our show was about more than marriage, though. It was about the extraordinary troubles that individuals and couples alike had overcome in life with the help of our Lord Jesus Christ. It was basically a half-hour interview show: we (along with the producers) would find people with extraordinary stories and messages to share, and then Patti and I would interview them on-air and help them share those stories with the world.

We started out shooting that show at the TBN studios in Orange County, California, and our first guests were Pastor Jack and Anna Hayford from The Church on the Way. I talk about Pastor Jack a lot, because he's been such a positive influence in our lives. In some ways, outside of the Catholic world, Jack Hayford is like the pope. He is beyond reproach. Everyone goes to him for approval. It's no exaggeration to say that he reaches millions of people. Not a bad first guest!

The show also worked on a manageable schedule. We would shoot ten or twelve episodes, back to back over a number of days, and then be done for a while. It gave us plenty of time for all of the other callings in our lives—especially the theater, since Patti and I would continue acting, singing, and dancing from coast to coast. It also meant we could keep our primary home on Cape Cod, and fly in to California for short periods to work on the show.

We taped inside that studio for the better part of a decade, until Jan said, "I think you should go do it on a boat." Aha! Put the Captain on a boat! I liked that idea. So did our guests. Knowing they would get a fun boat ride out of it, guests flocked to our show in its last few years. The visual canvas opened up, too, and made for some beautiful television. Who else has ever set a talk show on the water?

The boat was in the harbor at beautiful Newport Beach. We'd go out and cruise around, and pass John Wayne's house four times a day.

For those who haven't seen the show, it basically went like this: You would hear the theme music and the announcer would introduce us, "Patti and Gavin MacLeod!" Then we'd say, "Hello. How are you? It's great to see you again." We were already seated on the ship, and we'd say, "Our guests today are so-and-so and so-and-so, who have finally been reunited." We'd tell you a little bit about their story, that they were married fifty years ago and something happened and he ran away, or she ran away, or whatever the tale may be, and then the guests would walk up the gangway and onto the boat. From there, they were the ones who told their stories. All we did was interview them a little bit to coax them along. The whole thing was shot as close to real time as possible, and it was only a half hour long. We'd stop once for a commercial they'd put in there. Then we'd wrap it up, the guests would go down to the bottom of the ship, and the next guest or guests would come up and we'd start taping the next show.

Jay Jones was our producer, and he and his wife, Marilee, are our dear friends to this day.

The show was easy. And guess what? Sometimes, that's exactly what the best things in life are: easy. Simple. Not everything has to be a struggle.

Patti and I met some inspiring people on that show—people who had been through everything you could imagine. There was a guy who had left his wife to live a homosexual lifestyle—and he talked about how his whole life had changed when he gave his life to Jesus. The desires he had disappeared, and his wife took him back, and they started a whole new ministry.

A former Miss America came on too: Cheryl Prewitt, whom I voted for when I judged the Miss America competition in 1980! In her case, she had been born with one leg shorter than the other. And she told us about the time that someone took her to Kenneth Hagin Ministries down in Oklahoma, and he prayed over her, and—believe it or not—she actually saw her leg grow.

She was a wonderful, inspirational individual. I remember lobbying for her with the other judges. There was something special about her. During the talent competition, she sang, and her microphone went out, but she kept right on going. She didn't let it throw her. I thought, *Wow, she's got something!* Little did I know, she had the spirit of Christ in her. The same spirit I would discover for myself four years later, and then discover in her when she and her husband came on our show. In addition to the miraculous story of her leg, Cheryl and her husband talked about losing their daughter, which had been incredibly difficult for them. It was quite an emotional show.

On a side note: her husband's sister married Oral Roberts's son, Richard. There was a birthday party some years ago thrown by our mutual friend Samantha Landy, and only a handful of people were invited. I was able to reacquaint with Oral and his wife, Evelyn, whom I had met once before. Patti and I took a picture with them. It's one of my treasures. It was quite a night being in his presence, especially knowing his backstory and what he overcame. The people I've been in the presence of is just incredible to me sometimes.

Anyway, my point is, our show wasn't always about the relationship angle. It was about how you could deal with the death of a child or anything else that could happen to one or two people. Drugs were a big topic. A good number of our guests became pastors of enormous churches because of the drug scene.

Any kind of problem that might exist between two people we talked about on that program. Lack of communication, for example. Dean Jones came on with his wife, Lory, and they started to have an argument right in front of us—on camera! It turns out it was all planned. They came out of it and said, "This is what you *don't* want to do." They were great teachers.

Our guests weren't all actors, models, and well-known pastors. There were many guests we had never heard of before our producers brought them to our attention. People who travel the country as evangelists would come in and talk about adapting to life on the road. We met couples who shared stories about having problems with their children, or problems with in-laws accepting that one or both of them had become born again. Dealing with the fact that some people don't want to talk to you or accept you once you become born again was certainly a hot topic. But we talked about all sorts of things.

Mostly, our show was about how people's lives had changed: where they were before, where they were now, and how faith in the Lord had changed their lives.

The show was a big success. A lot of pastors and their wives advised us to start our own ministry. Patti and I were already on TV, reaching an audience, traveling to churches, and talking to people all over the country about the way our lives had been enriched and made complete through Christ. So in some ways, Patti and I already had our own ministry! We just never made it official. We never became a 501(c)(3) organization so we could claim exemptions on our taxes, or collect donations, or give ourselves salaries or any of those things. There are all kinds of write-offs we could have claimed as ministers—and every once in a while when Patti gets concerned about money issues (as happens in just about every marriage), she'll say, "Well, maybe we should have done it!" But finding tax exemptions and write-offs was not the reason to get into it for us. Sometimes, I'm afraid that the money issues in certain ministries muddy the water of what it's really all about.

The fact is, we have a ministry. We had viewers all over the world, and now everywhere we go there are certain people who know us from that show. We touched a lot of lives. Patti and I were becoming ambassadors for Christ, in a big way!

I'm not saying this to be boastful. It just goes back to what the apostle Paul says in the Bible: once you become born again, you become an ambassador for Christ. As years went by, I grew more comfortable with that role of "ambassador" in every facet of my existence.

Earlier I mentioned that once you become a celebrity, your whole life becomes part of the act. I didn't like that act very much, because it involved a lot of showing off—showing up with prearranged celebrity "dates" on your arm, and the intrusion of the press into your family life. Well, serving as an ambassador for Christ is similar in that your whole life definitely becomes part of the act—but that's the only similarity. With Christ, it's no act! It's all truth! And I love it. Your belief and your gratitude and your grace are all tied together with the life you lead, in every moment.

I've been an ambassador for Princess Cruises, but the most important thing I've ever done is to become an ambassador for Christ. And I will always remain his ambassador.

The well-known evangelist Joyce Meyer says, "Sometimes, the only Bible people will read is watching *you*." So you have to be aware of what you're doing. You have to believe in what you're doing and to try to

It's more than a cruise—it's the *Love Boat*! My first day at Princess Cruises, 1986.

Sophia Loren on the *Crown Princess* in NYC— I can't believe this really happened. Wow!

Max Hall, former vice president of public relations at Princess Cruises and my traveling buddy

Prime minister Margaret Thatcher on the *Regal Princess*— an unbelievable honor!

What a special moment to be in this president's presence!

Erin Moran, Susan Olson,
Me, Florence Henderson,
and Marion Ross—
at the christening of the
Emerald Princess, Piraeus,
Greece, May 13, 2007

Cruising in the good old days with Lee
Mimms (my Princess manager) and Patti

Celebrating my eighty-
first birthday with
Joan and Lee Mimms
and my darling Julie

2012 presidential summit aboard the
Grand Princess in the Mediterranean

One of our best friends in the world, Nancy Sinatra Sr., New Year's Eve in Palm Desert, California

Sealed with a kiss—at Mary's Juvenile Diabetes Research Foundation event in New York City

Tony Orlando, our manager, Susan, Patti, and me at his Yellow Ribbon Music Theater in Branson

My beautiful, talented manager, Susan Munao, also known as "My Gina"

My inauguration dinner as honorary mayor of Pacific Palisades

Renewing wedding vows on the *Crown Princess* with
Captain Di Stephano on Valentine's Day

The *Love Boat* welcomes
a *Love Story*—me, Ali
MacGraw, and Ryan O'Neal

"Welcome aboard!" What a great job. Thank you, Lord!

The Zalin-Steele family BBQ on the fourth of July in Pacific Palisades, after a great parade

The Zalins—Mack, Stephanie, Mark, and Angelica

Brotherly love (older)— on Cape Cod

The Steeles—Jade, Jill, Drew, and Shelby

Pink party— The See Family

Together with Pastor Jack and Anna Hayford at a King's University event

Oral and Evelyn Roberts at his special birthday dinner

Kenneth Copeland at his Eagle Mountain International Church

Pastor Ray Wilson of West Coast Believers Church—a true shepherd

As Jonathan Sperry in the
God-inspired role of a lifetime

My role as a Christian
professor in a thought-
provoking film with
Hal Linden &
Jennifer O'Neill

Celebration of my eightieth birthday luncheon aboard the *Golden Princess*, 2011

Julie Benson, vice president of public relations. What a beautiful boss—and she likes hot dogs too!

John Chernesky inspired the award-winning video *The Life and Times of Gavin MacLeod*—thanks, John!

All aboard for my party with family and friends

help people. You may lose your temper in the moment sometimes, and people may say, "What's going on? He calls himself a Christian?" People are watching you all the time once you profess your belief. Well, let me tell you, when you combine that belief with fame, it gets pretty interesting. You're watched twice as closely! I have a lot of eyes on me wherever I go, but that's not a burden to me. That's a gift. An incredible gift! I try to own up to that. I try to be the best ambassador for Christ I can be.

In the early 2000s, after our run on TBN ended and after I came off the road from *Copacabana*, Patti and I sold our house on Cape Cod and set up our home base in Pacific Palisades—in the same gorgeous area where Ted Knight had found his dream home.

I loved it there. So much so that I became the honorary mayor of Pacific Palisades. I hosted parades, spoke for the community, and dedicated my time to that tony town as best I could.

Patti and I started spending more and more time in Palm Springs as well. It was easy to commute back and forth between the hustle and bustle of LA and the relative quiet of that desert oasis. We enjoyed that. And settling down on one coast meant we could spend more time together, simply "walking the walk," as people say.

Patti and I had touched so many lives with our TV show, and we continued to touch so many people through our faith even while juggling my duties for Princess with my theater work and occasional guest roles on TV shows. I thought I was doing pretty well!

I wasn't fully aware yet of the power I could have as an ambassador for Christ. I didn't realize that I had one more step to take to bring all of my talents—and maybe my whole life's journey—together in the name of Jesus.

25

NOT SO GRACEFULLY

G ETTING OLDER IS NO PICNIC, LET ME TELL YOU.
I've tried to approach the closing doors of old age the same
way I've faced all the other closing doors in my life: always
knowing that another one's about to open.

The thing is, the best way to get through all of this stuff is to laugh!
You get old, and stuff stops working. As I've stated, I've been through a
couple of heart attacks and a quintuple bypass. I have stents in the arteries in my legs just to keep the blood flowing. When I lived in Pacific
Palisades, I suffered an infection in my spine that nearly paralyzed me
for life. I had to skip out on a big TV Land salute to *The Love Boat* because
I was laid up with a horrible, nearly permanent back injury.

But you know what? I'm still walking. And all I can say is, "That's
great!"

Every morning I thank God for my waking up. I thank God for the
ability to *get* up. I thank God for the day, and I thank God for my life—
each and every morning.

Without him, this ship called MacLeod would have sunk a long time ago.

I could have died from that first heart attack, or the second one. Four stents for my circulation, a thing in the left atria of my heart that's there to prevent me from having a stroke, my second eye will have to undergo a cataract operation soon . . .

When you get older it's "patch, patch, patch." You just try to keep this vessel of a body from sinking!

For heaven's sake, don't ever ask an eighty-year-old man how he's doing. He'll talk your ear off with every medical malady under the sun! I won't do that here. (Or have I done that already? I'm sorry!)

What I hope is that through the example of my life, and the fact that I'm still going strong at eighty-two as I write this book, maybe I'll take away some of the fear of getting older. It really is a fascinating part of life's journey. You think you know everything when you're a teenager, but you don't. You think you've got it under control in your twenties, but you don't! By forty, you feel all full of yourself, as if you know what you're doing. Guess what? You don't! You just keep learning, and hopefully you just keep getting better at this thing called life.

When it comes to death? It's all okay when you know what's coming next.

And I'm not just talking about where your body's going to be lying—although there's a funny story in that.

Remember back on that fateful morning in 1984, when I prayed to Christ to give my mother more time? Boy, did he ever listen. He gave my mother nearly twenty more years on this earth. We found her a beautiful assisted-living home in the Palm Springs area, so my brother and I were both able to be close to her and to spend time with her, through her very last days.

When my mother finally passed away, my brother and I went down to Forest Lawn Cemetery in Cathedral City. We wanted to ship her body back to New York so she could be buried with my father, and in order to do that we had to pick out a casket. I tell you, when you first go into a room full of caskets, it's kind of morbid—but like anything else, you stay there for a few minutes and it's okay. You can touch the caskets, and they get less scary, and you just get used to it. So we picked out one for mom, and then I got curious. I saw this wall on the inside of the building, a sort of mausoleum. I said, "I like this wall."

Looking up, I saw the final resting place of Dinah Shore, and all of these other people I had worked with. So I asked the cemetery guy, "If I wanted to get into this wall over here after I die, what's the story on that?"

He handed me a brochure. "I'll tell you what's available, because some are already gone. You know John Phillips? Of the Mamas and the Papas? That's him," he said, pointing to one of the blank slots. "His name isn't on it yet."

It was strange, but fascinating. "Now, you could be *next to* John Phillips, or *on top* of John Phillips. It depends on the price," the man said.

I said, "What's the difference?"

He said, "It costs more, the higher up."

"The closer to heaven, you charge more? This is interesting," I said. "Well, how much to be *next* to John Phillips?" It was like eight thousand dollars for that little rectangular slot in the wall. It's California real estate—it's pricey!

I went home to Patti and said, "How would you like to spend eternity next to John Phillips?" and she said, "Can't you get me a bigger name?"

Long story short: We got it. I own it. Patti and I are going to be buried right there next to John Phillips.

And I did mention it's California real estate, right? No joke. A decade later someone offered me sixteen thousand dollars for that spot. I declined, but it's nice to know I made a good investment.

It's funny, I wound up sitting next to Mackenzie Phillips—John Phillips's daughter—on a plane to New York for the seventy-fifth anniversary party of CBS in 2003. I told her I would be spending eternity next to her father. I think she thought I was nuts.

This is as good a place as any to talk about that seventy-fifth anniversary party, though. Such an extraordinary event, to see so many great stars and great friends together in one evening!

I talked to Candice Bergen, whom I hadn't seen since we were on the set of *The Sand Pebbles*. I saw my buddy Tom Skerritt for the first time in ages, and we laughed about the way my kids would react when he used to call the house. I looked back at one point and waved at Angela Lansbury. (I did a guest role in *Murder, She Wrote* back in 1990.) And Patricia Heaton, who was a huge star at that moment on one of TV's biggest shows, *Everybody Loves Raymond*, came over to our table and said, "So! This is the 'A' table!"

That made us smile. Of course, our whole gang from *The Mary Tyler Moore Show* was there. Everyone except for Ted. Boy, did we miss him.

What a treat to be invited to gather with all of those fabulous people in the same room and to pose for a photo that encompassed seventy-five years of entertainment. That picture of all of us, dozens of stars from all those different eras all gathered on one stage, will be admired for decades to come.

In many ways, that night was like revisiting my whole career. It got me thinking about a lot of things—like about what I wanted to do with my future. (Yes, there is always a future to think about, no matter how old you get.)

While I dedicated most of my time to live theater, I made a bunch of guest appearances and performed a few one-off television roles through the 1990s and 2000s. David Letterman had me pop onto his *Late Show* numerous times while I lived on Cape Cod. I did some funny stuff. I flew in over the audience dressed in full captain gear. I danced with a chicken. He and I played as if we were college roommates in one sketch. I even married a couple on Valentine's Day. My kids thought I was crazy to do it, as if somehow making those appearances amounted to Letterman making fun of me. I didn't see it that way at all. What good is anything if you can't laugh at yourself? I was honored to do his show, and it was easy for me. He'd call me up, I'd pop into the city, I'd do the show; then

I'd stay at our apartment on Fifth Avenue and head back to the Cape the next day. (Funny story: Patti and I sold that apartment at one point, and then later decided we'd like to have a place in Manhattan once again. We looked all over and couldn't find anything we liked. Then one day, a real-estate agent, completely by coincidence, took us to see a place in very same building we had lived in before. We wound up buying another apartment in that same building! It was great. It was right across from the Metropolitan Museum of Art, and when the windows were open, you could hear schoolchildren in the playground nearby. Boy oh boy, did I love that sound.)

I played a role on a show called *Burke's Law*, a revival of the 1960s cop thriller, with Milton Berle near the very end of his life. Ed McMahon and Rue McClanahan were on that show too. I played a Catholic cardinal on an episode of HBO's gritty prison drama, *Oz*. I showed up as "Uncle Stu" on *The King of Queens* a couple of times. I did *Jag*, and *Touched by an Angel*, and as previously mentioned, I visited my old dressing room on the CBS Radford lot when I did a couple episodes of *That '70s Show*.

Yet of all the roles I did, only one stood out to me from that whole decade and a half: a role I played in a Christian film called *Time Changer*.

I worked with a director named Rich Christiano, whom I have come to love as a son. He believed he could tap into the nation's churchgoing public to find an audience for this independent film far from the usual Hollywood channels. The idea was intriguing. The film was good, and it found a footing. After a limited release, Rich marketed the film directly to viewers on VHS, DVD, and video-on-demand services. He had big ideas. He had big dreams. He really thought that marketing a film directly to a Christian audience could be powerful. He believed in the power of film to deliver the message of Christ. Potentially even to bring people to the Lord.

I wasn't sure where it all would lead, but I hoped he was right. And I hoped to find that sort of work again.

The thing is, I felt a longing inside. Not the longing I felt before. Not the emptiness. Not at all. I hadn't felt empty from the moment I gave my life to Jesus.

I guess it was more of a calling, really: I was beginning to long to do something with my work that would be far more fulfilling than any role on a commercial film or television show could offer.

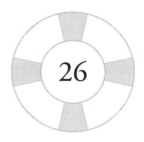

26

ENJOYING THE
BLESSINGS

I N 2008, RICH CHRISTIANO CAST ME IN A FILM CALLED
The Secrets of Jonathan Sperry.
At first I was a little put off by the fact that he wanted me to
play the part of an "old man." I still think of myself as young!

But then I read it. The script was beautiful. The story was beautiful.
The movie had a message—a biblical message—that was told with innocence, simplicity, and beauty. It was a period piece, set in 1970, about
three young boys who discover strength through the Bible, thanks to a
man named Jonathan Sperry.

The role of Jonathan Sperry was delicious to play as an actor. He had
depth. He had layers. He went through a range of emotion. I also had to
grow a moustache for the role. In all my years in the business, even with
all the stuff I did playing characters with and without hair, growing a
moustache was something I had never done before!

But Sperry was also great to play as a human being and a servant of the Lord. He was a kind old man who not only led a Bible study for these neighborhood kids, but he taught them—and a whole town—the greatest of Christian lessons through his actions. Not just words, but *actions*—in his life, and ultimately, his death.

The movie didn't follow the typical release schedule of a Hollywood film. Instead, Rich followed through on his vision to market the film directly to churches and churchgoers. Churches sponsored the film in hundreds of movie theaters all across the country upon its release in the fall of 2009. The following year, the film was released on DVD—and churches continued the practice of showing the film to large audiences, even as the film was being sold to thousands of individuals who would watch at home on TV.

I started going to some of these screenings, and I can hardly even describe the emotional impact this film was having. In some cases, for certain people, this film was as powerful as that moment when Patti led me into our old apartment and handed me a Bible with my name on it. This film, through its simple message, was almost like reading the Bible to people who were primed and ready to receive God's message—even if they had no idea they were ready to receive that message when they sat down in the theater! I saw lives change right in front of my eyes.

At some of the screenings, they held altar calls at the end of the film. I watched a ninety-year-old lady in one audience come all the way down from the balcony, ready to accept Christ in her life right then and there—*because of that movie!* I had a little boy come up to me after a different screening, and he recognized me and tugged on my shirt: "Mr. Sperry, Mr. Sperry! Can I tell you something? You have just changed my life."

It's hard to believe a movie can have this effect, but it can. I said to that little boy, "Do you mean that you want to do something for Jesus?" And he said, "That's what I mean!"

You can do a lot of *Love Boat*s, you can make all the money in the world—but that? That *never* happens. Or I should say: that never *happened*. Now it does, because this is what my life has become: a life spent delivering God's message through my work and sharing God's message through my day-to-day existence.

After seeing people brought to the Lord because of a role I played, I started to realize that nothing else mattered. I started to realize that this is what my life had been leading to. All of the ups and downs in my career, the twists and turns, the roles I'd played, the parts I missed, and the parts I'd been given—all of them were leading me right here. And now I don't want to do anything less.

Sometimes focusing on the work you want to do means saying good-bye to the work that came before it. That's not easy. But when it is time, it's time.

The time for me came in 2010.

I got a call to do a guest-starring role on the CBS drama *Cold Case*. I love that show. It's a great show. But they wanted me to play the captain of a ship.

The only other television work I had done after filming *The Secrets of Jonathan Sperry* was to make a guest appearance on the Disney show *The Suite Life on Deck*. It was a wonderful experience on a wholesome, great program—and those kids who starred in it, Dylan and Cole Sprouse, are two wonderful boys. But get this: the show was set on a cruise ship!

"Don't they have any imagination?" I said to Patti. "Who are these casting people? They see a 'captain' part and they always think of *me*?"

I don't want to sound ungrateful. I'm as grateful as can be! But as an actor, the reason I enjoyed doing guest parts on television shows was because they gave me a chance to stretch. I'd think back to those juicy parts I got to play in the 1960s, and all the TV roles I was doing now just started to feel boring. It seemed like so many of the roles I had been offered in recent years weren't allowing me to stretch at all. I felt as though I was being typecast.

But what really bothered me was I had been spoiled. I had seen what movies like *The Secrets of Jonathan Sperry* could do. Having roles with real purpose? That's all that mattered to me now.

I wondered if getting called in for that *Cold Case* audition was a sign—if perhaps God was telling me it was time to move on and focus on other things in my life.

The fact is, after many decades in the business, I was tired of having to go to auditions and read for people who were younger than my kids. Not that I thought I was above it; I just got *tired* of it. I was turning down a lot of roles, and it wasn't fair for my agents. They were working hard to get me work and I kept saying, "I don't want it. I don't want it."

So I decided this was it. I wasn't going to do it anymore.

I drove all the way in to the *Cold Case* offices in Burbank, from Pacific Palisades. I had a plan in mind. It was a great moment for me. I got to the studio and watched as the young actors came in and were picking up scripts and looking at lines, going back and forth. I said to myself, *I'm glad I don't have to do that.*

They called me in, and they were excited to see me. "Oh, I'm so glad you could make it, Gavin! You have a blue screen in back of you, now here's the camera, this is so-and-so the director . . ."

I said, "How are you? Nice to meet you."

"Okay, we're going to do this scene on page seven—"

That's when I interrupted. "I have to tell you something before we start," I said. "We're not gonna start. I just want to tell you I love this show, and I love the casting on this show, and I want to applaud all of you who are involved in it. I like you so much that I came all the way over here to tell you that I am not doing this anymore. I'm not going on interviews anymore. I'm not doing television anymore. I had a good run, I'm very grateful, so . . . adios."

They were stunned. They said, "Nobody's ever done this before!" I'm sure they went back and told their families that night: *You'll never believe what happened today! Gavin MacLeod quit the business, right in front of us!*

All I could think was, *Wow, did that feel great!* It was time. I knew it, and I followed through.

I drove over to see my agent. He said, "Well, how did it go?"

"It was great!" I said.

"No kidding?"

I said, "Yeah. I told 'em I'm not gonna do it."

He said, "What?"

I said, "I can't do this anymore. I'm eighty years old! I'm not gonna go out and read for parts."

I felt really good about my decision. I said, "You don't need to get me parts anymore, because I don't want to play them."

When I first came to California in 1957, all I wanted to do was to get an agent who would get me parts. *Any* parts. But the thing is, I did it. I've done all that kind of stuff. I'm older now, and there aren't that many parts for older people anyway. So I made a nice exit from showbiz. A dignified exit. I did it my way, and that felt good.

As I left my agent's office, I felt as though a big weight had been lifted from my shoulders. I was free to fly again.

Like I said, now that I'd seen what *The Secrets of Jonathan Sperry* could do, I'd been spoiled. *Jonathan Sperry* has brought so many people to the Lord. There's a man up in Canada who was so moved by it, he bought tens of thousands of copies to distribute to everyone in his community. Everywhere I go, in stores, or even my local post office, people talk to me about it. It's five years later now, and that film just keeps growing by word of mouth!

I'm doing God's work, as his ambassador. And it just doesn't stop. It continues wherever I go. That role of ambassador is what I wear, all the time. People stop me on the street to talk about *Jonathan Sperry*. One guy told me he gathered his whole family around the TV to see it. Another guy came up to me and said, "Where did this movie come from?" He was so moved by it that he got busy telling everyone he knew about it. He thanked me for making it.

Even people who *haven't* seen it are moved when I tell them about it.

I tell you, the wonders of this film don't end! I was getting my kidneys examined one time and when I was lying on the table the technician asked me what I was up to these days, and I told him, "I made a Christian movie called *The Secrets of Jonathan Sperry*. I'm a born-again Christian. I gave my life to Christ."

"So have I!" he said. He started telling me how his whole family had become believers. I tell you, once you start down this road it seems everywhere you go you hear stories of how people's lives have changed through Jesus. What a joyful way to go spend your days—interacting with people and sharing the joy!

Becoming an ambassador for Christ is the greatest role I've ever had in my life. I've been an ambassador for Princess Cruises for twenty-seven years, and I cherish that work. But being an ambassador for Christ is the ultimate. It's better than getting any Oscar, any Emmy, any kind of award there is.

I walk around in a state of perpetual gratefulness now. The people I've seen who are living good lives today, who are happy and fulfilled, are not the same people they were before they came to Christ. He's a wonder-working guy who can change you, and change you, and change you.

And this joy I'm expressing? It's out there for anybody who wants it.

I feel more fulfilled now than at any time in my life. Acting and entertaining was my purpose in the past. Now my purpose is to serve God. In fact, I googled my name recently (how's *that* for keeping up with the times?) and I saw myself described as "Gavin MacLeod: Actor and Christian Activist." I thought, *Wow! I've really made it!*

It's funny how if you're open, God can—and will—use you. He's given me a long life, and I want to use my life for him. I could have died from my heart attack or bypass surgery. I could have died from my back infection. It's a miracle that I survived and that I'm not on a walker. I'm grateful for all that. But getting to play the role of Jonathan Sperry, and seeing the result of that film, is the ultimate fulfillment and promise of everything else that preceded it.

It's startling when I stop and think about it: God led me through every twist and turn in my life to play the role of the Captain. A captain is a role of authority, a role that's looked up to. It's a fatherly figure, and that in and of itself is different than playing almost any other type of role on TV. It brings with it a certain level of respect, love, and responsibility. And no matter what other roles I've played in my life, I will always be viewed as the Captain.

You know what I think? I think God gave me that role. I think God was pushing me toward that role my entire life. I played the captain of the *Pinafore* in a Gilbert and Sullivan production in high school. I played a different sort of captain in *Androcles and the Lion* when I first went on the road out of New York City. I had millions of people watching me in ninety countries around the world as the Captain of *The Love Boat*. And then God allowed me to continue acting in the spirit of the Captain in all of my work for Princess Cruises, for all these years since the show went off the air.

Only after I had gained that notoriety, only after I had gained a certain amount of respect, only after I had traveled the world and met people of all stripes, from all walks of life, only *after* I had taken this long, fantastic voyage of a life did God put me in the role of Jonathan Sperry—because he knew that now, after all of that, people would listen to what the Captain had to say.

Isn't it interesting how God can use us? Looking back today, I can see the path he laid out for me, clear as day. God was speaking to me all along—even when I wasn't listening. God was guiding me—even when I wasn't watching where I was going. Sort of like the Captain of a ship.

I can't help but smile now and embrace it with open arms.

Patti and I still get invited to various churches to give talks, and I say yes whenever I can. When they screen *Jonathan Sperry* at various venues, a practice they continue to this day, I show up and talk in those venues as often as I can. What's so unique about this movie is that kids come to see it—and sharing God's influence with young people is such a gift.

One lady called me recently to let me know that after seeing the film with her daughter, they were home and she walked in and caught her little girl in her room, lining up all of her stuffed animals and preaching to them. The little girl was saying, "I'm Jonathan Sperry!"

The stories keep coming, and every one of them touches my heart.

Throughout my career, as I've mentioned before, whenever I had a death scene (those juicy scenes that I loved to play), it seemed that the director would shoot it first. They didn't do that in this film. But the movie *did* involve my character's death. (I don't mean to give too much away here, and I don't think it takes anything away from the film. After all, I haven't told you what Jonathan Sperry's "secrets" are!)

The scene at the cemetery was a beautiful scene. Rich had it all worked out so they could do it all in one take. It was like magic. The fact that they were filming my burial scene intrigued me. I wasn't actually *in* that scene. I didn't climb inside the casket as they lowered it into the ground. I'm not a method actor to quite that degree!

But I asked, "Do you mind if I come and watch my own funeral?" How many people get to watch their own funeral?

It was a gorgeous day. They picked out a beautiful casket for my character. I really liked it. And you know what? As they lowered it into the ground, it made me think about my legacy. I have amassed an amazing body of work. I've played an incredible array of parts as an actor. I'm proud of every single thing I've done, from *The Mary Tyler Moore Show* and *The Love Boat*, all the way back to that tiny appearance as a protestor in *Lamp unto My Feet*. (How wonderful, looking back, that the very first TV show I ever did had a spiritual bent to it!) I'm proud of every step I've taken on the stage, from the leading roles in musicals, to *The Connection* and *A Hatful of Rain*, and all the way back to my very first role on the school stage in Pleasantville, when I was just four years old.

But you know what? Out of everything, I like the *Jonathan Sperry* legacy the most.

I've had a couple of film offers recently, including an offer for another

Christian film—and I've turned them down. There's a part of me that keeps thinking, *Maybe* Jonathan Sperry *is the film I should go out on.*

I hope that doesn't sound morbid.

I won't say it's a promise. But if *Jonathan Sperry* were to be the last film I ever did—the one that would get mentioned as my final role when my obituary shows up in the papers—I certainly wouldn't complain.

After all, this isn't just a role. It's me doing God's work.

God knows he is the Captain of my world.

I think he gave me the role of the Captain so that I could serve as a stand-in "captain" to a few people here on earth—to help guide them on their way into his arms.

For that, I stand humbled. For that, I stand in awe. And for that, I know I will have no greater role in life than to continue to serve our Lord in any way I'm called, from now until that day when he finally calls me into heaven.

My work and my life are intertwined, yet I take it all a little easier now. Let's face it: life isn't all about work. I have my kids and step-children, whom I love. I'm blessed to have my first wife, the mother of my children, whom I love, still in my life. I have ten grandchildren, whom I love. I have my brother and his wife and their family, whom I love. I have my Princess family, whom I love. I have great friends, whom I love. Jesus said to love everyone. I have a wealth of experience and a million stories to tell. (Believe me, I've got more if you want 'em!)

And best of all, I have Patti. My beautiful Patti.

I may not live in a mansion anymore, but I tell you, I am a very rich man.

So while I'm still at it, and while I still can, I'm going to savor every last bite of this incredible voyage of my life.

In fact, if you'll excuse me, I think I'm gonna run down to the local diner—and order myself a hot dog.

ACKNOWLEDGMENTS

T HIS BOOK WOULD NOT HAVE BEEN POSSIBLE without the support of a whole bunch of incredibly talented people—all of them friends, some old, some new, whom I love—and I'm eternally grateful to each and every one of them.

First of all, I want to thank my manager, Susan Munao, one of the great motors of my life, whose friendship and partnership in my career for the last thirty years has meant everything to me. Without her creativity, taste, and perseverance, half of what I've talked about in this book (and the making of this book itself) would never have happened! Not to mention that I simply couldn't function without the tireless assistance of her sister, Anne Marie Merz—"My Girl Friday" (and Saturday, and Sunday, and Monday . . .). They are both my sisters in Christ, and I'm just so thankful for all that they do.

I want to thank Joel Kneedler, my literary agent (and thespian brother) at Alive Communications, who brought me to just the right publisher and is just a gem. My fabulous editor, Debbie Wickwire—I wish I could handle a horse the way she does! And of course Matt Baugher, who believed in this book from the very beginning, and who's quite the thespian in his own right—I wish I had his voice! And I send a special thanks to the wonderfully dedicated staff at Thomas Nelson Publishing.

Then there's my collaborator, Mark Dagostino, whose talents speak for themselves on every page of this book. He's become like a loving son to me—one who guides me and advises me and has become a little paternal to me as we've gone through the emotional process of reflecting on my entire life over the course of this past year. Thank you, Mark.

Honestly, this whole team has been a gift from God to me. They make writing a book seem easy!

I could fill a book with the names of people I'd like to thank. To borrow a bit from my friend Valerie Harper, who in her own book borrowed a line from an acceptance speech by the great Maureen Stapleton: "I'd like to thank everyone I have ever met in my life!" I want to thank every actor I've ever worked with, every director who ever directed me, every producer who believed in me enough to hire me . . . every person in every congregation I've ever been in who raised their hands for Jesus!

I want to thank my wonderful family at Princess Cruises, who've given me the opportunity to see the world and to share in so many journeys of a lifetime. Especially Julie, Karen, Suzanne, and Cynthia—all in public relations—and also one of my best friends, who manages my Princess Cruises appearances, Mr. Lee Mimms.

I want to thank Hal March for firing me and kick-starting my whole career! (Ha!)

From the bottom of my heart, I want to thank my first wife, Joan "Rootie" Rootvik MacLeod, for being my loving wife all those years, and for bringing me the four children I always dreamed about. I want to thank my children for everything they've given me, and for being the forgiving, loving, incredibly talented people they are. I want to thank my wonderfully talented and loving stepchildren for accepting me, and sharing their lives with me, and allowing me to love them too.

I can't forget my wonderful grandkids, all of whom I just adore. And my brother and his wife and my whole extended family. I love you all!

But most of all I want to thank Patti—my beautiful Patti—for everything. For loving me unconditionally and believing in me more than I believed in myself at times; for cherishing every facet of our life together, and remembering all those little details I couldn't remember as we tried to make these pages sing; and for being there. Always. I will love you, always and forever.

Finally, I want to thank my Lord and Savior, who kept me alive long enough to get these memories down on paper; who guided me (and continues to guide me) on this incredible journey at every step and every turn along the way.

PHOTO CREDITS

Unless otherwise noted below, photos are from the MacLeod family photo archives.

INSERT 1

Page 5   *A Hatful of Rain* handbill: © 1955 Playbill Incorporated.

Page 6   *I Want to Live!* photo: *I Want to Live!* (Feature) © 1958 Metro-Goldwyn-Mayer
Studios Inc. All rights reserved. Courtesy of MGM Media Licensing.

High Time photo: Archive Photos/Moviepix Collection/Getty Images.

The Sword of Ali Baba photo: © 1965 Universal Studios. Courtesy of Universal Licensing LLC.

Page 7   *The Sand Pebbles* photos: "THE SAND PEBBLES" © 1966 Twentieth Century Fox. All rights reserved.

Kelly's Heroes photos: Licensed by Warner Bros. Entertainment Inc. All rights reserved.

INSERT 2

Page 1   *The Mary Tyler Moore Show*, photos 1 and 2: "THE MARY TYLER MOORE
SHOW" © 1970 Twentieth Century Fox. All rights reserved.

The Mary Tyler More Show, photo 3: "THE MARY TYLER MOORE SHOW" © 1970 Twentieth
Century Fox. All rights reserved; CBS Photo Archives/Archive Photos Collection/Getty Images.

SAG Awards photo: John Shearer/WireImage Collection/Getty Images.

Page 2   *The Mary Tyler Moore Show*, photos 1 and 2: "THE MARY TYLER MOORE
SHOW" © 1970 Twentieth Century Fox. All rights reserved.

The Mary Tyler More Show, photo 3: "THE MARY TYLER MOORE SHOW" ©1970 Twentieth
Century Fox. All rights reserved; CBS Photo Archives/Archive Photos Collection/Getty Images.

Page 4   *The Love Boat*, photos 1 and 3: © American Broadcasting Companies, Inc.

MacLeod with Warhol: Photographed by Jim McHugh.

Page 5   MacLeod with Merman, Miller, Channing: Ann Clifford/Time & Life Pictures
Collection/Getty Images.

The Love Boat, photos 2–5: © American Broadcasting Companies, Inc.

Page 6   *The Love Boat*, photos 1–3: © American Broadcasting Companies, Inc.

People's Choice Awards photo: © CBS Photo Archive.

Page 7   TV Land Awards photo: Gregg DeGuire/WireImage Collection/Getty Images.

The Love Boat, photos 2 and 3: © American Broadcasting Companies, Inc.

Page 8   *The Mike Douglas Show*, photos 1–3: © Michael Leshnov.

Photo Credits

ABOUT THE AUTHORS

GAVIN MACLEOD IS BEST KNOWN AS CAPTAIN Stubing on ABC's worldwide smash *The Love Boat* and as Murray Slaughter on *The Mary Tyler Moore Show*. He and his wife, Patti, hosted *Back on Course* on TBN for seventeen years, and for thirty years, and still today, Gavin is the global ambassador for Princess Cruises. He dedicates his acting talents to the world of faith-based films, including his starring role in the beloved feature *The Secrets of Jonathan Sperry*, and is often called to emcee or speak at events. His website is www.gavinmacleod.com.

MARK DAGOSTINO IS A *NEW YORK TIMES* BEST-selling coauthor and one of the most respected celebrity journalists in America. For ten years he served on staff in New York and LA as a correspondent, columnist, and senior writer for *People* magazine, interviewing personalities such as Michael J. Fox, Christopher Reeve, Ben Affleck, Jennifer Lopez, and Donald Trump.